Eating Fire

Eating Fire

Family Life, on the Queer Side

Michael Riordon

BETWEEN THE LINES

Eating Fire

First published in Canada in 2001 by
Between the Lines
720 Bathurst Street, Suite 404
Toronto, Ontario
M5S 2R4

National Library of Canada Cataloguing in Publication Data

Riordon, Michael, 1944–
Eating Fire: family life, on the queer side

ISBN 1-896357-45-8

1. Gay couples—Family relationships. 2. Gay parents—Family relationships. I. Title.

HQ76.3.C3R55 2001 306.85'086'64 C2001-901903-3

Cover and text design by David Vereschagin, Quadrat Communications
Cover photo from EyeWire

Printed in Canada by union labour

Between the Lines gratefully acknowledges assistance for its publishing activities from the Canada Council for the Arts, the Ontario Arts Council, and the Government of Canada through the Book Publishing Industry Development Program.

Contents

Preface

We live in a relational universe. The sun flares, a hawk swoops over Manchuria, and in an ice-shrouded Ontario barn, a pig suffocates. These events, we know now, are connected by mysterious cosmic threads. Moving through our lives, we define ourselves not only as the insular I, but in relation to others: parent, friend, teacher, priest, lover, nurse, cop, boss, and all the rest. To navigate this crowded landscape, but without the usual map, we queer folk have to improvise as we go. This is a gift, and one of our talents.

In writing my previous book, *Out Our Way: Gay & Lesbian Life in the Country*, and in reading from it across Canada, I kept hearing how hungry we are to know more of each other's lives and survival tactics, both rural and urban. Along the way, people have often expressed amazement that my partner Brian and I have been together twenty years, yet still delight in each other. Luck of the draw, I say. Well, maybe 90 per cent luck; the rest is work. And there's no particular virtue in duration, I argue. We've all seen people imprisoned in marriages or their equivalents that should have expired years ago. Still, they say, it's encouraging to know that *our* relationships can work. A fair number of people have also said, "You really ought to write a book about that."

Here it is.

My journey with Brian is my starting point. But since I've never considered myself exactly a supermodel in the relationship department, I also set out to explore how others create and sustain the amazing range of connections and families with which we people our world.

To find stories, I asked a few well-connected folks to suggest potential contacts. Those contacts led to others, and they to others; this is family on a grand scale. Then I went on the road, and travelled about eight months, all told. This isn't a survey or a comprehensive study. I missed whole provinces, whole races, and many people in unique relationships that I'd like to have met. As always, I depended on the random kindness of strangers willing to share their stories. *Eating Fire* is a series of glimpses, brief encounters, most of them face-to-face, though a few people I could reach only by phone.

A book takes a while to create, in this case four years from first impulse to the package of words now in your hands. In that span of time, it's inevitable that some people whose stories fill these pages have moved on to other houses, places, jobs, relationships. Some of us, I'm sad to say, have died. All of us have aged, and I've added a compensatory couple of years to people's stated ages since I met them; I ask forgiveness if I've rendered anyone old before their time.

Years ago my elderly English godmother, who made bitter marmalade and had antimacassars on her overstuffed chairs, read an article I'd written. "Oh, Michael," she said to me in her rather mournful way, "why must you always talk about what you do in the bedroom?" Like most things I write, the article dealt with some aspect of injustice and resistance. Cousin Enid was one of the last people on earth with whom I would ever have discussed what I do in the bedroom. She would have had the vapours. Along the same lines, this book is a little about what we do in the bedroom, or wherever else we may happen to do it, and a lot about less technical, more elusive matters: who we are, what we do in other rooms of our lives, and what we offer to the world.

Where people have asked me to protect their identities, for their own sake or their children's, I've put pseudonyms in quotation marks the first time they appear.

Thanks to everyone who provided leads and contacts, the connections that make possible a book like this, and our lives. I'm especially grateful to the folks who trusted me to convey their stories. Thanks to Between the Lines for its stubborn survival and independence in an increasingly grey world of mindless conglomerates, and to both the Canada Council and the Ontario Arts Council for continuing to support work like this which doesn't even register on the screen at the mindless conglomerates. Thanks also to the Lesbian & Gay Community Appeal of Toronto, for supporting a project whose boundaries went far beyond that city. And to Maureen Garvie, who edited the manuscript gently and with finesse.

My deepest gratitude to Brian, my Brian, without whom – well, I can't imagine.

Michelle Hart provided the title. During our brief encounter at the Black Orchid in Calgary (see chapter 18), Mike Hart told me that's what Michelle does on special occasions: she eats fire. As proof he sent me a spectacular photo: there she is, a dragon in a vinyl sheath, uttering a huge tongue of flame. Next day on the Greyhound heading north to Red Deer, swishing through rain-soaked, spring-brown undulating fields, it occurred to me that here was the perfect title to embody the thrills and perils of family life on the queer side: *Eating Fire*.

Fruitful Couplings

In the year 2001 the Canadian government finally passed legislation it could no longer avoid, rendering same-sex couples equivalent to the hetero variety in a wide range of existing laws. But under intense pressure from right-wing primitives in its own and other parties, at the last minute the reigning Liberals tacked the "defence of marriage" amendment onto the bill. It defines that institution, which previously made no mention of gender (everyone just *knew*), as a legal relationship between "only one man and one woman, to the exclusion of all other."

To hear them tell it, they saved the traditional family and western civilization, and just in the nick of time. But what exactly were these people defending – the missionary position?

A few years ago, when anglophone activists in Ontario were harrumphing that bilingualism would kill the English language, I said in some forum that the only serious threat to English came from the people who spoke it. Same sort of thing goes for marriage, I'd say. Divorce statistics show so many heteros abandoning ship, you'd think it was the Titanic.

In charting an original course for our relationships, we face a startling array of fundamentalists, not all of them brandishing crosses. Some queer activists argue that any homo who's monogamous has to be crazy, and the search for Mr or Ms Right is practically a mortal sin. Well, burn me at the stake. Though I wasn't aware of looking for him, I stumbled onto Mr Right twenty years ago. He still is, if not perfect, at least just right.

I agree that *enforced* monogamy is a prison, and I dutifully slept around for a while to prove it. But I also found that as my co-mingling with Brian deepened, other playmates seemed a little – how shall I say it? – redundant. No doubt I've forfeited many thrills, but neither have I skiied down Mount Everest, and in this lifetime probably never will.

At another place on the spectrum, we meet in these pages two men who were married in 1974, by an actual minister in an actual Canadian church. In their compulsory marriage-preparation course, Chris and Richard informed the startled minister that they would both continue to have sex with other men. A quarter century later they are still married, still happily, by their own account, and they still have sex with other men.

So there we have it. No map. Sail on.

1 War and Peace, and Celery

THE OTHER DAY BRIAN AND I HAD A FIGHT. AS IT USUALLY HAPPENS between people, and nations, the fight was not about what it seemed. What it seemed to be about was celery.

We were having our breakfast by the fire; in winter, as warmth spreads from the woodstove, so do our activities. We were discussing what vegetables we might plant this year. Brian said, “I’d like to grow celery.”

“Sure,” I said, “what does it need?”

“It’s a challenge,” he replied. “If it doesn’t get enough water, it goes bitter.”

This was the wrong thing to say. Though entirely surrounded by water, Prince Edward County is notoriously prone to drought. Most summers our well runs dry, or close to it. We have fifteen rain barrels lined up under eavestroughs, in an elegant tandem array that Brian conceived to capture every precious drop. But by August, without rain . . . “Why,” I asked, “would we want to grow something that needs a lot of water?”

“Because we’ve never planted it before, and I’d like to see how it grows.” I could hear a slight edge stealing into Brian’s voice, and mine.

“You know how it grows,” I replied. “You just said, without water it goes bitter.”

I had a vested interest here. It’s mostly me who waters the garden, by hand with a watering can, as day cools into evening. In our garden Brian is the sorcerer and I his apprentice, but with a twist. As we run out of water, I start rationing it, budgeting. How much can I stretch it, how little can I afford to give each plant, how does the beauty of flowers rank with the food value of vegetables? I apologize profusely to the unfortunate plants that will have to wait till tomorrow, or beyond.

A little later, when the gardens begin to register the effects of insufficient water – smaller plants, blossoms falling off before turning to fruit, end-rot spoiling the tomatoes – Brian notices. "These plants haven't been getting enough water," he says, then adds quickly, "I'm not criticizing you." But it's too late, I've failed again. Each summer, deep in the drought, we have the same fight. The more things we grow, I argue, the less water each of them gets, and I end up responsible for it. Why don't we plan better, and grow less? To Brian, the sorcerer, planning is anathema. "If watering is the problem," he says, "I'll help."

"That's what you always say," I say. "Anyway, the problem isn't watering, it's *water.*" And so it goes, back and forth. At the end of it, we agree: next year we'll plan better. We'll mulch more, and this won't ever happen again.

Last year we were given *Dry-Land Gardening,* a fine, sensible book by Jennifer Bennett. I treat it as a bible, the source of our salvation, but Brian hasn't had time to read it. And he wanted to grow celery. By now I was steaming. "While we're at it," I said, "why don't we grow bananas?"

"There's no need for sarcasm," he said. "Why are you so angry? I just want to try something, is that a crime?"

"Ah," I retorted, "so now this is about me thwarting you. You propose, I get in the way, is that it?"

"All right," he said, "we won't grow celery."

"Why not? Because it's a stupid idea or because I thwarted you?"

"What does it matter?" he said. "The point is, you got your way."

I went skiing with the dog. He went to work in the shop. The snow was smooth that day, the air crisp, and the light perfect. I came back mellow, went into the shop and said, "Sorry, I should have shed the anger before dealing with the celery question. I'm not apologizing for my anger, though. I think it was justified." Less mellow than I thought.

"Obviously it's still there," he replied. "Why? You got what you want, no celery. What more do you want from me?" We wrangled again, until he snapped, "Fine. You plan the garden."

I snapped back, "Grow what you want." Impasse.

I itched to storm out, make some grand gesture, at least slam the door behind me. So, I'm sure, did he. But we stayed put, eyes connecting then sliding away. In due course we talked, and talked; the heat gone from our voices now, we chose our words with more care. This is what emerged:

In the garden, as in any realm of tangible things, Brian is a sparker, a generator. Let's grow shiitake mushrooms, he'll say, or why don't we build a greenhouse, a grey water lagoon? I, on the other hand, am a planner: what are the specific steps needed to make this fantasy happen? Inevitably, the sparker's role is more glamourous than the planner's. Brian didn't remember the argument we had in mid-drought last year, nor the conclusion we reached. I did; filing such things for future reference is in the planner's job description. "The effect of ignoring that is to dismiss my role in the garden," I said. "I don't mind you leading, and I'm happy to give you credit for it, but the repetitive, invisible daily work – the watering and weeding that sustain the garden – that also deserves credit."

"But I do value your work in the garden," said Brian. "Maybe I haven't made that clear enough to you."

"Well," I said, "one practical way to value my work is to take it into account in planning the garden; for example, by not growing things that need a lot of water until we come up with a better way to provide it."

And so it went. In the end we came to this: we'll plan the garden together, we'll listen to each other, we'll honour our different strengths, and this will never happen again.

What can I do but love this man? With him, for the first time in my life, I'm learning how to fight fair.

2 Dancing with Widows

ON THE ACADIAN SIDE OF CAPE BRETON, I'VE STOPPED BY TO SEE "Maria" and "Cassandra" with my friend Judy Burwell, my driver and companion on this Maritime trek. Pockets of snow still linger in the hollows from an April blizzard. Two days later, a *souete* roared in from the Atlantic side. Its 140-kilometre winds took the roof off a house just up the road, peeling it off like loose skin, but spared Maria and Cassandra's trailer home and their little clutch of tourist cabins. The cabins look tiny and vulnerable on a narrow strand by a cove still clogged with ice, and beyond that the blank grey expanse of the gulf. Across the cove, the town straggles along its sheltered harbour, with small fishing boats, a wharf piled with lobster traps, the looming stone church and the school next door where Maria took her lessons, and her faith, from the nuns. Behind the town a dense, cold mist shrouds the Cape Breton highlands.

Inside the warm, compact trailer, Judy settles with a book while I sit at the kitchen table with Maria and Cassandra, to hear their stories. Maria's unfolds like a variation on *The Sound of Music*.

"The word homosexual is not in the Catholic Bible," Maria told her local prayer group in the early 1980s, reading from a statement she'd been preparing for weeks. "Homosexuality is a state of being someone different, rather than acting differently from the normal way of life. I know what I am talking about because I am one." The group stirred uncomfortably, but following the priest's example, continued to listen. "All through school I had mad crushes on my women teachers, never on the men. I was the smartest kid in class, I excelled and studied like crazy to please my teachers. When my girlfriends took walks on Sunday afternoons to meet the boys, I went with them a couple of times, but I was bored to death. After that I stayed home and played with cars I had built out of wood. Later, I decided to join the convent, to find out if I had the calling to be a nun." For centuries the convent provided women the only sanctioned alternative to marriage.

"But," Maria continued to read, "there were some very pretty girls in the convent. I wrote an innocent note one day, Mother Superior found it in my desk, she packed my bags, told me I was damned, and kicked me out." Maria was seventeen.

In 1957 she moved to Boston, where one of her sisters lived. Maria went out on dates with men. "It was fun as long as we were just friends, " she recalls, "but the minute things got serious and a little petting started, it made me so nauseated, I had to go home. Since I was very secretive about my real feelings, I began to feel very lonely and out of place." She turned to a familiar refuge. Every evening after work she went to church and prayed for guidance. "One night the Lord told me you can't go on hurting these guys, it's not right. You have to stop lying, he said, you have to accept who you are."

Maria came out to an older woman she'd just met. "This woman was very nice to me. She told me I wasn't alone. That was a surprise for me, and a big relief." At a discreet house party Maria met her first partner, with whom she lived for the next seven years. With a second partner she moved back home to Cape Breton in 1970. "My parents were getting quite old by then, and my father was needing more care than my mother could provide," she says. "I'd had enough of living in the city by then, so it wasn't hard for me to move."

With her partner's help Maria opened a TV repair shop on the main street, using the electronics course she'd taken in Boston. Business was slow. "There were two problems: First, TV repair wasn't something that women did around here, and second, definitely not two women together. But after about a year, when people started to realize we did good work at a fair price, more of them started to call." The business thrived for the next two decades.

Meanwhile, Maria's mother kept trying to find a man for her, believing that if she had one she wouldn't have to work. Maria laughs. "I kept telling her, look at all the women who get married, and how many of them still have to work!"

The tourist cabins also thrived, and in the off-seasons Maria serviced electronic equipment on the fishing boats. After fourteen years together, in 1982 the partner returned to the U.S. to care for her ailing mother. A year or so later Maria took up with a woman who lived nearby. "But this woman was so ashamed, so guilty about being gay, she would even hurt you in order to disguise the relationship, so it never really worked." Then a friend passed on the address of LYNX, an Ottawa-based group that links lesbians across Canada. Maria joined immediately.

In Calgary, Cassandra Britton also happened to see a poster for LYNX. She paid her dues, got her first newsletter, and responded to several correspondents on the list through a box number at LYNX. "Maria's ad called to me," she says. "She said she liked a campfire by the ocean, a walk in the woods, and dinners by candlelight. I thought that sounded very romantic." It appealed to Maria that Cassandra wanted a monogamous relationship. The two wrote back and forth for a year or so, then ran up enormous phone bills. In April 1995 Cassandra flew to Halifax for the Easter holiday.

In the surge of travellers at the airport, they spotted each other from photos they'd exchanged. "I was very nervous," says Maria. "I didn't know what to expect. She could have taken one look at me and got back on the next plane home."

Maria had booked a hotel room. First they went out to dinner, exchanged gifts – flowers, little things – and talked. "All I can remember of it now is that we drank an awful lot of tea," says Cassandra.

Maria laughs. "So much tea! I guess we were afraid to go up to the room."

They roamed Halifax for a couple of days, then drove north to Cape Breton, crossing to the Acadian side on the Gulf of St Lawrence where the Darveau relatives had gathered for Easter. "It was a big culture shock for me," says Cassandra. "I had some French from high school, but I'm not too confident about speaking it. And I couldn't believe how many cousins she has. But everyone was nice to me." Easter morning they all trooped off to mass, and Cassandra heard Maria sing in the choir, a fine mellow tenor.

A month later Maria flew to Calgary for the wedding of Cassandra's younger daughter, and in June Cassandra moved to Cape Breton. "Neither of us was getting any younger," says Maria. "Still, it was very brave of her to just pick up and move like that."

"What else could I do?" says Cassandra. "I wanted to be with Maria, and she couldn't leave here because of her mother." Though Maria's father had died in 1987, her mother, now ninety-three, needed help to continue living at home. "There was really nothing to hold me back," Cassandra adds. "The children were all grown, I had no other family, and possessions don't mean much to me. They can always be replaced. It's not so hard when you know you're moving to true love and happiness."

From a certain wariness in her manner and voice, Cassandra strikes me as someone for whom neither love nor happiness has come easily. All she says of her childhood is that both parents were strict fundamentalists and physically abusive. On her honeymoon she discovered that she'd married an alcoholic. "But I didn't have the self-confidence to end it," she says, "not for almost fourteen years." By then they had three children. One day a neighbour offered to take her to a service at the Salvation Army. "I talked to the minister there about my husband, and because they don't approve of drinking, finally I had an ally." The minister persuaded her husband to get treatment. It didn't work, but for Cassandra a door had opened. "Eventually I asked him to move, and then we got a divorce. For several years after that I raised the kids on my own, mostly working as a nanny."

In 1987 Cassandra happened to catch a Donohue show about lesbians. "I said to myself, My God, *that's me*! It was amazing, as if a light had suddenly come on." When her current charge grew too old for a nanny, she applied to work for another couple. They were Christians, they said, and they liked to be completely open and honest about everything. The new nanny told them she was a lesbian. They fired her, explaining in a letter that God considers homosexuality to be a wicked lifestyle, and they didn't want their daughter corrupted.

Cassandra took the letter to the Alberta Human Rights Commission. Sorry, said the Commission; the provincial human rights code doesn't protect homosexuals. (The Alberta government finally included sexual orientation in the code more than a decade later, when ordered to do so by the Supreme Court of Canada.) Determined to get a hearing any way she could, Cassandra wrote to the *Calgary Herald*, which covered her story, as did the local CBC Radio station. Suddenly at forty-six Cassandra Britton, mother of three, was a lesbian activist.

Her younger girl reacted positively, her son less so. "But he was very nice to me when I came for the wedding," says Maria. "I think he made it his job to take care of me." Cassandra's older daughter still won't talk about it. On the other hand she did come to see them in Cape Breton, a visit that Cassandra describes as "strained." Now that direct flights are available from Calgary to Halifax, they're hoping the younger daughter will bring her new baby for a visit.

Much more of a strain was Cassandra's prickly relationship with Maria's mother. Because the elderly woman hated to be alone after dark, Maria would spend nights up at her house. When Cassandra arrived from the West, and Maria moved into the trailer with her, her mother was furious.

"It wasn't personal," says Maria. "She always took an immediate aversion to anyone I got close to. Instead of seeing it as sharing, she felt she was losing me." Maria was her youngest daughter and the only one of her children who lived nearby.

"So every night the two of us would go up there and stay with her," says Cassandra. "That was so hard when we were trying to get acquainted with each other, but her mother was very stubborn."

At the same time, Maria was studying business administration and computer technology at the regional college. "It was a very hard course with a lot of assignments, so I'd be at school all day, then I'd come home, grab supper, and hit the books. I had no choice, it was either that or I'd fail."

Cassandra nods. "I understood, but even so, I felt like a widow." After Maria's mother had a stroke in 1996, the tension mounted. "She started to have falls at night," says Cassandra, "and she would fight with any caregiver we hired. Everything was such a huge battle with her – changing a furnace filter, it was like World War III. We'd be so wrought up we couldn't sleep."

"And I was caught in the middle," says Maria, "trying to be the peacemaker and make everybody happy. I could see how hard it was on Cassandra, but at the same time I also knew how much my mother hated to give up control of her house."

How did they come through it intact? "It wasn't easy," says Cassandra. "If I didn't love Maria as much as I do, I wouldn't have put up with it, not at this point in my life."

Says Maria, "We talked a lot about things, as much as we could. I think both of us tried hard to understand how it was for the other one."

Cassandra adds, "I don't know what we would have done if we didn't have this place to get away to." When Maria's mother needed round-the-clock care and they couldn't afford to provide it at home, she went to the local foyer, the home for seniors, where she died eighteen months later.

Cassandra makes tea, under cheery hearts cut from wallpaper and pasted to the cupboard doors. Twilight has yielded now to night and fog. On the bookshelf there's a tidy row of mysteries, and a Bible. Maria's guitars are propped in a corner. A cat purrs, curled on her lap; the other has retired to the bedroom. Since one got killed on the highway and another disappeared for seven weeks, the cats now go out only on leashes.

The cabins are open from mid-June to mid-October. Off-season, hardly any tourists come up this way. But during those four months they work long hours, seven days a week. "We're quite relieved when it's over," says Cassandra, "but you do get to meet some great people. A lot of musicians come through here. They'll bring their instruments, Maria will take her guitar or her harmonica, and we'll have a bonfire down by the beach. Guests write to us that this was the highlight of their whole trip."

The rest of the year Maria works a couple of hours a day at the college, not far from here, and Friday and Saturday mornings they both clean an office building in the town. "We enjoy the time together," says Cassandra. "We make a good team."

On Wednesdays they deliver Meals on Wheels to the elderly. "It's nice," says Maria. "Most of them already knew me from the TV repair, but this is a good way for them to get to know her too."

For Cassandra, moving here from Calgary was like changing planets. "Besides a different language, a different religion, and an intense quiet unlike anything I'd ever experienced, I also found the people here very reserved with me. They still are."

Maria smiles. "Strangers don't come around here too often, except for the ones that pass through in the summer. People want to know if you're going to stay before they open up to you."

In Calgary Cassandra had got used to being out. "It bothers me when we have to hide our affection for each other," she says. "We're a couple too, and we shouldn't have to do that."

Maria is more of a known quantity here. She plays guitar for prayer meetings at the seniors' foyer, and sings in the choir. "They're all very accepting of me," she says, "even the priests. We've been lucky with the priests here. None of them has ever said anything against us."

Cassandra hesitates a moment. "I don't have any close friends. Not yet." In fact her most enduring connections, aside from Maria, are with people she has never met. Twelve years ago she sought penfriends through an English newspaper, and some have been corresponding with her ever since. "We've become quite close, as if there was no ocean between us. Now they include Maria in their letters and birthday cards. Who knows, maybe one day I'll go visit some of them." More recently, Cassandra has started corresponding with Canadian peacekeepers on duty overseas. "That's added a whole new dimension to my life, and I hope it brings some joy to theirs."

Now and then Maria and Cassandra get a yen to dance. At local straight youth-oriented dances they feel doubly out of place. The nearest gay dances are in Sidney, a two-hour drive each way through the mountains. But right here, five minutes up the road at the seniors' club, they can dance together, slow dances and all. "It's all widows there," explains Maria. "You have twelve women to every man, so the women all dance with each other. The point is to have a good time. So if we go, no one looks twice if we dance together."

Cassandra laughs. "Thank God for the widows!"

"You don't see that so much in the English communities, only the French," says Maria. She smiles, a little mischievous. "Who knows, maybe the women here are killing off their men."

3 The Hired Hand

At 5:10 a.m. the alarm rings, seven days a week. It's January, won't be light for another two hours. They throw on some clothes, one of them stokes the woodstove, then they're out to the barn. They milk twenty-six cows and clean up. If all goes well, they're back in for breakfast by 8:00, their hands red as raw meat from the icy water.

Gary baked last night, so there's fresh bread. They're out again an hour later for more chores: clean the stables, haul hay, feed and water fifty-five or so head of cattle and the Appaloosa horses, a hobby of Ron's. The vet arrives to tend a mare who injured herself last night in her stall. After lunch Gary listens to music for a while on his door-sized electrostatic speakers, so sensitive you can almost hear the musicians' hair grow. His musical orientation is baroque, a taste acquired in his teens. Ron planned to catch up on farm accounts today, but instead he'll have to work on the tractor – it broke down blowing out a huge dump of fresh snow from the neighbour's drive.

By 3:30 they start the afternoon chores: milk, feed, straighten out bedding in the stalls. In summer there's less barn work but more field work: tilling, planting, mowing, baling and storing hay, tending to the chickens, turkeys, and vegetable garden, harvesting and canning. They could be in for supper by 7:00, or not. "We don't punch a clock," says Ron. "You're done when you're done." And soon it's time for bed. In a few hours the alarm will ring, again.

Ron grew up farming this deep land in southwest Ontario where he was born fifty-seven years ago. In his early thirties he set up house in a village down the road with a man he loved. But on snowy days he couldn't get to the farm by six for morning chores. So he built his current house, close by the barn and across the yard from his mother's house.

By age twelve Ron was having sex with other boys. "I knew that's what I wanted, but I always felt guilty about it too. I was pretty involved with the United Church back then, Sunday school and the choir, and they said it was a sin. If they knew, they wouldn't have had anything to do with me. I could've put up with that, but I didn't want to shame my family." In his early twenties his mother caught him kissing a fourteen-year-old boy. "She really told him off, but she never said a word to me about it. Things like that just don't get talked about in my family. And my mother knows if she confronts me straight on, I just dig in my heels." Square and sturdy, he looks hard to move.

Doing what family and church expected of him, Ron dated women, the last one until he was twenty-five. "She wanted to have sex, and she was pushing to get married," he says. "Finally I couldn't do it any more, so I wrote her a letter saying I was sick of living a lie. It wasn't fair to either of us." She still drops by for a visit now and then with Ron's mother next door.

Ron's young lover refused to be tied down, either to Ron or to the farm. "I'd given up too much by then to get where I was," says Ron. "I wasn't about to throw it all away for him." Then he met Gary.

Tall and lean, Gary is forty-two. He also grew up on a farm. "From a very early age I knew I was attracted to men," he says. "At five or six I can remember watching the guy that brought us feed from the co-op mill. He usually wore a t-shirt, and he had these gorgeous bulging arm muscles. I liked that, it was beautiful to me. But of course as you grow up, you learn to keep those thoughts to yourself." In high school he dutifully dated a girl. "I felt sorry for her, but more than anything I kept wondering what was wrong with me – you were supposed to like all that, and I didn't. The first time we kissed I could hardly stand it."

When he was twenty Gary read *The Sand Fortress,* a novel about gay life in the big city. "If that was it – drugs, parties, multiple sex partners – it was not what I wanted, not at all. As I read I became more and more depressed. At the end of the book this young guy kills himself. It seemed like his only way out." Gary swallowed a bottle of sleeping pills and left a note telling his parents he was gay. "I'd always been quite close to them, but didn't see how I could tell them anything about what I was going through." To his surprise, he woke up. His parents had already found the note. "Both of them were very upset that I'd felt bad enough about myself to do that. My mother also blamed herself for the fact that I was gay, but I told her I was just born this way, and this is the way I would always be. She worried about what the neighbours would think, that sort of thing, but over time she got to be quite accepting."

So did Gary. "I figured if I was going to be gay, I had to do something about it. So I forced myself to go to the bars and the baths. But in the back of my mind there was always this hope that I would meet someone. I actually did meet a guy in Toronto and fell in love – I guess it was more like being infatuated – but it didn't mean the same to him at all. That hurt, but of course you get over it and you move on." Mutual friends introduced him to Ron at the Robin's Nest, a gay club up the road in Cambridge. They went home to Ron's place, and a couple of months later Gary moved in. "I knew right away this was the type of life I wanted," Gary says. He was twenty-two.

Twenty years later they're still here. "In the early years we had some pretty stormy battles," says Gary. "I actually packed my bag and walked out of here a few times. Then after three or four days I'd come back and we'd sort it out." Gary is the hired man. Ron pays him, as an employee. This arrangement has tax advantages, but perhaps more important, says Ron, "People around here accept it as perfectly normal. It's not unusual to have a hired hand on the farm."

"If I was just living with him and working somewhere else," Gary adds, "people would see that as weird."

I wonder how it feels for the hired man. "We share the work equally," Gary replies, "and when I'm dealing with something, whether it be a cow or a piece of machinery, I don't look at it as if it were his and therefore I don't care about it. I treat it as if it was my own."

"We talk about everything," Ron adds, "and we make most of the decisions together. Maybe not something like when to breed a cow, but most everything else. I treat him pretty much like an equal partner in the farm."

Yet he's not a partner, he's the hired man. How do they deal with that? "As far as I'm concerned, this is Ron's farm," says Gary. "He was here long before I was, and he's put a lot more into it than I have. Ultimately it's him who's responsible for the farm, so he likes to have the ultimate say about it. I don't have any problem with that."

What would happen to the farm, and the hired man, if Ron were to die? "That's a hard one," Ron admits. "When Gary first moved in here, I would never have considered leaving everything to him, everything that I worked forty years for. How did I know how long he'd stick around? And then if anything happened to him, whatever I'd left to him would go to his family, not mine. Of course the longer he stayed, the more complicated it got. I only see my nieces and nephew once or twice a year, and they're not getting everything, that's for sure. But it was my father who paid for this farm, not me – though I certainly did my share – so they ought to get something out of it too. It does create a problem."

And there he stops. For Gary, passing it on is less complicated. "I don't own nearly as much as Ron does, but with no kids coming on, who else would I leave it to but him?"

Ron has never lived far from his immediate family. His mother, just the other side of the yard, thinks the world of Gary. But she's less discreet than her son might wish. "I shouldn't say this, but sometimes she doesn't know enough to keep her mouth shut," says Ron. "I'd just as soon she didn't say anything at all to people about me and Gary, so I don't tell her much. What you don't know, you can't talk about."

Her sister, Ron's aunt, has always been nice enough to Gary but wouldn't quit pushing Ron to get married. "You just smile," says Gary. "You look stupid, I guess, and you hope the subject changes."

"You also get kind of fed up with it," says Ron, "so after a while you tend to avoid people who do that."

They're not out to the neighbours. "Some of them must've realized something by now," says Ron. "They'd have to be pretty stupid not to. But people round here aren't real neighbourly anyway. They're nice enough when you run into them, but they don't get that close." Since they have no time to clean the house, a local woman comes in every two weeks. Has she mentioned the calendar on the kitchen wall, each month displaying a different man, half-stripped, all muscle, tan and possibilities? "She's never said anything," says Gary. "Anyway, look, I'm sorry, but no one has the right to tell us what we can or can't do in our own house."

Now and then they'll go out to a local event, Ron says. "But we don't really feel like we belong. Around here you're supposed to have a wife and kids, it's not supposed to be any other way. And most of the things that get people together – church, school, scouts, hockey practice – they all revolve around family and kids. If you're not into that, you really don't fit too well into their little scheme of things."

For Gary it can be even harder. "At least Ron can talk to the other farmers, but if you don't have your own place and you just work on somebody else's, they look down on you. As far as they're concerned, you're nobody, and you have nothing much to say."

Once a year a neighbour invites them over for his pig roast. "You go in there, you say hi to the ones you know, and that's about it," says Ron. "They walk away and go talk to their own group."

"And then you just sit there by yourself," Gary adds. "I don't think of myself as taking the feminine role, or any particular role at all in our relationship, but I do sometimes identify with another farmer's wife. She's working on the farm just as I am, but he's the one that's really running it. You'd think I could go over and have a good talk with her, but I can't because I'm a guy, and it doesn't work that way."

"When you get home, you wonder what was the point of it," says Ron. "Then after a while you don't want to bother anymore."

Gary adds, "We might just as well stay home."

So what do they do for a social life? "Not much," says Gary, with a short laugh. They have a few gay friends within an hour's drive or so, and occasionally they'll get to the club up in Cambridge. "We used to go more often," says Ron. "We'd sit and talk with friends. But most of the people you meet there really don't have any interest in our kind of lifestyle."

"Besides," Gary adds, "when you have to get up shortly after five every morning, you can't afford to stay out that late!"

What do they do on a Saturday night? "Well, usually we'll go out to supper," says Gary. "We go to a mall in London and get a hamburger at Wendy's or someplace like that. After that we do our grocery shopping, and then we come home." He laughs, and adds, "Same old thing, every week, it's domestic bliss." Friends have suggested the reason they've stayed together so long is lack of temptation, since they rarely encounter other men. "But then you could just as easily say that being together as much as we are is quite a test of our relationship."

Evenings after supper they'll sit and talk. Ron may work at his rug-hooking or watch TV until he falls asleep. "I can always tell when he's nodded off," says Gary, "because normally he mutes the advertisements." Gary listens to music upstairs or devours any gay novel he can get his hands on. "Ron says once I get into one of them, the world could fall down around me and I would never notice." If the night is clear, Gary might be out in the observatory he built behind the house, with his eight-inch telescope taking in the heavens. He warns stargazer wannabes not to be fooled by the coffee-table books with their dazzling, night-long exposures from billion-dollar telescopes. "With an amateur telescope, often you'll be looking at something that's not much more than a fuzzy spot. It teaches you to appreciate things that you normally wouldn't even notice. Then you start thinking about how long it took that light to get here. When it dawns on you how immense and beautiful the universe is, it gives you a great sense of humility. And patience," he adds. "It teaches you patience, which is something I can certainly use."

Last time I checked, they had sold the dairy herd and started raising beef instead. With no cows to milk, they don't have to get up *quite* so early. But still, with animals, chores have to be done, without fail, every day. And the alarm rings – again.

4 Finding Home

ON A MOLTEN SUMMER AFTERNOON NANCY ARRIVES HOME BY BIKE from her job at the Mississauga Public Library. We sit in the well-groomed garden behind their house, one in a small circle of tidy bungalows at the end of a suburban street. To accompany the gingerbread that Nancy made last night, Kenna brews barley tea, a traditional beverage in the land of her birth, South Korea. Both women speak softly, their voices disappearing now and then under jets thundering into the airport a few miles to the north. Their young beagle-terrier, Mocha, barks fierce warnings at some unseen intruder in the deep, wooded ravine beyond the garden.

Seated in one of the garden chairs she built, Kenna looks as sturdy and enduring as the furniture. She grew up in South Korea, with Christian fundamentalist parents. From early on, she says, she preferred boys' clothes and games, but her mother did her best to raise her as a proper little girl. Kenna wanted to be a TV producer, but her mother thought it more practical for her to train as a nurse. Kenna became a nurse. "I always danced along to her rhythm," she says. "I followed the planned route, I didn't know anything else."

When her mother announced it was time for her to marry, a matchmaker arranged for Kenna to meet a series of eligible bachelors, their credentials pre-approved by her parents. If neither party was impressed, that was the end of it. But when a man wanted Kenna and she wasn't interested, the pressure on her mounted. "Think about it," her parents urged, "give him another chance."

"I had no sense then of being a lesbian, only that I didn't want to be doing this," says Kenna. Finally a Korean emigrant turned up from his new home in Canada, determined to take a wife back. "It wasn't really what you'd call a forced marriage. It's just that I wasn't strong enough to say no. I didn't know how."

They married and she came to live in his Toronto apartment. After eight months she asked him to leave. "He had relatives, but I had nowhere to go."

Was there physical abuse? "Yes," she nods, and leaves it at that. Come home, her parents urged. Kenna was torn. "I'd never had to take care of myself or worry about money before. I was raised high middle class, driven to school by a chauffeur. I was so embarrassed I would ask him to let me out a few blocks away – some of my schoolmates even had trouble paying their tuition." Kenna's mother told her that by ending the marriage she had brought shame on the family, and her father-in-law demanded to know what she had done to make his son hit her.

Kenna was twenty-four. "I decided if I didn't want to go back inside their egg, I would have to survive here, one way or another." She had no family in Canada, no friends, no income, no English. She started to drink, and thought of suicide. "It felt like I was on a dead-end road. But now, looking back, I think that's when my life really started, when I finally became responsible for myself." She signed up to study English at night school, applied to the College of Nurses for accreditation in Ontario, and got a job washing dishes in the cafeteria at a toy factory for $3 an hour.

Nancy smiles. "She's hardly ever washed a dish since."

Nancy grew up in Hamilton, a little to the west. Shortly after she was born, her mother was hospitalized for severe depression, and for the next twenty years subjected to shock therapy and antidepressant drugs. "Of course I felt responsible," says Nancy. "And my father was very argumentative – it was his way or no way, he was that kind of person. So there was a lot of yelling in our house. My brother and I learned quite early it was safer to keep our feelings to ourselves."

In kindergarten she absorbed two other life lessons. First, she was clearly more interested in girls than boys, especially her classmate Melanie, with whom she loved to sit close. One day the teacher scolded them sharply and separated them, and the second lesson registered: whatever mysterious offence she and Melanie had committed together, it was a big one.

In her mid-teens, Nancy and a small group of friends got into drugs and alcohol. "Right from the beginning I drank more than anyone else." In and out of treatment programs, she has come to understand that she drinks in order to drown the unruly emotions, including her dangerous interest in girls. And though she knows it can't be done, not without killing her, still she keeps trying.

In March 1988 both Nancy and Kenna happened to come out to the same friend, so she introduced them. Says Nancy, "Kenna struck me as very quiet and innocent. Of course I wasn't anywhere near ready for a relationship, not even with myself, but I'd have been the last to know it."

Kenna recalls, "The sexual attraction came first for me. By then I'd had some bad experiences with both men and women, so I wasn't ready to commit to anyone."

Nancy adds, "I was terrified. I had no experience of relationship at all, except for one time with a bi couple who were experimenting, which was a disaster for me." Beer, lots of it, smoothed out their first date. Within eighteen months they had bought a house together, on this quiet suburban street.

From the beginning Kenna anticipated that her journey with Nancy wouldn't be smooth. Nancy worked increasingly long hours at a series of jobs, up to sixteen hours a day. Often when Kenna arrived home from her evening shift at the hospital, Nancy would still be out drinking with co-workers. "She tried to please everybody," says Kenna. "She would always want to pay for everyone's dinner, then she'd have to go to the second-hand store for her clothing. She couldn't set priorities, everyone else came first."

"It's true," Nancy nods. "I felt so guilty for my mother's illness, all I could do after that was try to be as nice and as good a girl as possible. Of course when you add being gay to that, you have to be even better."

None of this was spoken at the time. Says Kenna, "We didn't know how to talk to each other. I get mad easily, but I keep it to myself, inside, until I've solved it."

They tried a trip to Korea, stayed with Kenna's parents, travelled the islands. For Nancy it was less a vacation than another nerve-wracking test.

One night in December 1993 Kenna got home just after eleven. No Nancy. She waited up, anxious and increasingly angry. Around two a car pulled up and sat idling in front of the house. Kenna watched from the window. After a while the car drove away. No Nancy. "I was furious," says Kenna. "Of course I imagined all kinds of things, where was she, what was she doing?" When Nancy finally showed up, Kenna demanded answers, but Nancy was beyond talking. "I slapped her," says Kenna, "not that hard, but it really freaked me out that I could get angry enough to do that. At that point I knew that our relationship didn't work."

Nancy says, quietly, "In fact nothing happened that night, nothing sexual. I was out drinking with a co-worker, and when I got home I was afraid to go in, afraid that Kenna would be angry because I'd had too much to drink. So we went to a doughnut shop and talked some more. It was an awful feeling, like being a kid again, scared to face my dad." Shortly after, they made an appointment with a lawyer. They would sell the house, and go their separate ways.

But there was a problem. CC, their beloved dog, was at least ten when they'd adopted her from the Humane Society, and now she'd been with them almost four years. She wasn't well, she was fading. If they split up, what would happen to her, who would be responsible for her, how would she survive the stress? They negotiated a compromise, one of their first. They would stay together, but only until CC died.

Nancy was seeing a counsellor at the time who suggested that Kenna come along for a session or two. "I thought that was nonsense," says Kenna. "Korean people don't believe in that, we don't even have a name for it. If you have a problem, you sort it out for yourself."

Nancy prevailed, and Kenna went. "But I refused to talk," says Kenna. "I wasn't even prepared to listen. I was quite arrogant about it." Nancy happened to mention a book she wanted to write, about her family and depression, but she couldn't do it on top of her job. Without hesitation Kenna said she would do anything she could to support Nancy in such a project. "At least that would solve one of the problems," Kenna laughs. "I would know exactly where she was!" For the next four years Nancy stayed home and wrestled out the first draft of her book. She's already had favourable responses from more than one publisher.

As the afternoon fades in Mississauga, so does the heat, a little. Kenna and Nancy both keep a wary eye on Mocha. Last week she romped too long in the sun and nearly died of heat prostration. We compare notes on parenting small, foolish animals. Then we come to the subject of Kenna's mother, and The Letter.

Recently, entering Canada as a landed immigrant, her older brother stayed with them for a month while he looked for an apartment. "He was always a spoiled brat, and he has a violent temper," says Kenna. The same day they found him an apartment, he picked a fight with her, backed her against the fridge, and choked her, at which point Nancy intervened. Kenna ordered him out of their house. Shortly after, an aunt and uncle visited from Korea. "As guests they were very demanding, and apparently my hospitality wasn't good enough for them. I expect that both they and my brother blabbed to my mother about the situation here, with Nancy and me."

You have hurt and shamed us, her mother wrote, so much that we are disowning you. God disowns you too, so you are going to burn in hell. Kenna's brother has the same first initial and at first reading she thought the letter must be aimed at him, "for being such a bad boy instead of a proper big brother to me." But then no Christmas card arrived, and no call on New Year's Day, both highly unusual lapses. The second letter removed any doubt. Citing Sodom and Gomorrah, Kenna's mother wrote that her relationship with Nancy was a sin, especially when she put this woman before her own blood. And what would her teenage grandsons make of Kenna's wickedness? As well as being disowned, she and Nancy would get what they deserved: they would die of AIDS and burn in hell.

Kenna was shattered. "Suddenly everything that I'd accomplished counted for nothing. I couldn't believe how easily I crumbled. I had no idea how much she still controlled me, even after I'd been away from her half my life."

Nancy adds, "That kind of fanaticism is really frightening. Imagine how unhappy her mother must be to fear and resent her own daughter's happiness so much."

"Everything was poisoned," says Kenna. "I became very angry and bitter." At work she began to see her mother in co-workers. "They would talk about being such good Christians, and then I would see them behave like devils toward the patients. It's the same thing my mother did in the name of her god. She made her own daughter into an enemy."

Kenna's counsellor – by now she had one of her own – suggested that she write a response. In it she accused her mother of attacking her only daughter to protect an abusive son. If I had accepted his violence without protest, she asked, would you still love me? "I would never send this letter, but it was a good way to get my feelings out." She and her mother, now seventy-three, had not spoken or written in over a year, but just before my visit Kenna received a parcel from her – no letter, but a supply of seaweed, kelp, and a particular kind of Korean anchovy that's hard to find in Canada. Kenna took it as a peace offering. "But I don't feel strong enough to talk to her yet. I'm afraid that she could still control my emotions and make me feel guilty and ashamed. If it happens while we're both still walking on the earth, that would be nice. But if not, so be it."

A few months ago Kenna took a leave of absence from nursing. She tends the garden, builds furniture, and does some photography – their last Christmas card featured a wintry, painterly photo of the creek at the bottom of their ravine. "Sometimes I just sit here and do nothing, for hours. I've never felt so content. I wish I could live like this for the rest of my life."

Nancy works part-time at the library. "We have less money now, but both of us have come to realize how much more important our sanity is than money," she says. With both of them home more, they're learning how to read each other better and how to work things out. For the few hours I'm with them in their garden, they seem gentle and careful with each other. Their wounds remain close to the surface.

Kenna still struggles with the idea of God. "I can't believe in the same god as my mother. Christians like her say that if you're not Christian you will go to hell. How can it be that all the non-Christians in the world will end up in hell? This is fascist. It's what the missionaries have done. And what's the difference between Christian missionaries going to Korea selling Jesus and the Yankees going there to sell Marlborough cigarettes?"

If she can't believe in her mother's god, who then, or what? "I don't know," she says. "I'm afraid to just come out and say I don't believe in God. Maybe I'm still afraid of being punished. Anyway, I hope that when I get over letting my mother control how I think, I'll be able to move into the area of spirituality more freely." At their first

Toronto Pride day, when the Metropolitan Community Church contingent passed by, Kenna sat down on the sidewalk and cried. "I do know that there is some being that watches over me. That's all I know."

Nancy continues to wrestle her own demons. In the past twenty-two years, she says, despite AA meetings and treatment programs, she has only managed about two full months of sobriety. A month before we met, she drank herself sick and unconscious. Kenna watched her through the night to see that she didn't stop breathing.

"I can't do this any more." Nancy's voice trembles. "My system has changed, so now alcohol acts on me like poison. It can only go two ways. Either I go on like this until I die from it, or I live. I don't want to die." She's signed up for another treatment centre not far from where they live. In the meantime, she and Mocha both drink a lot of water.

CC, the dog who can be credited with keeping Kenna and Nancy together, died in 1998. She's buried by the Korean gingko they planted for her in the garden. It's a handsome, well-shaped young tree, and in time will grow to an impressive height.

5 Where the Boys Are

Driving Professor Friedenberg On a cool spring afternoon Edgar Z. Friedenberg and I take a drive around the peninsula just south of Hubbards, where he lives, about an hour down the coast from Halifax. The Atlantic is quiet today, not surly, its broad leaden mass blurring into clouded sky. This is an outing for Edgar and a courtesy to me, the visitor from Upper Canada. I drive, he talks, crumpled in his seat. After nearly eight decades in the world, he's giving way to gravity.

He took his middle name, Zodiag, from his mother's line, and the small department store that supported the family for five generations in Shreveport, Louisiana. About as far from cosmopolitan New Orleans as you can get in Louisiana, Shreveport is a short drive from east Texas, and only three miles from a huge Strategic Air Command base from which fleets of bombers sally forth to keep the world safe for capitalism. "It's a bad place," says Edgar. But it also carries a certain attachment; his e-mail address is shreve@.

Edgar Friedenberg was born in 1921, twelve years before his only sister. "I must have been a mistake," he says, in a soft voice with a trace of southern langour. "My mother's fantasy, which she never realized, was to live in a nice hotel where she could ring bells and have things brought in. Not that she didn't care for me, I just don't think they welcomed the intrusion." He taught himself to read by the time he was four. "I came to discover that most of the things you weren't supposed to know were written down somewhere." He laughs in short bursts that sound as if he might need more air.

Due to "unspoken anxieties" in his parents, young Edgar was not sent to school but tutored at home. In those days lynchings of slaves' descendants were still not uncommon in the South, and Jews were reviled almost as much by the white, God-fearing majority. But at thirteen Edgar finally insisted that he *must* go to school; instead his tutor suggested that he try the entrance exams at the local college. He passed, easily.

"I was rather scared when I got in," he says. "If I'd been older I'm sure I would have been brutally tormented as a faggot by my peers, who were four to eight years older, but perhaps no one could imagine a faggot so young." On the contrary, he wrote in a wry, elegaic 1998 memoir in the British journal *Sexualities*: "The boys, to my astonished delight, often basked contentedly in my yearning gaze, even as they teased me about it. Straight young men may, and often do, enjoy the response they arouse in gays; our rapture attests to their evident virility." He was eventually elected president of various clubs and became associate editor of the student paper.

Unlike some other well-known older gay men who argue, for example, "I'm not a gay writer, I'm a writer who happens to be gay," Edgar Friedenberg considers his sexual orientation to have been centrally formative to his life and work. "It has certainly influenced every important contingency in my life. If I had not, even as a child, been attracted to boys – preferably good-looking, rough athletes – I would not have become a teacher. Teaching was the only obvious, legitimate way I could imagine to stay where the boys are." A delighted child's smile lights his face.

He sailed with straight As through a Bachelor's, then a Master's degree, both in chemistry, as his tutor had suggested. "It didn't even occur to me to ask what being a chemist might be like, with its customary acceptance of the values and conventions that lead to success in industry," he writes. At Stanford University in California a professor in the School of Education encouraged him to switch faculties; he jumped at the chance. But midway through his PhD studies, late in World War II, Edgar was drafted into the U.S. Navy.

Here again the voyage was smoother than he had feared. Training as a radio technician, he never saw combat, and other men helped him out with the tasks he couldn't manage. "And I found that only a small percentage of young men are appalled by the idea that another man feels affection for them," he says. "In fact I had learned quite early that most boys had been given very little of it and need all of it they can get. I got mine through the erotic equivalent of photosynthesis, depending on young men for their warmth and energy, breathing in the maleness they naturally put out."

PhD in hand, he got his first teaching job at the University of Chicago. One of his functions, a decisive factor in accepting the job, was to be assistant resident in a dormitory unit for male undergraduates. He kept a cookie jar always filled in the lounge, replacing it each time it was stolen. When a man came home drunk, Edgar covered him with a blanket, and sometimes with excuses. "The guys came to me when they were in trouble, not for advice – they knew they had more street-cred than I did – but because I cared for them, which made it easier for them to care for themselves. I became what I had feared nature could never allow me to be: a Jewish mother."

At this point he got his first sharp lesson in the dissonance between homosexuality and formal education. After compliments from colleagues on his first year in the job, he was suddenly dumped from the dormitory post, and a year later from the faculty, in both cases without explanation from the authorities. There had been no charge of sexual misconduct, and none had occurred. "What I stood condemned for was something far worse in the ethos of this university," he writes. "I was emotionally involved with my students. The fact that I was in love with a few of them was not really the problem. What was intolerable was that I was babying them, interfering with their growth."

This was his crime: "The university's job, as the authorities see it, is to train competitors. If you develop any sort of emotional commitment to someone who might be your competitor, you might just screw up the whole game. A taste of that commitment was what those young men got, and were in grave danger of learning, from me. It became quite clear that by our very nature, the university and I were toxic to each other. All my life I've had an absolute aversion to hierarchical institutions of any kind."

A few years later Edgar distilled what he had come to understand about these two guiding passions of his, youth and the abuses of authority, into his first book, *The Vanishing Adolescent.* The first publisher he sent it to, Beacon Press, brought it out immediately in 1959. Though in a preface to a later edition the author called his slim volume "a love story," it takes the form of a fierce, acerbic critique of a culture geared not to freedom but to grinding its innocent young into pliant grist for "an absurd, dangerous and rather contemptible economic system." Throughout the late 1950s the mass media that served this system whipped adults into a froth of terror and indignation over "the youth problem," and "juvenile delinquents." To Edgar Friedenberg, delinquents were boys who had been broken – or, alternately, boys who had managed, despite the terrible forces bent on breaking them, to keep intact some remnant of the tiger spirit that so caught his imagination, and sometimes his breath.

He writes, "Adolescents both comfort and terrify me by their very nature and existence. I once described to an acquaintance what I had seen at a large track meet, especially during the time *between* events when an endless procession of tall, calm-looking boys in snug, glowing warm-up suits jog or lope around the track in pride and self-absorption, singly or in two and threes, or lie in the infield, aloof and immanent. When I paused, he wanted to know who had won. If I had told him that I had just heard the Budapest Quartet playing Mozart, I suppose he might have asked me the same thing."

Coming out when America was half-asleep on too many episodes of *Father Knows Best,* the book is astonishingly radical, and on many levels. At the climax of his argument, the author asks: Why do the men who run things keep brutalizing boys into becoming just like them? "The adolescent boy is likely to be a double threat to the insecure adult: in his own right as a creature of some intensity and a threat to order and, simply by being young, as a stimulus to repressed homosexual feeling in adult males." (Girls and women have little place in his argument. It's not that he lacks respect for them – "They are more courageous than men over the long haul, and better able to stand up for what they believe in under pressure," he writes – but simply that his attention lies elsewhere.)

More than a decade before homophobia was named, he identifies its malevolent force, both within and without. "Homosexuality," he writes, "makes almost unbearable demands on personal character. Perhaps the most painful consequence of that is that it involves the aging homosexual in passionate love that cannot conceivably be requited – and that could not decently be accepted if it were, since a man who genuinely loves a boy cannot encourage him in a manner of life that will bring such bitter sanctions upon him."

The mass circulation *Newsweek* took note of the book and its author in a cover story on the crisis in education. In 1957 the Soviet Union had launched the world's first two artificial satellites, throwing the U.S. establishment and its media into a panic: how could a primitive band of Reds and peasants have outdone the world's most powerful nation? Clearly the American education system wasn't doing it's job! Virtually overnight Edgar Z. Friedenberg became a star, in high demand across the nation as an expert and consultant on youth and education. Even *Playboy* interviewed him on growing student dissent. Because the Library of Congress listed his book under sociology, he received a deluge of job offers from university departments in that discipline, though he had never taken a single formal course in the subject. Over the next decade he taught as a full professor at three universities in California and New York.

By the end of the 1960s the United States had sunk into a brutal, escalating assault on a tiny, distant country, as well as a domestic war against many of its own citizens of African origin, and increasing numbers of its more privileged dissenters of all ages and races. In 1968,

Edgar noted that while the American people elected Richard Nixon as their new president, the Canadian people elected as its prime minister Pierre Trudeau, who declared that "the state had no business in the bedrooms of the nation." Taking quite literally the right-wing bumper sticker, "America: Love It or Leave It," Edgar Friedenberg left. In 1970, just before he turned fifty, he moved to Halifax, where he would teach for the next sixteen years in the Department of Education at Dalhousie University.

"A citadel of sanity," Edgar called Canada. But six weeks after he took up residence here, Prime Minister Trudeau invoked the War Measures Act, effectively suspending civil rights and due process for large numbers of Canadian citizens in Quebec. It was a spectacular first entry in a file that, ten years later, would spill into Edgar's fifth book, *Deference to Authority: The Case of Canada.* The decade, and his book, featured a series of stunning revelations: routine break-ins, mail tampering, and dirty tricks by Canada's national police, as well as elaborate justifications for these illegal practices from leading politicians and the establishment press.

Written with the clear-eyed empathy of a life-long outsider, *Deference to Authority* offers a warning to his fellow citizens in a country which remains, to his chagrin, a colony. "Canadian society is deficient not in respect for law but in respect for liberty," he writes. "And the fundamental function of secrecy in Canadian governmental practice is not concealment but the cultivation of docility. . . . Peace, order and good government in Canada depend ultimately on the deep acquiescence of the people in the idea that they have no inalienable rights; ultimately, the final decision rests with the cabinet." While some critics attacked the author for his American gall, others acknowledged his meticulous reasoning and uncommon good sense.

When pressed to identify his politics, Edgar called himself a radical conservative. He served as president of the faculty union at Dalhousie and for several terms as president of his local New Democratic Party riding association. In "The Resources of Gaiety," his memoir in *Sexualities,* he dismisses any contributions he may have made to the gay liberation movement that grew up around him at Dalhousie. "I never denied, concealed, or regretted my attraction to young men, though it frightened me," he writes. "But I thought genitalia were dirty and embarrassing, and was even more unwilling to embrace a stigmatized identity than I was eager to be embraced – or better yet, spanked – by a hot, sweaty fullback or tight end." And yet he professes, "In spite of all temptations to belong to other nations, I remain gratefully queer as, to the best of my knowledge and belief, I always have been."

After he came out formally in 1971, he chaired a committee of the Gay Academic Union that would take on cases of discrimination against gay or lesbian faculty members. "I interpreted this to mean that it would be my duty to convene the other members of the committee to investigate and act on complaints we might receive. When none of these was forthcoming for a year or two, I was relieved, in both senses of the word; and replaced by a more active and accessible colleague."

His legacy as a queer national would find expression in other, subtler realms.

Dinner Apparently Professor Friedenberg was famous for entertaining favoured students at dinners with delightful food and talk. While he potters about the kitchen preparing ours, he invites me to sit and read – in other words, I assume, to keep out of his way. I notice his hands shaking a little as he cuts the chicken, his breath short from effort and concentration.

The house is old and looks well used. Thick beams support the upper floor. When I settle into a worn leather chair in the corner of the living room, it groans. Beside it, *New Yorkers* in a stack come easily to hand. He calls out from the kitchen, "Under the new editor it's become right-wing in a peculiar way. A recent piece on schools argued that drugging students with Ritalin is a good thing, because it allows them to be trained better to take their places in the free world." *The Vanishing Adolescent* lives.

Over dinner we talk about love and sex. "I have always assumed that the people I was attracted to wouldn't be attracted to me," says Edgar, "and if they thought I was trying to come on to them, they would be put off by it. That negative assumption allowed me to go to the limits that my cowardice would permit. It also kept many doors open to me – I've had some awfully enduring friendships, and even some love from people, some of them straight, who wouldn't have liked it if I'd made a pass at them." I find his candour startling, and clear of apparent complaint. "I did have erotic fantasies about some of them, and they probably knew it, but that was only fair." The puckish smile erupts. "I'm probably the oldest living virgin with dual citizenship."

I listen, occasionally supply a question, and wait. He's still for a while, watching me, then he stirs in his chair. "I'm quite capable of being manipulative," he says. "I know that people can feel trapped by me, but not in such a way that they'd feel unable to escape, just tired. I liked leading someone on who was tense or frightened, but smart enough to be interesting, to the point where he'd be so bored he'd fall asleep." He chortles.

He doesn't strike me as manipulative, but then I'm not a rough athlete. What does he mean? "I learned from my mother to anticipate every wish of the person I wanted to please. It's so easy to confuse being helpful with being intrusive." I listen to his shallow breathing for what seems a long time but is really no more than a minute. It must cost him to talk this much. "On the other hand," he says, "I don't think I've lost more than three or four friends in my life, except through death. They really shouldn't have to go to such lengths to get away from me."

The self-deprecating irony, the filigree phrasing – somewhere deep in this man, a southern belle practises for the cotillion.

The morning after While Edgar fries bacon and eggs for our breakfast, I ask him about Steve. I met him when I arrived, a man in middle age, plainly dressed, who lives in the small house across the yard. I nattered about how hard it was to find the place. He nodded, smiled, and directed me to Edgar's door. "He's expecting you."

In 1971, not long after Edgar bought this place, two hitchhiking students phoned from a gas station up the road to ask if they could stop by for a visit. "I was much more immediately entranced with Ross, a beautiful physical object, and in the beginning I rather undervalued Steve," Edgar says. He invited them to stay a while, in the bedroom off the dining room where I slept last night. The two young men were lovers. When Steve, a gifted pianist, was offered work at a recording studio in Los Angeles, Ross decided to go with him, and Edgar agreed to let another student, a woman, live in the cabin.

Then Ross changed his mind: He wouldn't go west. "Steve came by that evening to talk," says Edgar. "I've never had such overwhelming feelings as I did that night. I told him that of course they had every right to go, it's the American way to move on, and whether or not they made it wasn't my responsibility, it was entirely beyond my control. At the same time, I said, the basic problem here was that one of us simply wasn't being honest. He thought I meant him. Finally I told him that if he left, I would go insane. I had just turned fifty, and I had never met anyone remotely like Steve, no one who affected me that way, neither before nor since. I believed that if I was not able to respond to that, if my own cautions prevented it, it could very well be the last time anything like that would ever happen to me." Steve moved into the house across the yard.

I take it from Edgar's remark about being the oldest living virgin that the two of them haven't been lovers. "No," says Edgar. "The relationship is ... the language for this is so difficult, it's been spoiled by Christians and sentimentalists – it's *organic*. We understand things about each other even when we don't communicate in person. He is my heir. I suppose you could say we live as a family. Considering the difference in age, it has elements of a father-son relationship. Since he arrived at the height of my fame, I think he believed I'd be able to help him more, to open more doors for him. He was disappointed, and angry, I think, when he thought I withheld support of that kind. But I've never had that magic available to use myself, let alone for anyone else." For several years now he has been trying to find a literary agent and someone to publish his autobiography. So far, though he has six books and a long list of articles in major magazines to his name, no doors have opened for him.

Steve comes by in the morning to check on how Edgar is doing and ask if he should take Casey for a run. Casey is a young foxhound; he strikes me as a canine version of the rough athletes that Edgar favours. Edgar consents, gratefully, and Casey is out the door in a flash.

As we sit down to breakfast, Edgar says, "I can't imagine what my life would have been like without Steve. Certainly I would have overeaten, and very likely I would have gone from one superficial relationship to another. A lot of people that I rather liked, Steve couldn't stand. He hates people who strike him as phony. I don't hate them particularly – there are so many of them."

So Steve determines who he should and shouldn't see? Edgar shakes his head. "With some I maintained friendships anyway, with others not. He's also brought in some people, and none that I've ever regretted. Without Steve I would have continued to bounce along, trying to get nectar out of artificial flowers. He, on the other hand, is absolutely real."

Edgar said earlier that if Steve had taken off, he would have gone insane. Yet Steve has done exactly that several times, gone to New York, where Edgar says he had some success as a playwright and screenwriter. "I found that I could let him go. I've even helped him to get away. It comes down to the old cliché: if you love something, let it go, and if it loves you it will eventually come back." Each time the prodigal Steve has returned. "But even though I can let him go," Edgar continues, "I could never foreswear him, that would not be surgically possible. I don't think he could do so with me either. I hope this is not a case of simple dependency. We're careful to live so as to minimize that possibility." A third small building on the land, the Chalet Riel, was once Edgar's study; now it's Steve's.

As if to frame the picture he's painted, Edgar quotes a character in T.S. Eliot's *The Cocktail Party*: "Why speak of love? We're used to each other. I never thought I should be happier with another person."

The one thing I've been shy to inquire about is Edgar's health. But given my nosiness in other matters at least as personal, and his remarkable candour, that seems foolish. His condition is called congestive heart failure. It sounds catastrophic, but he says it's actually a reprieve. By the mid-1980s he could hardly walk a city block without losing his breath, and in cold weather he had to wear a respirator. Then in 1986 he had a pacemaker installed and underwent bypass surgery to head off a heart attack. "Though it's certainly uncomfortable to have your breast cut open like a chicken, and veins extracted from your thighs, the relief was immediate," he says. "This way the capacity of the heart just gets less and less, until eventually you die of what used to be called the old man's friend, pneumonia. I'm told it's one of the best ways to go."

Does he fear death? "I'm horrified by it," he replies, "but it doesn't seem rational to be afraid of absolutely nothing, does it? I can't get over associating it with darkness and imagining it as extremely lonely. Loneliness has always been a factor in my life. If I could get over thinking of death in those ways, I don't suppose I'd be afraid of it."

But wouldn't each of those experiences, darkness and loneliness, require some degree of consciousness? "Well, that's the thing. It doesn't make any sense at all." Suddenly his boyish smile appears. "In a *New Yorker* cartoon two people are talking, and one of them says, No, of course I don't want to live forever, but I don't want to be dead forever either." He laughs his breathless laugh.

On 2 June 2000, Edgar Friedenberg's heart stopped.

Afterlife "What is homosexuality, anyway?" Edgar asks in "The Resources of Gaiety." "It is infinitely variable; while the very act of treating it as a phenomenon to be explained is itself an act, conscious or not, of bigotry. Homosexuality is not a phenomenon. It is a view of reality that has serious consequences. It can be and often is enormously subversive, for it calls into question our prevailing concept of maturity. Ultimately, straight society needs our perception that maturity itself is as much a political as a biological concept."

Here was Edgar Z. Friedenberg's most subversive, most enduring work. With his cookie jar always full and his blankets laid protectively over the vulnerable young, he chipped away at the stony heart of the beast that forces boys to mature into generals, popes, and CEOs. This, he believed, was his calling, both as an educator and as a queer national.

The Vanishing Adolescent ends with a plea that is no less compelling in our own dark age than it was in 1959: "What is needed is no program of technical training-cum-indoctrination, but the patient development of the kind of character and mind that conceives of itself too clearly to consent to its own betrayal. The greatest safeguard to any democracy is a continuing community of self-respecting young people who understand and accept their relationship to society. The basic unit of such a community is a stable self to respect."

6 I've Looked at Life from Both Sides Now

The gender apparent SHORTLY AFTER ANITA MOSHER learned to talk, she informed her mother that she was a boy. "No, Anita," said her mother, "you are a girl."

"No,"Anita insisted, "I a boy."

Ultimately such things were not debatable in a strict Roman Catholic household in small-town Nova Scotia, certainly not in the late 1950s. They were decided by God, not by small children. And too much candour could have terrifying consequences; an aunt of Anita's was put away frequently in the mental hospital. "I knew if I dared open my mouth too much, that's where I'd end up too," Kent Mosher recalls. "I knew I wasn't crazy, but I also knew in some fundamental way that I wasn't a girl." Anita became the neighbourhood tomboy, an acceptable role for a young girl. She would grow out of it, everyone agreed, when puberty hit.

She did and she didn't. Says Kent, "When I was about nine years old, terrible, terrible things started happening to me. I started menses very early, and was absolutely horrified by it. Things started growing that I didn't understand, and didn't want. Trying to stop it, I wore bras so tight that I still have the scars to show for it." It didn't work. By the time Anita was twelve, boys had already assigned her to the realm of girls and would no longer play with her. At the same time, she remained too much a tomboy for other girls, who were quickly absorbing the lessons of proper womanhood. Very soon Anita had no friends at all, and thought of suicide. Instead, says Kent, "around thirteen I decided, all right, if that's what you want, then that's what I'll do, I'll be a girl. I let my hair grow, wore dresses, dated boys, I did the whole thing."

Anita had no problem getting dates. "I was a good-looking female, I passed quite well. I became quite active sexually – in fact, I was fairly promiscuous. But I would do everything I could to avoid being completely naked. I couldn't bear to see myself like that. If I looked in a mirror, undressed, I tried not to see anything from the neck down. I also tried to accept that body, but all that happened was the gap between my mind and my body kept getting wider."

By the time she was twenty, Anita's career as a girl had become intolerable. Then she heard the astonishing news that doctors now had the means to change a person's sex, but this option remained far out of reach. "I had no information about it, I couldn't have begun to afford it, and I didn't feel anywhere near strong enough to find out more, let alone *do* anything about it." Her brother's wife worked in a psychiatric hospital, and the horror stories she told were sharp reminders to Anita that when people's sense of reality conflicts with the dominant one, they do well to bite their tongue.

No longer able to be a girl, and not seeing how she could become a boy, for the next decade Anita did her best to be neither. "Basically I was asexual. I figured if nuns like the ones who taught me in school could do it, so could I." She cut her hair as short as she dared. She gained weight. "I did it quite deliberately to de-emphasize the breasts, both so I wouldn't have to look at them myself and also to turn off men." Kent laughs. "Didn't work. Couldn't shake them off, those men."

Almost thirty years after she'd told her mother she was a boy, Anita finally came out to someone else: the family doctor. He sent her to a psychiatrist in Halifax who made only one comment that Kent can recall: You'd look ridiculous as a man, so you might just as well drop the whole idea. "After all I'd gone through, I was so shocked to be dismissed like that, I walked out. That was another turning point for me, or I guess you might say a lesson. If that's all I could expect from medical types, well, then, forget it. I was back where I started, more or less."

Another decade passed. Anita/Kent went to sea as a marine research technician, then trained as a nurse, moved to Alberta in the '80s boom, and found work at the hospital in Grande Prairie, a few hours' drive northwest of Edmonton. On his fortieth birthday Kent put a classified ad in the local paper: Transsexual interested in meeting others. Two transvestites called. One of them put him in touch with the Illusions Club in Calgary, a support group for male cross-dressers and transsexuals. At their recommendation he contacted Dr J.J. Miles.

In September 1994 Dr Miles did an assessment and ran a series of psychological tests. He found that Kent had a deep hatred of his current body sex ("Surprise, surprise," says Kent) and was, the doctor concluded, a true transsexual. Kent Mosher had what psychiatrists call a Gender Identity Disorder.

My bag of tricks Though Russell Stephen Schofield's gender journey would veer sharply in middle age, the earlier stages went more smoothly than Kent's. Russell grew up comfortably in North Vancouver and followed his father's footsteps into sales and marketing in the male-dominated technical service industries. At twenty-one he married Barbara; they moved to Kamloops and Russell fathered a daughter, Sarah, and a son, Justin. In his own father's eyes – his parents separated when he was seventeen – Russell was a model son, a success in every way. He had a good career, a good relationship with a lovely wife, two fine children, a big house, two cars. As a man in a man's world, he passed with flying colours.

From the inside, however, the view was a little different. "I always felt like an interloper, a trespasser, somehow in the wrong place," says Stephany Lynn Schofield. "I've always preferred the company of women, and I've never had much interest in men, either as friends or as role models. But I didn't know why. I could never have identified gender as the issue. I didn't have the information then, or even the language." Russell's family certainly never encouraged candour in such matters. "We weren't accustomed to dealing with complex issues of any sort. So all this vague, undefined confusion I felt, I could never speak any of it for fear of ridicule and rejection." Career, marriage, and children added further barriers. "It was unthinkable to do anything drastic that would majorly disrupt all that. So there you are, stuck. You live a false existence, and you keep putting off the changes you have to make if you've ever going to be you."

On business trips he carried what Stephany calls "my bag of tricks," the make-up and clothes he'd accumulated on the sly, the means to turn Russell into Stephany. "The only time I'd ever do it was in my hotel room. I would have been terrified even to think of venturing out, for fear I'd be spotted as a pervert. I relished those times so much, the chance to be myself, but as soon as it was over I'd feel dirty and perverted again." In his forty-third year Russell told Barbara that he needed to try living on his own. "I was still much too ashamed to tell her the real reason. But I did think that by then the kids were old enough to survive any upheaval that a trial separation might cause."

On his own for the next eighteen months, Russell continued his transformation. He signed on with a psychologist, the same woman his wife was seeing. After an interview with transgender activist Roxanne Hastings (more on her in chapter 24), he joined the Illusions Club in Edmonton, where he had moved with his family several years before. He devoured books, magazines, anything he could find on transgender. "I kept bursting into tears with the recognition, as all these things that I'd buried started to surface. It was an incredible sense of awakening." On Tuesday night, 6 January 1996, for the first time he stepped out of his apartment as Stephany. I expect to hear butterfly metaphors, but Stephany laughs. "I shudder to think what I must have looked like, it must have been ghastly!" She survived her debut at the gay bar and went back, again and again, eventually working there as a bartender.

In due course Russell decided to come out to his wife. It was a classic exchange. I have something to tell you, he said. Is it another woman? she asked. The other woman, said Russell, is me. He handed Barbara a photo of Stephany. Barbara was speechless.

"You have to understand," says Stephany, "this had been a pretty traditional type of relationship. After the kids were born, my wife stayed home, she baked cookies and played housewife. This was a huge shock for her." He could have argued, but didn't, that as a man he had been faithful; in the few sexual encounters he'd had with men, he had been Stephany, "a girl in a heterosexual relationship."

Over the next few months the psychologist worked with each of them. One evening Barbara invited Russell home for a birthday dinner. She took him aside and handed him a gift. The card read, "To Stephany with love from Barbara." The gift was a pair of panties, in the correct size. "Of course I burst into tears," says Stephany. "This was a degree of acceptance far beyond anything I had expected."

After dinner, Russell told the kids. "I'll never forget the look on Sarah's face. She went absolutely white and just stared. Justin looked away, looked back, and then he asked, 'Does this mean you're gay?'" Russell explained that his struggle with gender identity was quite separate from sexual orientation. And that was that.

Russell and Barbara decided to reunite and bought a house in Edmonton. In his work life as a consultant on control systems for heating and ventilation facilities, Russell continued to function as a man. "That's a very male-oriented industry, and there's no way I could go in there as a girl. It would have made both me and my clients very uncomfortable." But in the sanctuary of his own home, he lived more and more as Stephany, in her clothes, her wigs, and her make-up, shaving her body. Within a couple of months the tension of this daily shape-shift began to tell on both Russell/Stephany and Barbara. Finally in late summer 1997 Russell went to a psychiatrist specializing in gender identity. After a series of interviews and tests, he was diagnosed as having a Gender Identity Disorder. Stephany puts it more simply: "I was born one way, and programmed another."

Transition I arrived rather nervous for my encounters with both Kent Mosher in Red Deer and Stephany Schofield in Edmonton, even more so than usual with strangers. In our prior contacts by e-mail, both seemed pleasant, confident, and open. But I had never actually met a transgendered person face to face, at least as far as I knew. The qualifier is relevant; a startling number of heteros still make the same claim about homos.

It's not the politics of transgender that make me nervous. Until 1973 the influential American Psychiatric Association still included homosexuality on its list of mental illnesses and disorders. It took two decades of effective pressure to get us off that damning list, and though some primitive shrinks still cling to the disorder notion, the vast majority have come to understand that the only real disorder associated with homosexuality is the fear and loathing of it. On the matter of transgender, our society and its mental arbiter, official psychiatry, have evolved to about where they stood on homosexuality before 1973. Given the parallel, I have nothing but respect for the courageous individuals who will nudge, push, and kick the remaining barriers out of the way.

Still, I was apprehensive. From birth we learn the markers of gender before any other human distinction. Though colour or race might give it close competition, it is surely the first thing we notice about each other. Girl/boy, man/woman – these categories are highly charged. Two women friends report that when people mistake their cherubic curly haired boy-baby for a girl, some fall over themselves apologizing – I'm so sorry, I should have known – as if they'd committed a huge indignity against both parents and child. Though we homos, some of us at least, can play exuberantly on the borders of gender, we have the comfort of knowing where they are, more or less. The butchest of dykes still registers in some mysterious way as a woman, the flamingest of queens as a man. Transgender is something else.

Kent Mosher meets me at the Greyhound station in Red Deer. He's a large man, still carrying much of the weight that Anita gained to ward off men, and soft-spoken, clearly on the gentle side of the male spectrum. The house he shares with his partner, A.J., is newly built and sits on the edge of a large construction site backed by muddy fields. The house next door is half built, and the fields will soon be plowed under and planted with more houses. It's been an unusually wet spring for southern Alberta, with steady rain day after day. The two shi-tzus don't get out much – they'd be up to their long-haired necks in mud.

Born in the United States, A.J. taught French for a while, then signed up with the U.S. Army for five years, "basically playing games," she says, in West Germany. "Though I hadn't done anything about my sexuality up to then, I was attracted to the army partly because I knew somehow that I'd find other gay people there, people like me. I guess I was a little naive. It was terribly stifling, with the constant threat of witch-hunts keeping everyone, including me, deeply hidden."

After leaving the army she trained as a dental hygienist in Georgia, then happened to spot an ad: the United Church of Canada was seeking a dental hygienist to work in Newfoundland. She got the job, travelling from one outport to the next with the church's dental program for kids. "I still kept putting my sexuality off as something I would get to when the time was right," she says. Out of a job when her contract ended in 1986, she took the route of many Newfoundlanders, moving west to look for work. In Grande Prairie, unemployed, she finally decided the time was right. She contacted the local gay group, and a member introduced her to Anita Mosher.

"For me it was love at first sight," says Kent. He was still passing as Anita (coincidentally, the same first name as A.J.), but a couple of weeks after they met he came out to her as Kent. He told her he did not identify as gay and that his attraction towards her was that of a man for a woman. Some day, when the time was right, he said, he would pursue a sex change. Apparently A.J. absorbed these revelations with remarkable calm. "I come from a background where tolerance for everyone was valued," she says. "Since I was really interested in this person I'd just met, I figured why not hang around and see what they're like. Also, I was just coming out myself, just getting used to this new label, 'lesbian.' In Kent I found someone willing to accept me as I am, so I thought he deserved no less from me in return."

A work in progress In January 1996, Kent began hormone therapy. These complex, potent chemicals regulate secondary sexual characteristics such as body hair, breast growth, voice, and the distribution of muscle and fat. Bi-weekly intramuscular injections of testosterone, in a suspension of food-grade oil, produce noticeable changes within a few months, each of them a herald of physiological maleness. Body hair starts to appear first and continues to crop up in new places for several years. Muscle and bone density increase fairly rapidly. The clitoris grows. The voice begins to deepen, and settles to its new level within a year or so. (Kent sounds to me like a light tenor.) Fat distribution shifts, usually from thighs and hips to sides and gut. Recently Kent has been diagnosed as prediabetic and told that he has to shed weight, but so far the protective bulk he put on as Anita just won't go away. "Trouble is," he says, "testosterone raises the insulin level, and insulin fosters the depositing of fat, which makes it that much harder to lose weight. But I haven't come this far just to die, so I'm working on it."

Injecting testosterone carries other risks: migraines, high blood pressure, liver and heart disease. Also, since ligaments and tendons develop more slowly than the muscles and bones they connect, the risk of injury in the first two years of hormone therapy is considerable. Kent has to be particularly careful; six years ago, pre-testosterone, he injured his back and since then he's been on long-term disability. There are other discomforts. "The gear I have to wear to flatten the boobs makes it harder to breathe," he says. "Right now, so I could talk comfortably, I've taken it off." But he considers discomfort a small price to pay for the evident changes. "I've masculinized quite well. Now I've reached the point where I can pass as a male in the outside world. This is exactly what I've always wanted."

Kent Mosher strikes me as a work in progress. But he and I have just met, we have no history, no great expectations. A.J., on the other hand, defines herself as a lesbian. She entered this relationship, her first, with a person that she assumed was another woman. Surely such profound changes in her partner must challenge her capacity for tolerance. "Well," she says, with a little pause, "maybe this sounds odd, but when the changes started I had already bonded with the individual, so the physical thing, the body, has really had secondary importance for me. And this person has what I would regard as both male and female characteristics, which perhaps makes it easier. He's very intuitive, he can size up people and situations pretty fast. And his philosophy, his belief that things will work out, that's very comforting to me too." She smiles, and shrugs. "What can I say, I like the guy. He's on a real interesting journey, and I'm happy to travel along with him."

I just want to be a girl Stephany Schofield started her hormone therapy in September 1997. "The first night I took estrogen, I could read the disturbance on the faces of my wife and daughter," she says. (Justin was away.) "They wanted to know where this would end up, how would it affect us? I had no idea. All I could say was, at this point I have to do this, I can't go back." For Stephany the effects were immediate and tidal. "Within forty-eight hours I felt as if I were being flushed of something huge. It was quite strange, like an out-of-body experience, which is not surprising when you introduce such a powerful foreign substance into your body."

To complement the estrogen, her endocrinologist prescribed a drug that stops the uptake of testosterone, further reducing such male characteristics as body hair. Though her breasts didn't grow, they became more sensitive. Then progesterone was added to the regime. "Due to my age, the doctor was very cautious with that," says

Stephany. "After all, you're trying to reverse forty-five years of hormonal impact in a couple of years. They watch closely for a tendency to blood clots, and at the first sign of that, you're cut off immediately." Stephany sailed through.

The emotional journey was not so easy. For Barbara, the changes became too unsettling, and over the next ten months their relationship disintegrated. "It didn't end well," says Stephany, "though I don't know there's much either of us could have done differently." In December 1998 Stephany moved out of the family home and found an apartment for herself in the valley of the North Saskatchewan River that cuts through the centre of Edmonton. The place looks as if it had been furnished more by function than design, with things to sit on and eat off, a table for the computer. It has the temporary feel of a stopping-off place for someone who's passing through.

"Those first few months on my own were hard," says Stephany. "I wavered between joy over the enormous changes I was experiencing, and loneliness and pain over the loss of a twenty-five year relationship with my best friend. I also felt terribly guilty about the chaos I'd created, both for her and my children. Several times I thought of suicide."

The changes kept Stephany going. With her testosterone down to the normal range for a female, her breasts were growing. Approval for surgery came through, which meant that provincial medical insurance would fund the costly operation. "Normally they make you wait two full years before surgery, during which you have to live full time as a woman. They call this the 'real life test.' But if you're okayed by two psychiatrists and your endocrinologist, one year will do it."

When I meet Stephany, she's wearing a loose dark shirt over tights, her hair casually tangled. Her life has levelled out. It has also changed immeasurably, she says. "I went from being quite career oriented, with a big house, two cars and so on, to working six days a week at the Leather Ranch, earning $5.65 an hour and barely able to get by. Beyond rent, food, and the clothes I wear, that's it, there are no extras."

Over the past few years she had sent out more than 100 applications for jobs, starting with the sales and marketing positions so familiar to Russell. No one called back. As she evolved into Stephany she went after jobs with less public contact, in administration and marketing support. Still no calls. Finally she resorted to the employment office and eventually found the Leather Ranch. "They knew I was transsexual," she says. "I believe I was hired on my ability and experience, but I also suspect they may have seen me as something of a tourist attraction." With a $40,000 debt, and earning minimum wage, Stephany saw no alternative but to declare bankruptcy. "That," she says quietly, "was a very hard pill to swallow."

In shedding Russell, she also left behind his social life. "It became impossible to stay connected to the couples from my married life. These are people who sit around in upper middle-class living rooms and talk casually about how we should load all the homos onto a barge and send them out to sea." At the Illusions Club she got to know some of the people Russell's former friends would have dispatched, especially the transvestites and transsexuals. "When I was working at the bar, I had a lot of fun with some pretty crazy drag queens. But I realized after a while that the bar scene wasn't the right place for me either – too late, too many cigarettes, too much drinking. Basically I just want to be a girl, with a normal life."

Her daughter, Sarah, lives with her now, and Justin will join them next week. As I arrive to talk with Stephany, Sarah is heading out on a date, with her girlfriend. Stephany smiles. "That's the other side of all the turmoil I caused. It also gave my wife and children an opportunity to explore in ways they might never have done otherwise. When Barbara realized that some aspects of my femaleness actually attracted her, she was able to acknowledge her own bisexuality. Justin went out with a transvestite for a while, though now he's with a woman. And Sarah has come to terms with being a lesbian. It seems the changes I was making allowed them to feel okay about exploring too. That's the best gift I could have given them."

In year one of hormone therapy, Stephany responded to a want ad at Alternative Connections, an Internet matching service: Forty-seven year old male in Sacramento, California, seeks relationship with mature female-to-male transsexual. "Unlike some of the other ads, this one seemed interested in more than the exotic, more than just a chick with a dick." She sent an e-mail, he wrote back, and within days the e-mails were flying. They exchanged phone numbers, ran up some heavy bills, sent photos. Stephany invited him up for a visit. "I wasn't overwhelmed by his looks from the photo," she admits, "but Richard has a wonderful energy, he's kind and gentle, and we really hit it off. We made love for a whole week. I was on cloud nine. He had no interest at all in what hangs between my legs."

Towards the end of his visit Richard said he'd like to see the famous West Edmonton Mall. Stephany agreed, then started to have doubts. "I don't pass all the time, I have no illusions about that. I don't wear wigs anymore, but I'm still in transition, and I'm no centrefold. That's okay when I'm on my own, but with Richard – well, anyway, out we went. As soon as we got on the street, he grabbed my hand, and that was that. He never blinked, he never faltered for a moment in validating me as a girl."

A certain amount of anxiety over passing is clearly not out of place. "Though I've never been assaulted, I have had horrible remarks thrown at me," Stephany says, "and friends of mine have been beaten up, right in front of gay bars. Late one night in a restaurant I was sitting quietly with another transsexual and someone threw a lit cigarette butt into her hair. I'm not naive. I could be killed for being who I am." For a while Stephany joined the campaign for transgender rights, going to rallies, writing letters, working with the provincial NDP gay, lesbian, and TS caucus. "But I'm fed up with fighting," she says. "I just want a quiet, normal, everyday life, with my family around me for Christmas, that sort of thing."

Richard came up for another visit over Christmas and met Sarah. They got along just fine, says Stephany. When she flew down to Sacramento in February, Stephany's legal name-change hadn't come through, and she crossed the border as Russell. "It was so strange," she says. "It felt like I was doing drag." She was comfortable with Richard's two kids, who are about the same age as hers. "I'm in love with him," she says. "It's a fairy tale. I could never have imagined anything like this. I really thought I'd end up alone." When Richard asked her to marry him, she accepted. "On one stipulation," she says with a grin. "I'm going to the altar as a virgin. In white."

The business of the penis Early in Kent's transition a woman came by the house to collect data for the Canada census. A.J. went to the door and answered a few questions. "And the man of the house?" the woman asked. "Well . . . " said A.J., unsure how to proceed. This was Alberta, where the government steadfastly refused to include sexual orientation in the provincial Human Rights Code, let alone transgender. The woman asked again, so A.J. called Kent. The woman took one look at him and her eyes widened. She gulped, closed her file, and fled.

By now Kent and A.J. tend to be regarded as a heterosexual couple. "They don't have a clue," says Kent. "I guess that's what people do, they read the cover, not the book. We just sit back and chuckle." In fact he's delighted to be acknowledged as a man. "When I take the van into the garage for repairs, and the mechanic says 'Hi, guy,' it really makes my day." The only downside he's discovered so far is in the men's washroom. "They're a *mess.* It's not a lot to ask – please, fellas, couldn't you learn to *aim* better?"

At which point I bring up the business of the penis. Technically, Kent has three choices: to live with an enlarged clitoris, or to undergo a metaoidioplasty or a phalloplasty. In a metaoidioplasty, the simpler of the two surgeries, the enlarged clitoris is freed up to function more as a penis, and a scrotal sack is constructed with testicular implants. A urethral extension can also be built to allow peeing from the penis, but this procedure carries a heightened risk of infections, fistulas, and further surgery to deal with the complications. A phalloplasty is a series of operations using tissue grafts from other parts of the body to construct a penis. Since the new penis doesn't get erect or flaccid on its own, Teflon inserts or pumps can help in achieving erections. Phalloplasty costs a lot more than metaoidioplasty, leaves extensive scarring where the grafts were taken, and can take much longer to heal.

Knowing all this, and also that before any surgeon would agree to operate, Kent would have to lose a significant amount of weight, I wonder if having a penis is worth all that to him. I've never understood why men, both gay and straight, worship the phallus. Since I'm not much concerned about sowing my seed, I experience my own penis as sometimes convenient, sometimes quite vulnerable, and capable of both giving and receiving pleasure. These do not seem to me grounds for worship. Easy for me to say, I suppose, having had the thing since birth.

Kent nods. "One of our FTM community leaders argues that it's not the penis that makes the man, it's the whole package, the whole being. But even if you're a genetic male, and let's say your penis is blown off in a war – technically speaking you would still be a male, but wouldn't you want it back?" He raises his eyebrows: it's not a rhetorical question.

"Well," I answer, "probably. But I'd also want my hand back, or my eye. More so, I expect."

"In any case," says Kent, "it sure would make the man that I am feel complete and whole to have one."

Someone's wife The appendage that Kent wants is the same one Stephany will shed in her surgery. "Essentially they castrate you," she says, casually, in a tone that implies nothing more daunting than a good enema. "They use portions of the scrotum to create the labia, build a vagina out of the hollowed-out penis, inverted and stuffed up inside you into the cavity we all have." The procedure takes four to eight hours. Over the next few months, while the incisions heal, she will have to use a stent, a medical dildo, to ensure that the new vagina doesn't collapse. "I'm told that sexual performance varies with the individual," she says, "but I don't particularly care, now that I've discovered I can achieve orgasm in my own way. I know that whatever I do – the surgery, the years of laser to get rid of facial hair – I'll never be a genetic woman. So what? I just love being, and being accepted as a woman."

She and Richard will marry in Edmonton, and Stephany will move south to live with him in Sacramento. "Imagine that," she says. "I'll be someone's wife! I'll become a U.S. citizen, we'll buy a house, and we'll have a normal suburban relationship. Richard would be happy for me to stay home, but though I do like to cook and bake, I don't think I'd be satisfied to be a full-time housewife. I think it's healthy for both people to have things going on outside their relationship that challenge them. I expect I'll write."

In their parallel journeys from one gender to another, Stephany and Kent have each made a similar discovery. "It's a man's world," says Stephany, "Men make all the major decisions, they rule the world. You don't notice it when you're a man, it's just normal, the way things are. Now I see it from a totally different perspective."

So does Kent. "As a female I often felt victimized and taken for granted, I hardly ever felt like I was taken seriously. That's not been my experience at all as a man. In most situations you're just automatically treated with more respect. And that's especially true if you're fat. A fat male can expect to be treated *much* better than a fat female. So there you go – to become a feminist I had to become a man!"

I have to ask each of them: any regrets, any sense of loss? "The lost years," says Kent. "But there's nothing to be gained by dwelling on that, is there? I know I'm here for a reason, and my time isn't over yet. I still have work to do."

"If I could have made these changes in my teens, I would have avoided thirty years of hormonal patterning," says Stephany. "And I'd be free of things that keep reminding me how long I carried that other gender. But what's the point of obsessing about all that? Outwardly I don't mind if people think of me as a transsexual. Inwardly, I'm just a girl. That's all I ever wanted."

7 Mr Right

Hal and George IN MID-WINTER OF 1989, HAL HINDS, A PROfessor of biology and botany at the University of New Brunswick, went out with some friends to Dance Trax, then the only gay bar in Fredericton. At fifty-two he was "between people," separated from his wife, and his male lover having married a woman. "I watched this lovely bearded man for some time and finally I asked him to dance," he says. "He turned me down flat!"

George Flanders, the lovely bearded man, suggested they go someplace quieter and have a beer. He was twenty-two, on a student exchange from his hometown in Maine, studying international affairs at the university in Fredericton. Says Hal, "So we started an international affair right away. I asked him if he wanted to see my waterbed."

The waterbed is George's now, but mine for my brief visit. It's my first ride on one of these contraptions, and I imagine that sex on it must require a fine sense of balance.

When he was four, in rural Massachusetts, Hal began to discover the joy of sex with other boys. "Nothing was forced. I enjoyed nearly all of it; in fact it was usually me who'd start it. I don't remember ever having felt any guilt about sex, but as I became older it got harder to find buddies willing to do it with me. And then I began to see that some people had a real hang-up about it, and therefore you had to be discreet."

His other love was the forest. "I practically lived in the woods, became very agile in the trees, and got to know all the plants and birds." After a tour of duty in the U.S. Army, he taught at Smith College, worked summers as the first naturalist on the Cape Cod seashore, and wrote his first book, *Wildflowers of Cape Cod.*

There were sexual adventures, and a passionate love affair with a man that collapsed after a year or so. "What I really craved but couldn't seem to find was one long-lasting relationship, a marriage really." He found it in his first romantic liaison with a woman, Judy. They married and had two children, and in the early 1970s moved north to a run-down farm in central New Brunswick. There they lived off the land for the next few years. By then Hal was missing his work as a botanist, so he got a job demonstrating in the botany lab at the University of New Brunswick. Soon he was managing the university herbarium where specimens of the provincial flora are housed, and working on a massive book project, a technical guide to the flora of New Brunswick. It would take a decade to complete.

Meanwhile, at a bar in Saint John he met Dan. The younger man drove up to the farm on weekends. "It must have been awful for Judy, not knowing why this distance was growing between us," Hal says. After nine years the marriage finally dissolved; Judy and the kids moved to Maine. "It was hard to be without the children. It felt almost like a death in the family." Dan came to live with him on the farm, then went off to marry and have children himself. In time Hal and Judy renewed their friendship, and the two children spent their growing-up summers with their father, tagging along on botanical searches.

In the early 1980s Hal sold the farm and moved to Fredericton, where he helped start FLAG, Fredericton Lesbians and Gays. Through most of the decade FLAG organized educational and social events, including dances that drew people from all over the province.

In mid-decade, with more and more gay men in the province getting sick and dying of AIDS, several people gathered in Hal's living room to launch AIDS New Brunswick. It was a grass-roots movement to counter the vicious discrimination that people with HIV and AIDS were encountering, to lobby for government funding, and to keep medical professionals up to date on treatment options as they evolved. Hal also launched the Nature Trust of New Brunswick, to protect significant and vulnerable areas, and a province-wide mushroom club. "I'm big on starting things," he says with a laugh, "but not so good at sustaining them." Along the way, he met George.

George Flanders had been sexually active since grade school, usually drawn to older boys and men but never without shame. "With Hal I finally started to see for the first time that there was no reason to be ashamed. That was a big change for me." There would be others. Not long after George checked out Hal's waterbed, Hal informed him that he'd recently tested positive for HIV.

"We had been very careful, very safe," says Hal, "but when things started to get serious, of course I had to tell him."

This was George's first encounter with HIV. "I was quite alarmed," he says. "I was fearful for myself, but even more so for him. But I guess I got over that fairly quickly. I knew it might cause difficulties later, but by this time I was falling in love with him, and it was too late."

Hal smiles. "I think George was very brave. He never shirked, not once. He's always been there, no matter what happened." A month after they met, George moved into Hal's house, a short walk from the university.

In 1991 they exchanged vows, and earrings, at a commitment ceremony in their backyard. Three years later George applied for landed immigrant status on humanitarian and compassionate grounds. "They accepted me as an independent immigrant, but really it was on the basis of our being a couple. We had letters of support from friends and from my family, and we were able to show how we shared our finances." George volunteered at AIDS New Brunswick and now works there full time.

At sixty-four, Hal has survived two serious bouts of illness due to the HIV. He's a little gaunt but otherwise looks fine. "I'm pretty pragmatic about treatment," he says. "I do what seems to work." That includes a complex round of drugs to be taken every eight hours, some of them prophylactics to ward off infection. He plans to go on a drug holiday in the early summer to give his body a rest. "It means facing a lot of unknowns, but I'm in relatively good health, and as a scientist I feel I should test the possibilities rather than simply going along with the existing regime. For example, I sometimes wonder if by stressing the body, the drugs themselves might actually make you more susceptible to opportunistic infection."

George has reservations. "I absolutely understand his desire to be free of the drugs, but I want to make sure he talks to his doctor first."

Hal nods. "I will, I will. I know that if anything were to go wrong, of course it would impinge on George. So I do recognize the need for caution."

A really nice coexistence Early in their relationship Hal and George chose to be non-monogamous, and they've sorted out the rules as they went. "If he's away on a trip, I feel it's important that he enjoys company and sex with nice people," says Hal. "The same goes for me if I'm away. Life is too short to miss out on opportunities to experience other people." The away rule is to avoid small-town gossip, he says, which can be far more upsetting than the actual encounter. "The way we work it, you can tell the other about the encounter or not, whatever seems right. The guiding principle is that it mustn't compromise our relationship."

While Hal and George were on a vacation in Vancouver a couple of years back, George found that he wanted to spend more time with a man he'd met at the baths. "Basically my hormones took over," he says.

"I could understand that perfectly well," says Hal. "Our age difference is a factor, I know that, it's why I can forgive and forget. But in this case, suddenly he didn't want to be doing things with me, and that took away from our vacation together. I felt he was being really inconsiderate, and that very nearly broke it. I moved out of our hotel room. We managed to talk our way slowly back, but it was close."

To talk peace, there has to be some recognizable common ground. What was it for them? I ask. They look at each other. Neither says anything. I try another tack: What makes their relationship work, what sustains it? George laughs, embarrassed. Hal says, "I'm interested to hear what you have to say about that."

After a moment George replies, "The most important thing is that we love each other. He's had quite a profound positive influence on my life. He helped me to accept myself, and I think I've matured a lot with him. We've developed a really nice co-existence."

"Oh, it's more than that," says Hal. "I've never been much attracted to younger men, but it's been a delight to have this sweet young thing around. He's handsome, he's intelligent, and we can converse as equals, not having to talk up or down to each other. Each of us has included the other quite intimately in his life. It would be really traumatic to pull that apart. I know such things happen, it's always a possibility. But . . . " He leaves it at that.

In early spring Hal works half days in his greenhouse off the kitchen, starting hundreds of seedlings for the garden that rambles up a long, gentle slope behind the house. He specializes in primroses, growing hundreds of varieties from several continents. The rest of the day he works in his office, revising his book on the flora of New Brunswick.

I watch the two of them cook dinner together, smoothly dividing tasks. From George's wine cellar, a cool room they built in a corner of the kitchen, he selects a favourite Chilean red. Wine is one of George's passions. "Good concentration," he says. "Do you notice the hints of coffee, even mint?"

Tim and Richard In 1975 Richard Fung and Tim McCaskell met in a place far removed from the smoke and heat of a bar – the Marxist Institute in Toronto. Tim was coordinating a night course on gay liberation, and Richard signed up for it. His journey began in Trinidad, where he grew up Chinese and Catholic, then took him to private school in Ireland, then to Toronto where he sought aversion shock therapy to "cure" his homosexuality. The therapist helped him to another kind of cure, coming out. "I was very lucky and just happened onto a good therapist," he says. "Last year, twenty-five years later, I sent him a thank-you note."

Richard came out intellectually and politically before he did sexually, and found his first sex partners in the gay studies group. At first he assumed Tim must be straight. "He was so butch, in boots and plaid shirt and jeans, I didn't see how anyone so aesthetically challenged could be gay!" In due course he invited Tim to dinner at his apartment. "We had sex that night," says Tim. He looks at Richard. "Didn't we?" Richard nods.

Tim McCaskell grew up in rural Ontario and went to Carleton University in Ottawa where he joined the anti-war movement. He worked for a radical newspaper in Toronto, then travelled in the Middle East, India, and South America, searching for sparks of revolution. In the summer of '74, back in Toronto, he came out. When his communal house unravelled a year later, he and Richard formed a new one with Tim's sister Lisa and two other friends. Over the next fifteen years, with various members, it became well known as a vibrant hub of gay community organizing. I remember parties at 188 Seaton, a giddy mix of cruising, gossip, and radical ferment. "The house provided most of our social interaction," says Richard. "Also, because each person only had to cook once a week, it gave you lots of time to do the things you really wanted to."

Their work evolved in parallel along the border between culture and politics. Richard worked in community cable TV and development education. For more than a decade he's been writing, making independent videos on race and sexuality, and teaching at various academic and cultural institutions in Canada and the United States. He calls his long list of writing credits "academic lite."

"Which means," says Tim, "that you can actually *read* it."

Richard smiles. "Tim is not my toughest critic. Usually he'll just say 'Oh, it's fine.' But I always test out my views on him, which is very helpful for my work in general."

For nearly two decades Tim has worked in the Equal Opportunity Office at the Toronto Board of Education, addressing inequities due to race, gender, social class, and sexual orientation. In the dark age of Tory Ontario, his program, now more safely titled the Equity Studies Centre, has to contend with slashed funding and more aggressive opposition but continues to do what it can. "I like young people," says Tim. "I like their idealism, and I enjoy helping them to focus their energy on changing the world." He credits Richard with broadening his own perspective. "Without him it would have been much harder to develop the understanding I have of how and why racism works, which is pretty central to what I do at the board."

Both of them have also been immersed in community organizing. While Richard helped establish a support network for gay Asians in Toronto, Tim has been deeply involved in the legendary gay liberation journal *The Body Politic,* the Right to Privacy Committee, formed in 1981 after massive police raids on several Toronto baths, and then AIDS Action Now. "By 1987 so many people were sick and dying, it was clear that the Canadian state needed a good kick in the ass to deal with the crisis," he says. "It was also clear that we needed a new kind of AIDS organization to ensure that the real issues got articulated – discrimination, hospital care, research, access to experimental treatments, all of that."

AIDS would have a seismic impact on their world. "My circle has changed radically," says Richard. "Most of my friends from the late '80s and early '90s, a whole generation of gay Asian activists – all but two of us are dead." Tim was diagnosed HIV positive in 1986 but believes he contracted the virus at least a couple of years before. "Though I didn't have much of an immune system left by then, for some reason I didn't seem to get particularly sick. We had so little information, no one knew what to expect." He maintained the vegetarian diet he'd started at nineteen and the exercise regime he'd followed for almost as long, took heavy vitamin supplements, and resisted anti-viral drugs with their brutal side-effects as long as he dared. "I've tended to direct my own treatment from the start. You could probably say that AIDS Action Now saved my life, by keeping me up to date on all the research advances."

Tim's diagnosis frightened Richard, but with the passage of time it has become a simple fact of their life together. "There are certain things you just do," says Richard. "We try to eat dinner by seven, for example, so Tim doesn't have to get up in the middle of the night to take his pills. There's also this sense of his own invincibility that's pretty typical of Tim, with his Presbyterian-rock type of personality. That seems to be infectious, so I've just come to assume he's invincible too!"

Post-monogamy As long as marriage has been with us, so has monogamy, whether voluntary or enforced, and so have its explosive offspring, infidelity, jealousy, and reprisal. Post-Stonewall, many gay liberationists regarded monogamy as a huge chastity belt, a monstrous device by which the patriarchy policed our sexuality. I recall Tim McCaskell arguing in the late '70s that it was a capitalist plot rooted in the evils of private ownership and that screwing around was a revolutionary duty. I can also remember noting that some of the most vehement critics of people desperately seeking Mr or Ms Right had themselves already found and in some cases were living with an intimate partner. In any case, monogamy is still with us, as are its prickly challenges.

For Tim and Richard, an open relationship was the only kind they could conceive. Says Richard, "I don't think that either of us felt it was forever. Many people I've known who formed a couple on that assumption ended up splitting – the terms were just too rigid. We didn't want to follow the old script. If our relationship was to work, it had to work on our own terms, which to some extent we had to make up as we went along."

"We're both pretty reasonable people," says Tim, "and the relationship has never seemed to put a limit on either of our lives. Some relationships get into trouble when they pose a barrier to something either person wants to do, or to some way they want to grow."

"Tim has always encouraged me to do things," says Richard, "like pursuing opportunities to travel, to teach, and to get fellowships for research and so on."

"On the other hand, we really enjoy spending time together," says Tim. "Richard is good company, we have wonderful conversations. He also keeps me connected emotionally to other people."

Richard explains, "Tim tends to have an instrumentalist approach to people. He sees them primarily for what they can bring to a particular issue or struggle."

Still, I'm curious about the emotional nuts and bolts of their non-monogamy. What about jealousy? Though it seemed a major flaw in anyone aspiring to be a proper gay militant, I've always been dangerously subject to it myself. "Tim is remarkably unjealous," says Richard. "I was more jealous in the beginning, until I realized how unnecessary it was."

"It's probably significant that our non-monogamy has been sexual, so both of us could feel fairly secure emotionally," says Tim. "As gay men we have so many options for sex without strings."

They used to go to the baths together, when they had the stamina for it. "I still have occasional flings when I'm travelling," says Richard. "Some of them have become something like family friends. But I wouldn't be inclined to do that here. It would complicate my life too much."

"Basically," says Tim, "we trust each other. That's crucial."

Richard nods agreement. "So often you hear of relationships ending with a breakdown in trust, when someone finds out they can't believe what the other one says. Tim told me way back that if he was ever going to leave, I would be the first to know. I believe that he would never do anything cavalier to our relationship."

Through hard, sometimes bitter experience I've learned what a critical role honesty plays in sustaining relationships. I asked Richard and Tim if, or how, they fight. "According to our family backgrounds," says Richard. "Mine is volatile, often on edge with lots of stormy intrigue, but in Tim's family emoting isn't allowed, everyone is an island. Tim refuses to fight with me. So we don't have big fights, we just bicker. I probably bicker more than he does, but then he does more of the irritating things that make me bicker. Like saying he'll water the plants while I'm away, and then forgetting." They exchange a look. Richard is just back from a three-day video conference in New Brunswick, and the plants look quite thirsty.

"No matter how volatile he gets, I know he really doesn't want to kill me and I know it will eventually pass," says Tim.

"Listen to you, how patronizing!" says Richard, with just a trace of volatility. "You might as well say I'm on my period!"

Tim smiles. "I do get crabby sometimes," he admits.

"But even when he's crabby, I suspect he's easier to get along with than I am," says Richard. "And though I can't imagine I'd ever want to be one myself, that Presbyterian levelness of his does have advantages. It's nice to get up every day with someone who says good morning so cheerfully. Anyway, we've been at it so long, like two stones in a river, we've smoothed each other out."

Richard and Chris Richard North picked up Chris Vogel at the Mardi Gras on a warm June night in 1972. Certain bars and cafes along Portage Avenue had served a discreet homosexual clientele since the 1920s, but by the early '70s the Mardi Gras was the favourite among emerging gay folk in Winnipeg. Downstairs was straight and upstairs gay, with a curtain drawn between by the owner to discourage recruiting.

Richard was twenty-one and Chris twenty-five. In the second year of their relationship, mid-winter 1974, they decided to get married, in a church. Though neither was inclined to be religious, says Richard, "We thought it would be a good way to focus public attention on the fact that homosexuals can have significant, long-term relationships. There just weren't any visible models at the time. Lots of invisible ones, but not any that you could see."

Before the minister at the Winnipeg Unitarian Church would agree to marry them, he insisted that, like any other couple, they take a formal marriage preparation course. In several sessions they discussed responsibility, conflict, commitment, the need for support and, rather unusually for such courses, their intention to have sex with other men. The minister was a little startled. Richard explains, "Free love was a popular idea in the straight counterculture at the time, and we thought it made a lot of sense for us as well."

Chris adds, "In our community there was and still is way too much conditioned belief that we shouldn't have sex outside the primary relationship. We've seen so often that people do it anyway and then lie to each other, or if they don't do it they end up resenting that they've missed something. Either way it can destroy a relationship. So why not be open right from the start?" The minister accepted their reasoning and married them. For more than two decades theirs would remain the only same-sex marriage to be sanctioned by a mainstream church anywhere in Canada.

In 1974 the newlyweds set about building a gay life for themselves in their prairie city of less than half a million people. They bought a comfortable old house in the Wolseley neighbourhood, close to downtown. They joined a gay group just born at the University of Manitoba and over the next few years organized socials to raise money for meetings and pamphlets, a peer-counselling phone line, a speaker's bureau, and a library. Richard produced a weekly program on the student radio station, the *Gay Christian Forum,* until the station closed in 1980. At that point Chris rallied volunteers to produce *Coming Out,* a weekly half-hour program on cable TV. Before it lost its time-slot to station cutbacks in 1994, it had broadcast more than 700 programs.

In the late 1970s Chris and a few clergy people launched the Council on Homosexuality and Religion, one of the first federally registered gay charitable organizations in Canada. It held worship services, sponsored reading tours and workshops, and won federal funding to publish a report on anti-gay violence – another first for Canada.

Winnipeg had no bars, no baths, "no scene to build on," as Richard puts it. The only game in town was a private club. Since they found it too conservative – it didn't have an exterior sign, for starters – and too exclusive, Richard decided to start a new one that would combine social services with a licensed club. After a series of fund-raising socials, it opened in 1982 across the street from the older club, with a sign outside that boldly proclaimed the Winnipeg Gay Centre.

"Many people doubted we'd be able to raise enough revenue to keep it going," says Richard.

"It was a constant struggle, but in the first three years we actually managed to raise and spend a million dollars," Chris adds. Now called the Gay and Lesbian Resource Centre, with paid staff and government funding, it's a familiar presence in Winnipeg.

While Richard was working full time on unpaid gay community work, Chris's government job supported them, with an occasional emergency boost from their families. By 1987, when the Manitoba government finally agreed to include sexual orientation in the provincial Human Rights Code, and Winnipeg held its first Pride parade, Richard had run out of organizing steam. He withdrew from the fray, joined AA, and returned to school to learn computer programming, his current work. "The way I see myself now," he says, "I'm just sort of an average guy, and that's what I'll likely be from now on. In fact that's probably what I wanted to be all along. But being homosexual, either you had to be a gay liberationist or stay in the closet and feel bad about yourself."

Chris still serves as treasurer at the Resource Centre. Occasionally he'll fire off a letter to the editor on some gay issue or use his extensive media contacts to help organize a community event. "There's quite an irony here," he says. "When I was young, I was very conservative, quite the stuffed shirt. I would never have dreamed of doing any of these things if it hadn't been for Rich. But having been dragged into it kicking and screaming, I found I really liked it. I got to be someone. And now I can look back and say I actually accomplished something."

Richard laughs. "I had all these bright ideas, and the good sense to recruit Chris. He just kept plugging away at it for the next twenty-five years. He's really amazing."

"Dumb persistence," says Chris. "That's all it takes, dumb persistence."

The bottom line I asked Chris Vogel and Richard North about the rules and regulations that govern their open relationship. "We don't have any," says Chris. None? "None. As far as I'm concerned, the rules that other couples have are only meant to disguise or limit something that doesn't require it. Some have a rule that you can't bring anyone home. But I'd much rather Rich brought them home, especially when he was drinking, because then I'd know where he was. Some have a rule that you mustn't talk about it, or you can only do it when you're away, presumably out of fear that you'll become emotionally attached to someone else and therefore your own relationship will fail. Well, there were three guys that Rich became emotionally involved with. It made no difference at all to me, and it was very good for him. I met them, they were neat guys, in fact I had sex with two of them. My motto has always been that our relationship has its own life, and it will stand or fall on its own merits, depending on whether or not we still love each other. All the rest is irrelevant."

Chris makes an annual pilgrimage to the baths in Toronto. Being partial to SM and leather sex, he prefers the Barracks, which has no equivalent in Winnipeg. "A few years ago it occurred to me that this is ridiculous – a week full of sex, then nothing at all for the next twelve months? What a stupid waste!" Fortunately a gay male phone line has opened in Winnipeg. "Now finally it has enough guys on it that you can be quite successful," says Chris. "I feel I'm making up for lost time before I get too old."

"The bottom line," says Richard, "is it's pretty hard to have more fun than sex. We've been able to have our cake and eat it – we have a nice home life, good relationships with our families, and all the sexual freedom that's available now to gay men."

What's their secret? "Right from the start," says Richard, "we've been very honest with each other. I think that's absolutely critical."

Chris adds, "I'd say it's the real meaning of fidelity, when you know you can depend on someone to be truthful, to be supportive, and to take care of you."

"I've been really lucky," says Richard. "Chris is the ideal partner, he's always been very supportive, and I've never felt insecure, not for a minute. I don't think he can say the same of me."

"You've always been there when it counts," Chris replies. "Whenever I've thought who else I might have had a relationship with, I could never think of anyone. Rich is the finest man I've ever met."

Richard laughs, embarrassed. "At any rate," he says quickly, "it's worked out very nicely."

In 1998 their city made history by electing the first openly gay mayor in Canadian history. "The place finally feels like home," says Richard. With its quiet streets, big trees and solid old houses, their neighbourhood is quite gracious, and rather gay. "It's mostly couples on our street," says Richard, "must be half a dozen, mostly lesbians."

Chris adds, "Alarms are raised immediately when a straight couple moves in. You've got to watch these things, you know." Another year in the civil service, and he'll take early retirement.

"We intend to live here happily ever after," says Richard.

"With our three cats," says Chris, "whom we love very much."

8 A Balance of Powers

Human rights PATRICIA SEALEY DIRECTS ME TO A PARTICULAR chair in the living room. "It will be easier for Catherine," she says. Quadriplegic since birth, Catherine Frazee can't move much else on her own except the hand that moves the lever that operates her motorized wheelchair. When I comment on the ecstatic budding of trees outside the window, in order to turn her head she has to turn the whole chair. As the three of us talk through the morning, and I adjust my body this way and that for comfort, Catherine's equivalent manoeuvres are marked by brief electrical whirs.

In October 1985 Catherine advertised her urgent need for a personal attendant to come in on the weekends. Patricia Sealey applied, mentioning that she was a lesbian. "By that point the closet had become pretty intolerable for me," she says.

Catherine was startled. "I had led a rather sheltered life," she says. "I was asexual myself, or if I had to choose, I suppose I would have said I was heterosexual, though I hadn't been in a relationship of any sort that really mattered to me. The only lesbian I'd known was decidedly weird, so it kind of spooked me to think of hiring one." But Patricia was the only applicant, and she happened to be considering another job that would pay more. To sweeten the pot, as Catherine says, her Toronto employer, Imperial Oil, agreed to fund an assistant for her a few hours a day at the workplace. Patricia took the double job.

Two years later she decided to move on, to New Brunswick with a friend of Catherine's; the two of them became lovers. Patricia got a job supporting disabled people at a tourist information office, a government scheme to cut the welfare rolls. When Catherine visited her parents in New Brunswick, Patricia would come by and do her care. Their friendship deepened.

In the meantime Catherine had been working part-time as a commissioner, a voting board member, with the Ontario Human Rights Commission. In 1989 she was asked to become interim chief commissioner, then chief commissioner, a full-time, high-profile job at a particularly stormy time in the life of the commission. Says Catherine, "Other people could provide my personal care, but I really needed someone to work with whom I could trust completely, and who also had the intellect to discuss things in depth, to bounce ideas around – something not usually required of an attendant." She asked Patricia to come back.

Fortunately, Patricia was not attached to the New Brunswick job. "It was really frustrating. All that project did was set people up to fail," she says. "With Catherine I knew my role, and I knew I could do the work." She agreed to come, but just for two months. Then she would return to her partner in Fredericton. Catherine was thrilled. "At that point," she says, "we embarked on a roller coaster."

The two of them recall a blur of meetings, speeches, conferences, and media interviews, eighteen hours a day, seven days a week. In the midst of it the commission debated a very hot item, the Leshner case: after being denied benefits for his partner, a provincial civil servant had laid a human rights complaint against his employer, the government. Since Catherine and Pat still honour their confidentiality agreements, they won't tell me who said what in the closed-door meetings. But another commissioner, who asked not to be named, reports that the debate was ferocious, with right-wing commissioners, a majority at the time, arguing that it wasn't homosexuals who needed protection but the children they preyed on and infected with AIDS.

For Patricia and Catherine, this was trial by fire. "I had to be incredibly guarded so as not to betray any of my own feelings," says Patricia. "I just took massive amounts of notes, and avoided eye contact with other people in the room." Like other gay and lesbian people who worked at the commission, she was deeply shocked by the hatred she witnessed. "I watched Catherine closely to see how she'd handle things. She was so *principled* about it. She would just listen, then she'd figure out what was the right thing to do, and she'd set about doing it. People who had been hurt were taken care of, and people who'd said horrible things were challenged. I was so impressed. She handled it all like a real stateswoman."

The day after the Leshner case was dismissed, Patricia arrived at work with her head shaved, dressed as dyke-like as she could manage. Catherine laughs. "She could have been wearing a neon sign!"

Within a year OHRC staff had found a way to reopen the case, and this time the commissioners voted to pursue it, by a majority of one.

Patricia's agreed two-month commitment passed, then most of a year. "Intensity like that will either pull you apart or it will bring you closer together," Catherine says. "I don't know when, but at some point I started to fall in love with Pat. And in lust too: I grew more and more attracted to her." As was her habit with feelings, she revealed little of this.

Says Patricia, "For the longest time I had no idea Cathy saw me as anything more than an employee. I just figured she was totally focused on her work."

Their "affair to remember," as they call it, began on June 21, 1990. "It's easy to remember the date," says Catherine. "It was the longest day and the shortest night, in every sense of the word, and the beginning of a very torrid summer!" She let her other attendants go on leave of absence. "I didn't need anyone else to put me to bed," she says with a delighted laugh. At thirty-five, this was her first affair. "I had never had a relationship with anyone, nor even a physical life of any significance. And here I was, suddenly touched very deeply, in ways that I had never thought possible. It was overwhelming." I can hear it in her voice, a visceral memory.

The two continued to work together at the commission. "Both of us carried on as stone-faced as usual," says Pat. "Aside from a couple of people we trusted, no one had a clue." Catherine felt that her job demanded she be seen to be as neutral as possible. She also worried about her parents, whom she describes as middle-class establishment ("*upper* middle-class," Patricia inserts) and her father a senior player in the Canadian business world. "I knew it would be a huge shock for them if I came out in a public way," says Catherine. "I've wondered sometimes if I didn't betray gay people by not being out at the time, but this whole thing really was entirely new for me."

Meanwhile, Patricia's partner in Fredericton had been asking when she would be coming home. "We put it off as long as we could, but eventually we realized that we had a responsibility to this other person that both of us cared about," says Catherine. In late July Patricia set off for New Brunswick. Says Catherine, "I was so filled with hopes and dreams by then, I just assumed she'd come clean with Carla and then return. But I didn't say so, I didn't want her to feel any pressure from me."

Patricia was feeling more than enough pressures of her own. "I had no idea what was going on with Cathy emotionally, I just assumed she thought it was the right thing for me to go back, and that's where I should be. Aside from that, I was very ambivalent about getting involved with her. I knew from experience what a hard, complex thing it is to live with someone who has a disability. I didn't even think she knew me that well; for example, I had never let her see my crazy, angry side. Politically we weren't exactly in synch, I was way more out than her. There was this class thing too. We came from such very different places; I found it especially hard to deal with Cathy's parents, and them with me. And in the six years I'd known her, she'd always been my boss. What kind of basis was that for a relationship? It just seemed so much easier to go back and be with Carla."

Patricia and Carla bought a house together in Fredericton. "That's how I dealt with my own doubts – I got more entangled!" say Pat with a wry smile. "And Cathy thinks *she's* neurotic." Hoping she and Catherine could remain friends, she phoned often to chat. Eventually Catherine told her to stop. In fact it would be better, she said, if they broke off contact altogether. "I wasn't angry, I just couldn't stand it," she says. "I felt gutted. I had never experienced such deep pain, and I hope I never have to again. I continued to put on my public face and do my work at the commission, but I was a mess." Pat wasn't doing so well, either. "I couldn't bear the thought of never seeing her again. And after a few months back in New Brunswick it was clear to me that the relationship there wasn't going to work."

Pat returned to Toronto and moved into Catherine's downtown apartment. "There were no trees," says Pat. "There was nothing green to look at, and no way to get to it without driving. I thought we both needed a place with a nice view, and a balcony that Catherine could get out onto, so she wouldn't be housebound from September to May."

When she lost her Human Rights Commission job in a Tory purge, Catherine began spending more time at home, working primarily as a freelance writer. They found their balcony and a stunning outlook in a posh co-op apartment building beside a broad green expanse of park and a shady, forested ravine below. When they asked the concierge if any apartments were available, he told them, "No, but wait a little, it won't be long." Most of the tenants are seniors.

On paper the apartment would be owned by Catherine. "I was afraid that if we arrived as a couple, we would never get in, and I really wanted to live here," she says. "Now I'm inclined to think they probably would have considered my disability the greater threat. In this culture it's quite all right for a woman, especially a disabled woman, to have a companion, just so long as they don't know you're sleeping together. But we were hardly in the door when I started agitating to make the place more accessible!" As the sole owner, only Catherine was interviewed by the co-op board. "That was the wrong way to start," she says.

"In fact it has haunted us a little." Pat explains, "There are some lovely people living here, but there are also some really nasty ones. Right from the beginning the nasty ones could tell I don't belong here. Maybe they can sniff it on me."

The choreography of daily life Pat grew up in rural New Brunswick. Her father was a Welsh immigrant and a Baptist minister. "We were dirt poor," she says, "but because of his status as a minister, we didn't really fit in with other working-class kids. We couldn't go to movies or dances, and any music allowed in our house had to be religious. We were an odd, isolated little island of a family." When Pat was eight, her mother died of breast cancer. The island got smaller, and more dangerous. Her father exploded more frequently, hitting Pat and beating her brother and older sister brutally. "We'd always wait for the next explosion, but the awful thing was you never knew what would set it off."

Pat's history in relationships also included sexual experience with men in her late teens, a half year of marriage to a man at twenty-one, and three relationships with women, the longest lasting nine years. "I'd been around the block," she says with a laugh. "Well, a few blocks, you might say."

Catherine, on the other hand, came to Pat a virgin. "I had always lived in my head. Through careful control and choreography of daily living, I learned to manage quite well, both intellectually and socially. I was actually quite busy, which gave me the false sense that my life was full. And though I had developed some very artful ways of masking it, I've come to recognize how lonely I was before I met Pat. My relationships went just so far and no further. I had such a lot of catching up to do emotionally."

When Catherine met Patricia, her body mattered less to her than her wheelchair. "At first it was quite disturbing to discover that I actually *had* a body, and suddenly there were things I wanted to do but couldn't. It's ironic, that's really the first time I became so painfully aware of my disability. And though I didn't doubt that Pat loved *me,* I could also see how much she hated it too."

"Not the disability," Pat corrects, "its consequences, the limitations."

Catherine adds, "I realized that if I were to love myself fully, and she were too, that love would have to encompass my disability. That was a huge struggle."

Several years of struggle and therapy later, Catherine has made peace with her body. "I have the confidence now that comes from knowing a big piece of me isn't cut off anymore. My life and my work are much fuller for that, because finally I feel like a whole person. For me that could only have happened in the context of a loving, trusting relationship."

That feeling is nicely conveyed in several black-and-white photos around the apartment. When they asked a photographer friend to do the shoot, Catherine was determined that it would not only be the more mobile Patricia who did the embracing. "It was a challenge," she says, and they exchange a smile. "It took ages and a lot of ingenuity so I could sit up and Patricia could lie in my arms." And so they are in one of the photos, entangled, both of them clearly enjoying the arrangement.

The disability proved even more challenging for Patricia. If she wants to paint at her studio, she has to ensure in advance that Catherine has an attendant. "If not, or if something falls through, I'm it. I have to shop, come home, cook, clean up. There's no choice in the matter. If I don't do it, she goes hungry." Pre-Catherine, when Patricia needed a break she took a walk, went to a gallery, hopped in the car and drove to her sister's place. "I can't do that any more, not without giving Catherine notice so she can get someone in to stay overnight, which means I can't act nearly so much on impulse as I used to. But even though I've sometimes resented that, it has actually forced me to grow up. I've had to become a lot more self-aware."

So has Catherine. "Until I met Pat, I was always the one who needed care. I'd never had the responsibility of caring for anyone else, of extending myself in that way. The challenge for me now is not to get too complacent with that." Pat nods in agreement. But finding their way through this dilemma took some delicate balancing of powers. "What I *can* do," says Catherine, "is pay other people to do those things that I can't do myself. In the culture I come from, that's quite acceptable. So for example, I can have an attendant come in once a week to make dinner, and that's the night I 'cook.' I'm quite skilled at cooking by telephone," she says with a laugh.

"Power is such a fascinating theme through our relationship," says Patricia. "In some ways the thing is quite *un*balanced, so we have to pay very close attention to where the power actually is or isn't, and who that's costing. After ten years I think we've got much better at balancing the imbalances."

One of their most irksome imbalances has been money. "Basically, she had it and I didn't," says Pat. "For the first six years she was the boss, and I was her employee. That's not an easy dynamic to change."

Catherine adds, "And most of the people we knew saw us in those roles too, which only had the effect of reinforcing them."

Pat no longer pulls in any income as an attendant, nor much of it from the work that most impassions her: making art. "I've never even come close to making a living at it, and it's very unlikely I ever will. I'm just not interested enough in the business side of it, and I don't spend time developing gallery connections and outlets, the things you have to do to get yourself known. I guess I'm a bit of a mole." Her bold landscapes, watercolours, pen and ink drawings, and torn-paper collages hang throughout the apartment, a vibrant, varied body of work.

Hoping to generate more income, Pat trained in art therapy. Unlike the talk therapist, the art therapist encourages clients to express themselves by spontaneous drawing, painting, and sculpture. They look at the results together to see what light might be shed on the client's life. "It's fascinating work," says Pat. "But once again, I'm not much good at selling myself, which you really have to do if you want to build a business. And most places where art therapy might be useful – schools, women's shelters, hostels for homeless people – of course those places don't have any money to hire you."

By contrast, Catherine has never had to concern herself much over the cost of food, shelter, or health care, and barring further privatizing of the Canadian health care system, it seems unlikely she ever will. "My parents are quite comfortable financially, and I don't doubt that if there was ever a real problem, they would help me to the extent they could. It's true that I'm driven in my work, and I don't want to turn away any contracts. But I don't think of the income as being necessary for survival. It's more for discretionary things – expensive computer equipment, travel to lovely places – things that I want rather than need."

In her case the border between want and need is not that clear. If she's to live a full life, her needs are unavoidably costly: attendant care, a van and the equipment to board her wheelchair, devices like the mobile crane that lifts her from chair into bath or bed. She considers computer equipment a discretionary item, but since she can't use a keyboard, she needs sophisticated voice-recognition software to write and an infrared remote-control mouse that she can operate from her chair. "Those two small but rather expensive items really transformed my life," she says.

Recently the two of them worked out a way to address their financial imbalance. "We co-write," says Catherine. "I have the contacts and reputation to get clients, and I know how to interpret what it is they really want. But faced with the blank screen, I tend to freeze. Pat, on the other hand, writes a fabulous first draft." Catherine suggests edits, the piece goes back and forth between them, and gradually a finished product emerges. "In the beginning, I was quite uptight about even having her *look* at my work, let alone actually edit it," Catherine says. "I was also rather nervous about editing her work. But we seem to have got over that."

"It's been great," says Patricia. "It would have been hard for me to get this kind of work, but I'm quite capable of doing it."

"It's still not an independent income," says Catherine, "not yet."

Patricia adds, "But it does come pretty close."

Finding me when I'm lost All this balancing they do must be taxing. "Oh yes," says Pat, and Catherine smiles. From early childhood, one of her primary survival skills was to observe. "I watched how people functioned in all sorts of relationships. And because I was ready to listen, they tended to be remarkably forthcoming about their trials and tribulations. So even though it was indirect, I did gain a lot of insight into what does and doesn't work. As soon as I got involved in a serious, loving way, I knew that I would be willing to do any amount of work to make a success of it."

The same goes for Pat. "I totally love and respect Cathy. She can also drive me crazy. But the few times I've been tempted to walk away, I've reminded myself that this is the best relationship I've ever been in, by far. Since the only alternative I could imagine was to be alone, and I don't do alone very well, it seemed pretty clear to me that I better stay and work it out."

Even with the best intentions, working it out remains a challenge. "Our processes are quite different," says Catherine. "I tend to think out loud, and I make elaborate lists of pros and cons. From my perspective Pat goes all over the map and I think, for Christ sake, will you just tell me what you want?"

Patricia nods. "It's true, I still do have trouble saying what I feel. Either way, it's a scary thing. If you bring something up it could lead to a fight, and who really wants that? But if you don't bring it up, the thing just festers, it gets harder and harder to deal with in any reasonable way. Anyway, why should either of us have to guess what's going on with the other? We've tried that, it doesn't work. You end up making all kinds of weird compromises, and then no one ends up happy."

When it does come to a fight, the tussle is shaped by their differing abilities. If Pat is moved to storm out and slam the door, first she has to make sure that Catherine has an attendant due, or at the very least a phone at hand. "It drives me mental," says Pat. "When I'm mad at Cathy, the last thing I want to do is take *care* of her! But I do have to stop and think, what are the implications for her safety, and what's really at stake here? Ultimately I think that's not such a bad thing for someone like me who's always tended to be a grand gesture sort of person."

Catherine's anger usually expresses itself in quiet ways. She becomes rigid and silent. "But sometimes she'll just open her mouth and holler," says Pat. "She has a good, loud holler. Or she has been known to smash her chair into a door."

"But I have to be careful," says Catherine. "If I hit too hard, my head will fall forward, and then I'll have to ask Pat for help, which is hardly the point! No matter how furious I am, I still have to go through that mental checklist."

"Neither of us can ever really let ourselves go," says Patricia. "We have to stay that much more conscious of the ground rules."

Earlier in our conversation Pat mentioned her crazy, angry side.

Has the vulnerable Catherine ever been afraid of her partner? "I've never been afraid she would hurt me," she says, "but there have been a few times when I feared that she might hurt herself. One time I watched her head for the balcony. She was so angry, but I couldn't grab her, I couldn't stop her. I don't think I've ever felt so incredibly helpless. In circumstances like that you have to get un-mad awfully fast. Not having the ability to hold her physically, somehow I did it with my words."

Pat nods. "Cathy developed her verbal skills early on, for survival, but I think she's taken it a lot farther as a lover. She has ways of finding me when I'm lost, just with her words and her tone. It's quite extraordinary."

While much of the work has been done in the spaces between them, they also acknowledge that they haven't been alone. "When I first moved in with Cathy and we weren't sure when we could or couldn't be out, we found that after an evening with people who didn't know about our relationship we'd both feel exhausted and empty," Pat says. "There'd be this huge distance between us. That's the price you pay for hiding and faking it. Since neither of us wanted to feel like that, gradually we limited our social time more and more to people we could be out with, safely and comfortably."

"Until then," says Catherine, "I had never really understood why people felt it was so important to be out. Isolation can kill you, that's why. It can certainly kill a relationship. When you don't have to hide anything from people, you can talk to them candidly, and they can help. Our friends know us well enough to say you're going too far here, or you're being a bit too controlling there. They'll mediate, or they'll provide support for the one that's needing it most. Or they'll get one of us out of here for a while, to give the other a bit of space. Without our friends I'm not so sure we would have made it."

Catherine and Patricia are both in their late forties. They've decided it's time they moved to a smaller, less expensive city. The money they save will renovate a cottage Catherine owns in Nova Scotia, to make it accessible so they can live there part of each year, in the quieter, greener place they both crave. They have no illusions about the challenge of this double move. It will be intricate and daunting.

"We'll work it out," says Patricia. Catherine just smiles.

9 Passage to India

The last I heard from Jean-Philipe Wilmshurst, he was working as a volunteer at the Child Haven complex in Kaliyampoondi Village in southeast India. In his free time he travels a couple of bumpy hours by bus into Mallampuram, the beach resort on the Bay of Bengal. It was there that he first met Padmanaban, his foster son. The town is designated a UNESCO World Heritage site for its caves and astonishing boulder-sculptures, carved by hand between the fifth and ninth centuries. Jean-Philipe stays with Padmanaban's family in their small, quiet village not far from Madras, India's fourth largest city, where the young man recently graduated from the Government College as a temple artist.

With grandparents from England, Spain and the Channel Islands, and an early aptitude for languages, Jean-Philipe seemed born to travel. In fact, rather than insert vacations into his work life as most of us do, he did the opposite: worked three years, travelled as long and far as he could afford, then worked again, most recently part-time in the library at the University of British Columbia in Vancouver.

As a traveller, he has found it a distinct advantage to be gay. In most cultures it remains a basic fact of life that men have much greater freedom of movement than women. "My favourite way to get to know a city or country is to meet a young man who lives there, become friends, and spend time exploring with him," explains Jean-Philipe. "It's the shared experience of being gay that makes that possible. Also, since I want people to accept me for who I am, I try to do the same in return, which helps me to be open and accepting of other people and cultures."

Since 1985 when the Hunger Project assigned him to set up a computer system in their Bombay office, Jean-Philipe has considered India his second home. He returns almost every year, always in the cooler, drier season. Summer temperatures in southern India can top

40°C for months; the average low in winter is 20. On December 9, 1993, he was exploring one of his favourite spots, a beautiful white beach that stretches for miles from Mallampuram. As can often happen in India, three schoolboys engaged him in conversation. They suggested meeting again.

Next morning the eldest, Padmanaban, handed Jean-Philipe a card. He had written, "My sweetheart, best wishes to you." He and another boy offered to accompany the Canadian down the coast to Kancheepuram, famous for its Hindu temples, some of them built in the ninth century. At fifteen, Padmanaban had to ask his parents for permission to go away overnight.

Early Saturday morning they caught the bus to Kancheepuram and rented rickshaws to tour the ancient temples. That evening Jean-Philipe wrote in his journal, "Padmanaban is a delightful friend and companion, a real sweetheart . . . I had to keep reminding myself that our friendship is platonic. It is far too precious and special to risk by being premature. Any approach must wait until my next trip to India." On Sunday he wrote, "I didn't get much sleep last night, if any. It was one of the most magical nights of my life . . . [In the morning] I told Padmanaban that I hadn't intended this to happen – wanted it, dreamed it, encouraged it, yes – and hoped he was not upset or angry with me. With his beautiful smile and loving eyes, he assured me he was happy and still wanted us to be friends and brothers . . . Such a beautiful, adorable, perfect boy, in my arms and in my heart." Jean-Philipe was forty-four. He'd had other relationships, but none, he says, "with such an immediate, powerful mix of physical and intellectual rapport. I couldn't imagine a more perfect person to share my life with."

After Jean-Philipe went back to work in Vancouver, the two corresponded until he returned to India in spring 1995. Padmanaban met him at the airport in Madras and took him home to meet his family. They're neither wealthy nor poor, says Jean-Philipe: they own their own house, raise a few chickens and goats, and the father has a job with the local public utility. Padmanaban had a surprise request. With his parents' approval, he asked Jean-Philipe to adopt him.

Jean-Philipe interpreted this as expressing a desire for permanence and the only kind of relationship with an older man, especially one from another culture, that would be acceptable to his family and peers. "So by our own declarations, and with no state agency involved," he says, "we decided that from then on we would call ourselves father and son. The idea of a foster son is probably easier to understand in Canada."

When they're together, Jean-Philipe pays Padmanaban's expenses, and when he's in Canada he sends pocket money. "Given our relative economic states, I can afford it and he can't, so I pay, just as my father supported me financially until I graduated." In 1998 he invested 50,000 rupees, about $2,000 Canadian, in the family's brick-making business. Within three months Padmanaban had cleared 25,000 rupees profit, which he used to start construction on a small house. "With my capital and his contacts and business savvy, I'm sure we'll be able to set him up in business and have him generating his own income soon," says Jean-Philipe. As his foster son, Padmanaban will be his sole inheritor.

On Jean-Philipe's return to India in February 1997, Padmanaban had another surprise for him. Though the young man had been quite willing to experiment sexually when they met, he had now concluded that he was attracted to girls. "He said he still loved me dearly," says Jean-Philipe, "but he didn't want to have a sexual relationship with me anymore." And while he had no problem with his Canadian dad being gay, he didn't want his family to know, because they would conclude that he was gay too.

Jean-Philipe was devastated. "Finally I thought I'd met the perfect person for me, five out of five. Instead it was only going to be four out of five: love, affection, companionship, and a future together, but not the sexual side." It was clear he'd have to choose. Either he could have a loving, platonic relationship with Padmanaban, or he could keep on looking elsewhere for a five-out-of-five.

"I agreed to his terms. If he finds a girl he wants to marry, that's okay with me, and if I meet a boy that I want to have sex with, he assures me that will be okay with him too, as long as it doesn't supplant him or interfere with our relationship."

Padmanaban's parents are delighted that he has a Canadian dad, and Jean-Philipe stays with them when he comes for a visit. "They know that we share a bed," he says. "That's all they know. I'm considered part of the family." While Padmanaban, his brothers and sisters can all speak English, the parents speak only Tamil. Jean-Philipe is learning it as he goes. "It's a fairly difficult language, and I don't expect I'll ever be able to speak it fluently."

More than once with previous lovers Jean-Philipe had assumed it would be for life. But this would be his first relationship that carried on after the sex had ended. He tested the new arrangement when he returned to India for a month the following year. "It worked out fabulously. Our relationship was as solid as ever – loving, long term, everything I want but sex. I thought it would be frustrating to share a bed with him, but it's not – we snuggle, we sleep with an arm over the other's shoulder. That's the best part of sex for me, someone warm and wonderful to hold. The other, rub, rub, squirt, squirt, you can do that any time. Affection and connection are the most important things to me now, and I get those unreservedly from Padmanaban. The only rule is no touching below the belt."

Does he worry about what it might do to their relationship if Padmanaban were to marry? "He says he's not in any hurry to do that, so I don't choose to dwell on it. For now he wants to be with me, whether it's in India or in Canada." Just in case, he has a Canadian visa application in the works for Padmanaban. "With our ongoing, mutually dependent, documented relationship, we could easily qualify under the same-sex partner category."

In January 1999 Jean-Philipe returned to India once again, but this journey would be different. Aside from a quick trip back to Canada in the summer to settle a few things, he now planned to make India his home. The choice he faced was simple enough: he could live in Canada without Padmanaban, or he could live in India with him, or at least close by. "Basically I gave up virtually everything in Canada to be with this young man," he says.

He also loves India. "From my first visit I felt at home here. I definitely prefer warm weather to cold. The country is extraordinarily rich, both historically and culturally, it has a reasonable infrastructure for getting about, and I've found it quite easy to make friends here. I was probably Indian in another lifetime. And this is where Padmanaban is. What more could I ask?"

At fifty Jean-Philipe considers himself retired. He can live in India for about one-third the cost of living in Vancouver. He stays with

Padmanaban's family, travels with his foster son, and volunteers at the Child Haven International complex of homes in Kaliyampoondi Village, Tamil Nadu state, Southeast India. Established in 1988 by a Canadian couple who live in Eastern Ontario, the complex houses 250 young people, newborn to twenty-one years old. Based on Ghandian ideals including non-violence, no hierarchy by caste or gender, and simple living with a vegetarian diet, Child Haven provides education, skills, and work opportunities for both the children who live there and adults in the surrounding area. Volunteers like Jean-Philipe pay their own way, work for room and board, and live in the same conditions as the children.

This is the place, and the life, that Jean-Philipe Wilmshurst has chosen for himself. "I wouldn't recommend my choices to anyone else," he says. "But given who I am, and what's important to me at this point in my life, what I'm doing seems totally logical to me."

10 War and Peace, and Bullshit

My early lessons in war and peace weren't promising. The imperial power in my childhood was my grandmother, Isabelle, or Gommie, as we called her. I wish I could have known her as an equal, this primal force. But I was only a child, and she had been raised in the Victorian belief that children are little savages to be subdued and civilized. Ironically, this particular savage was inclined to be helpful, sensitive, and courteous. I walked my brother's dog, set the table, wrapped the Christmas presents – on occasion, even my own. But there was a will in me too, a spirit not unlike hers. If I had known that such a process existed, I would have been ready to negotiate, but it would have been as foreign to my grandmother to negotiate with a child as with the handsome Québecois men who tended our garden in English Montreal. With her as with most tyrants, every dissent became a battle, and every battle a test of her power.

When my father died, I was four. My mother had to go out to work, so my grandmother moved in to run the house, and us. Though she was nearly sixty when I came into her care, Gommie was three times my size, an experienced general with an impressive array of weapons. The first and subtlest of these was beguilement: you're my favourite, she would say, and I know you will never be disloyal. Disloyalty included speaking out on my own behalf to anyone, even to my mother. The same standard did not apply to Gommie herself, who constantly recruited allies. Nor did it apply on the question of lying, tantamount to a capital crime when I did it. One afternoon the high school vice-principal called me into his office to ask why I gave my grandmother such grief. She had phoned that morning, such a nice old lady, in tears. This time I was lucky. Since I came top in the school in the vice-principal's pet subject, Latin, I was able to convince him that the nice old lady was a pathological liar. This was only half true; she was quite capable of telling the truth if it suited her.

When subtler methods failed, Gommie escalated the hostilities to shouting and threats to send me to Shawbridge, a notorious reform school for delinquent boys. When that didn't work, and I was close enough, she wheeled and hit me across the face as hard as she could. The lacerating earaches finally receded in my twenties. Or she'd enlist my mother to hold me while she beat me with a hair brush or rubber strap. When I could no longer be held, my grandmother learned to execute a spectacular collapse, feigning a heart attack. Terrified that I'd killed her, I would capitulate on the spot. She'd sit up and light a cigarette.

All of this together formed my first major life lesson: all's fair in love and war, which, as far as I could tell, were pretty much the same thing. Not surprisingly, this early combat training did not make for the best adult relationships.

It's eerie how people recognize and select each other for complementary wounds. In a series of non-sexual but intimate liaisons, nearly always with heterosexual women, I've followed a similar trajectory. The women have all been intelligent, creative, sardonically funny, eccentric, and hungry. With the easy clarity of hindsight, I see now that their needs, probably sexual but certainly emotional, weren't being met by heterosexual men, who were absent from their lives, either literally or figuratively. My job was to provide the missing sustenance, like a mineral supplement. For example, at least once a week I used to have dinner with "Hannah" at her apartment. I was in my thirties, she in her forties, both of us single. After we'd done the dishes, she would retire to bed. I'd sit on or beside it, and we would talk, play cards, and watch TV until she fell asleep. Then I would go home. As with the other women, Hannah and I laughed, gossiped, commiserated, gave advice by the ton, and shared far more intimate secrets than we, or at least I, knew how to bear.

Much too late, I came to understand the tangled web we managed to weave. In return for providing the mineral supplement, I was granted a similar place in Hannah's life that I had in Gommie's. You're special, they would say, I can tell you anything and you won't let me down. But from Gommie I had learned that my special status was conditional on good behaviour. In the adult, good behaviour turned into a kind of seduction, the desired intimacy and compliance offered much too easily, and much too fast. At the same time, I knew that any overt expression of will or spirit on my part, especially one that involved dissent, was a potential threat that would have to be carefully monitored and probably concealed.

Jung talks about the shadow, the repository for powerful feelings that have been declared bad or unacceptable. Banished into shadow, these lumps of clotted energy don't dissolve and vanish. Instead they fester and stew, like lava boiling at the earth's core, and eventually make their way up through fissures in our composure, to erupt at the surface unexpectedly and with malevolent force.

A series of minor differences with Hannah led not to negotiation – I had no idea how to do that – but to escalating, mostly unspoken tension. When she told me that my new boyfriend, Brian, wasn't good enough for me, the shadow erupted. I shouted that she was exactly like my grandmother, I hated them both, and wished that Hannah, like my grandmother, was dead. She replied coolly that we'd better not see each other for a while. We haven't spoken since.

Other liaisons have ended in the same way, with a terminal eruption on my part that must have shocked the other at least as much as it did me. Later, I would keep the actual explosion to myself – well, I'd share it with Brian – but then distill the fury into a letter, an act of cowardice driven by some primitive instinct for survival: if I were to spill my storehouse of grievances face to face, surely the other person would have no choice but to kill me. So I did them in first, on paper, and made my escape. What a sad, wasteful end. After several of these disasters, I became more cautious about forming close connections, especially with women, who are ironically the people with whom I'm most inclined to form such connections. But I know how easily seduction comes, and how hard it is to avoid: if I'm a very, very good boy, how can you resist loving me?

Frightened by these deeply embedded furies, I've been dabbling in Buddhism. Probably it's more than dabbling – I meditate, read, go to workshops – but not yet disciplined enough to call a practice. It makes such good sense to me: compassion, being present, non-attachment. As I understand it, attachment means getting stuck in positions, attitudes, yearnings, illusions of all sorts: I'm right, you're wrong. The Bible was written by God. A fetus is a person, a fetus is not a person. Progress is a good thing. If only I had a new computer/car/job/boyfriend/look/drug, I would be happy. In *Tricycle,* an American Buddhist magazine, Anne Jeffries writes, "Attachment leaves you imprisoned, your horizons diminished, and thwarts your ability to investigate without bias. Your ears are stuffed with your own prejudices, preconceptions, and, like the proverbial Zen teacup that is too full to receive one drop of wisdom, your ability to hear the other side is consumed by self-righteousness. In short, you relinquish your freedom of mind." For a writer, that could be fatal.

Not long ago I was at dinner with friends of ours and friends of theirs. Early in the evening one of their friends pissed me off. The infraction was unintentional, rooted in ignorance, and in the big picture, of minor consequence. Still, for some reason – the planets, my mood, particular buttons – this person called up my demons. To the onlookers it must have looked like sulking, but in fact I imploded, spiralling into the pit of my own rage, then embarrassment, then shame, and round again to rage. I knew by experience that conflict doesn't sit well in this house, and at a dinner party it would be just plain rude. But what could have been ruder than my surly absence?

My verbal skills were no use at all; I hardly managed a dozen words the whole evening. I don't know where I was, but certainly not present. Compassion for anyone, including myself, evaporated. As Brian got more chatty, trying to talk enough for both of us, my silent fury encompassed even him. Non-attachment remained a mirage, a vague exotic mantra to be intoned at workshops. As we left, our hosts said kindly that they were worried, this was so unlike me. I know better, and so does Brian. He told me later how nervous he'd been, waiting for me to explode.

Non-attachment says don't linger and fret over a lost evening. It's gone. Compassion says you are not bad, and neither is the person who provoked you. Very likely you felt worse than anyone else, both during and after the event. There is a lesson here, pay attention. I'm trying.

Brian and I have had other fights, over things both greater and lesser than celery. Some friends get alarmed when we yell at each other, and call each other asshole and such. But that's just play, verbal rough and tumble. It's informed by two decades of knowing each other, discovering what hurts and what doesn't. In a real fight there's less sound and more fury. Once we were both perched on the roof, making a repair. I can't remember the issue now; likely it had to do with the balance of power – it usually does. But this time we both had hammers in hand, and the roof is steep. We got down, stowed the hammers, and had it out.

Sometimes a fight will lead to such huffy posturing that it can only end in hilarity. One time Brian hurled at me in mid-skirmish, "But that's what you always do!" Without missing a beat I hurled back, as maniacally arch as Lady Bracknell, "I never do *anything* always!" Brian stared at me a moment, then burst into laughter. So did I. Who knew my inner Oscar Wilde lay so close to the surface?

The balance of powers is a delicate thing. When we work together, usually it's on Brian's turf, in the realm of practical things: gardening, fixing the roof, packing cabinets for delivery. In situations like these, generally I'm content to be a good helper, attentive and cooperative. Brian is no tyrant, but he will have figured out how to pack the truck, how to get the steel safely up onto the roof, how to support the luffah vines as they soar and grab at thin air. Often his solutions seem just right to me, sometimes inspired. But now and then I get ideas of my own, and some of these, it seems to me, may be safer, or simpler, or – yes, why not? – better than his. Well, now we have trouble.

I can keep my idea to myself, or I can present it. If I present it, it can go two ways: he accepts it, or he explains why it isn't such a good idea as his. If he rejects my idea I can accept his argument, or I do not, and say so. There is a third option, to reject his idea and keep silent, but we know where that leads: I fume, he reacts, we fight. Of course there's a fourth option, compromise – but that often goes missing in action.

If I continue to promote my idea, Brian has two choices: give way, or further defend his own. Meanwhile, the task isn't getting done, so the tension mounts. If he escalates, I can back down or match him. I can remind myself that it's his task, he has more invested here, let go. But damn it, he didn't even *consider* my idea. Remember, Michael, non-attachment. But *goddamn* it! "Fine," I might say, "do it your way." Of course he can't miss the edge in my tone, bright and hard as lacquer. He might say, "Why are you getting so pissed off?"

"Why? Because you're not listening."

"I listened, I heard you, I just don't think it'll work that way."

"But why not?" And so we go, butting heads until we're tired of it, or it's time to deliver the cabinets.

When we're on my designated turf – words, ideas, politics – the roles tend to reverse. Brian presents his idea. I accept it or explain to him why it isn't as good as mine. He agrees, or accuses me of being arrogant and always correcting him. I see his point or retort that he's not thinking through the implications of what he's saying.

Some of these bouts echo one of our formative battles. In year one or two of our union we were arguing about something, and apparently it was going my way. In the middle of it he suddenly said, "This isn't fair. It's so much easier for you, you're smarter than I am and better with words."

I was stunned, effectively silenced, but only for a moment. "What am I supposed to do then? Do you want me to shut up, not have an opinion, pretend I'm stupid, tie one hand behind my back? What would make it fair?" He didn't know. We wrestled, it got fierce. I don't remember now exactly how it went or where, but along the way he came to understand that, despite all the word power he ascribed to me, I wasn't smarter than he was, only more verbal, and I really hadn't done that well in prior fights. I understood that he felt insecure about his own intelligence, which is of a different, less linear sort, not so useful in arguments. He also saw how he might be inclined to pursue unfair advantage by claiming a handicap. I saw how I could slip into being glib, arguing to win rather than to seek truth or common ground.

It was a wonderful, historic moment in our growing partnership. He said what he thought and felt, and so did I. Both of us survived, and both of us were surprised enough to try it again.

You'd think it's all we do, fight. In fact it's rare for us to reach the point of pitched battle. Just as well: we live at close quarters and both work at home, so we're in each other's face most of every day. I've watched couples of various orientations whose bonds have endured long past the Best Before date; they gnaw at each other, like animals trapped in too small a cage. Can the prospect of loneliness really be that much worse? In our own small world, I'm grateful for the ways we've learned to manage the difference and conflict that are unavoidable in human affairs. The bedrock, it seems to me, is respect for the other and the recognition that this is rare enough to justify a good fight now and then. Though I've never seen the point in marriage, to all intents and purposes we're an old married couple. Some days we'll sit at tea and hardly have a thing to say. There are only so many words in the universe. But after two decades it amazes me that Brian can still surprise me, make me laugh, and give me such delight.

Out there in the larger world, it's not so easy. Recently the elected council in my rural county enacted a dangerous bylaw. They claimed it would protect us from factory farms, a rapidly spreading blight that threatens groundwater, small farms, and the environment across Europe and North America. But instead of protecting us, we discovered, the bylaw effectively opens the door to such operations and makes it more difficult and costly than ever for citizens to oppose them. It struck us as especially outrageous in the wake of the tainted water tragedy in Walkerton, Ontario.

On a few days' notice, several of us raised the alarm in local papers, and we put together a presentation to council, raising serious questions and concerns about the bylaw. The councillors regarded us impassively as we spoke, then without a word of debate or a single amendment passed the bylaw as it stood, unanimously. Usually I react to insults and setbacks like this with a mixture of rage and despair at the arrogant stupidity of the tyrants and the deadly apathy in the rest of us. But this time, for reasons I can't fathom, no rage, no despair. Instead, I got an idea.

The next day I circulated to several friends and allies a proposal for a new initiative, the Safe Water Group, to do independent research, education, and action on water protection. With sixty in sight, I said at our first meeting, I'm tired of running after corrupt, incompetent politicians, I'm tired of losing ground to liars and thugs, and most of all, I'm tired of reacting. I want to act for a change, to initiate, to make sparks. It's silly, but some days I still believe we can save the world. So do others, apparently. After only a few weeks the group had carried off its first project, a municipal all-candidates safe water survey, and we'd already been called "a special interest group," a badge of honour these days. We'll make sparks, of that I have no doubt. But that's the easy part. It's the rest that worries me.

Hannah argued once that all my gay political activities were nothing more than the expression of an unresolved primal argument with my grandmother. Hannah was, I now think, about half right. Certainly the bigotry that kept us suffocating in the closet had to be opposed. It still does, and so do all the other tyrannies. But I have to admit that all tyrants do look a lot like Gommie: they confuse might with right, they don't listen, and if you talk back, they whack you. I suspect Hannah may also have noted the potential tyrant in me, as when, with surgical precision, I cut off a friend – an acquaintance really (well, we'd slept together more than once) who, rather than taking part in a Saturday afternoon protest I'd helped organize, chose instead to *shop*. Though I doubt he was greatly harmed, in retrospect I found my own ruthlessness a little chilling. I fear that if I had real power in the world, power over fundamentalists, for example, or corrupt politicians, I would in short order become the sort of person that I would have to oppose.

My mother often told me I was the noisiest baby in the nursery – a crank from day one. A cohort in gay liberation called me Jeremiah, a voice in the wilderness. I must say the image has a certain appeal, wild and free. It also carries a cost. The voice from the wilderness is easily mistaken for the wind, and ignored. Unheard, Jeremiah wanders ever deeper into the desert and self-righteousness. A friend once said she feared I'd end up in a basement somewhere building bombs. Fortunately, not since childhood have I had a proper basement.

I suppose that leaves compassion and non-attachment. In the Safe Water Group, non-attachment will mean listening to others, even the irritating ones, even though the tyrant in me knows perfectly well that my way is right. Inevitably it will mean compromise; I may have to forego the thrill of dumping a bucket of manure on the mayor's desk. Compassion will mean reminding myself again and again, tediously, that each of us is wounded in a different way, and each of us wants only to be happy. From watching the news I can see how easily hatred kills. From watching fundamentalists, I can see how easily it distorts and poisons the hater, sometimes even more than it harms the hated. From my own experience, I know how fury sours the gut, and the mind. If I hate the mayor or the most offensive of the councillors, all I do is increase the density of hatred in the world, and surely we don't have room for one more ounce of it.

All of this makes such good sense. Damn.

The other day I mentioned to Brian that I was writing about our celery fight. "Oh, that," he said. "It's not finished, you know." Pardon? He smiled. Mischief afoot, I thought. He said, "You thought you'd won that, didn't you?" By way of response I uttered something benign and expansive about wanting no winners or losers, only truth. But yes, of course I thought I'd won.

He folded his arms across his chest, armouring. "Well, that's the thing. I still want to plant celery."

I see. So this is what it means to love.

Family Values

FUNDAMENTALISTS OF VARIOUS BRANDS ACCUSE US QUEERFOLK OF bringing down the family. If only we could.

The particular bundle of atoms and DNA that got named Michael Riordon never felt at home in his family of origin. We spoke such different languages and understood the world in such opposite ways that we might have come from different planets. Of course, I came from the planet Homo. But long before I recognized this origin consciously, I knew very well that I didn't belong where I was. When I ask queer people about the process of coming to terms with their sexuality, nearly always they begin by saying, "I always knew I was different." It's familiar territory.

Then again, lately I've begun to wonder if any of the inmates in my family of birth felt at home. Was I the only one who noticed? As far as I can tell, the only people the nuclear family really serves are some men (and some women) who want a little one at hand to bully, and a few individuals who stand to inherit, untaxed, large estates that they haven't earned. The nuclear family has served the rest of us about as well as nuclear weapons. Perhaps that's why both are defended most vehemently by the same people.

Since I didn't fit in any of the formal structures into which I was pressed – family, school, the football team, church, university, heterosexuality, my first full-time job – I withdrew from each as soon as it became apparent that I could. With each withdrawal there have been costs, no doubt. If I had stayed with the Sun Life Insurance Company, for example, by now I might be a senior executive with a spouse/tax shelter, two or more houses, a cushiony RRSP, and a comfortable contempt for people like me, the actual Michael Riordon, who have none of these except for a retirement plan that looks like this: first you work, then you die.

Even in the complex web of intersecting orbits called "the gay community," I didn't find a place that felt like home. As I used to do with my birth family, for a long time I believed it was my fault that I didn't fit. Other times I've been as sure it was theirs. Either way, blame no longer serves a useful purpose.

And it must be said: Being an outsider isn't all pain, no gain. Far from it. I've traded the relative security of being inside the castle walls for the relative freedom of being on the outside, in the open air. Out here, I believe, I can see more clearly, and more widely.

At the same time I do understand and share the deep desire for authentic connection that family is supposed to provide ready made. As it should be apparent from the previous chapter, such connections – the real ones – haven't come easily to me, and for that reason I'm inclined to admire them whenever I find them. It's one of my primary motives for writing this book.

To me, the families that work best are prepared to risk being advocates for the child rather than a medium for the dominant ideology. Instead of providing the first formative lessons in social control – you can't do that, what will the neighbours think! – the adults construct an environment, a nest, really, in which the young can safely learn to fly, and fall, and recover, and almost incidentally along the way, to love. Enough families like this, who'd stand for nuclear weapons?

The chapters that follow explore a variety of inter-generation familial constellations that I encountered on my journey for this book. All of them are dynamic works in progress. None of them is immune from confusion, or struggle, or pain. With no template that fits, they all have to find their own shape, which in time may turn out to be their saving grace.

If, by some quirk of cosmic flux I had landed in a family that lived by values like some of these, who knows – I might still be there.

11 My Son the Queen

Each time Ellen Ryan makes the two-hour drive down from New Glasgow to visit her eldest son in Halifax, she brings a load of groceries. "She's quite determined," says Patrick: "One way or another, goddamn it, she *will* get me to eat!" At 160 pounds on a 5' 10" frame, he considers himself overweight. "I'm obsessed with my weight. I only eat once a day, and even then not much. It's so hard to maintain a female figure."

About three years ago a friend suggested that Patrick had the ideal features for drag: a light frame, good bone structure. With help from his drag mother, Penny Tration, he learned make-up, clothes, and drag etiquette, and he mastered the art of walking in heels. But the real shift came with the wig. "I can put on heels, the dress, even the make-up, and I'm still Patrick. But the minute that wig goes on, suddenly I'm Jayde, and the trashy bitch attitude that's so common with drag queens comes right out. When the wig comes off, it's over."

It's an expensive way to shape-shift. Jayde's current wig, though nothing fancy, set Patrick back $500: "It's amazing how much money it takes to look this cheap!" He works as assistant manager for a call centre that gathers money for charities. "You know, those annoying people that call you when you're trying to have supper? That's us," he says.

Where Patrick suffers most for his art is in the waist. He gets into his corset on the floor, then one or two friends with strong hands yank on the cords, lifting and shaking him like a bag of bones until the device has cinched his 32" boy waist down to a girl's size four. "You ever put on one of those bad boys?" he asks. No. "Well, it hurts like hell. Last weekend it was on me so tight my legs went numb in the car, I couldn't move them. I had to get my friends to loosen it." What about breathing? "It's not easy. Every time I put the thing on, I think why the hell am I doing this? Did my mother burn her bra for this?

But Jayde is an essential part of who I am. I've lived so much of my life according to what others expected of me, now that I'm finally out I wouldn't change for anyone."

As mothers will do, Ellen Ryan fears for her Patrick. "It scares the hell out of me to know he's out there, in drag, especially after the murder of Matthew Shephard [a young gay man in Wyoming]. But I wouldn't question his right to be Jayde, not for a minute. I went to my first drag show in Halifax a month ago, and I was *amazed,* Patrick is a great drag queen. You'd think he was born to it. Anyway," she adds with a laugh, "I always did want a daughter. After growing up with four brothers, who wouldn't?"

When Patrick nervously showed his parents a dress he'd chosen for himself, his father, who works as a security guard in New Glasgow, told him he ought to know better than to wear anything so ugly and handed him some cash to make a better choice. The two of them stuff Patrick's Christmas stocking with make-up.

Losing Bobby Ellen's pride in her son the drag queen didn't come easily. With their father serving in the Canadian Armed Forces, she and her brothers grew up army brats, moving from base to base across the country and overseas. In 1971, at nineteen, her youngest brother, Bobby, signed on for training as a medic at the Esquimalt naval base on Vancouver Island. "He wanted so much to belong in his father's world," says Ellen. "Anything to win his approval."

She remembers the phone call in 1973: Bobby was in military prison. He'd been caught having sex with another man. "That's how the family found out he was gay. I already knew – we never spoke of it, but we were that close. On the same wave-length, you might say." The accused men had two choices: dishonourable release if they put up a fight, honourable if they went quietly. "Bobby didn't fight it," says Ellen. "He had no fight in him, he was just devastated."

Back home on the base in Alberta, his father and brothers shunned him. He tried to rebuild a life for himself, even got engaged to a young woman. "Of course he knew it wouldn't work, but by that point he was so desperate to fit in, he would have tried anything." In October 1974, two months shy of his twenty-first birthday, Bobby Skinner killed himself. He left his sister a note. "He said he couldn't live any more with the shame and the rejection. I know we tend to romanticize people who've died, but I really do think the world lost an awful lot with Bobby. He was the most wonderful person I've ever known." Ellen fell into severe depression. Her parents had her committed to a mental institution where she was subjected to electric shock treatments.

Early in Patrick's life Ellen began to sense a certain kinship between him and her lost brother. "It was hard to define, but at one point I wrote a letter to Patrick telling him that in the music of life he was offbeat to everyone else. After seeing what happened to Bobby, I was scared to death of the consequences, so I did everything I could to push Patrick back onto the straight path – to play sports, to hunt and fish, to be tough like his brothers."

It worked, and it didn't. Aware of his attraction to boys from about age eight, Patrick acted on it through his teens, but after each sexual encounter he felt overwhelming disgust. At school, for self-preservation, he joined the ranks of the homo-baiters. Increasingly isolated, at fifteen he attempted suicide with sleeping pills. Ellen sent him to a psychiatrist. When Patrick admitted that he might be gay, the shrink replied that homosexuality was a horrible sickness that guaranteed him a life of misery. Patrick became celibate.

At eighteen, living in New Glasgow, he married Susan. "It seemed clear to me that this was the only proper way to live," he says. They produced two children, Emily and Travis. In the fourth year of marriage, Patrick's attraction to men resurfaced. Since Susan was a staunch Roman Catholic, he sought guidance from the local priest, "a nice man," says Patrick, whom he trusted. The priest told him that homosexuality was a filthy sin that assured him an eternity of agony in the flames of hell.

A year later the marriage collapsed, and Susan disappeared with the kids to British Columbia. "I was devastated," says Patrick, "but it turned out to be a blessing in disguise. Finally I was free to open up and accept who I really am." At twenty-two, after skirting the issue for several hours, he told his mother that he was gay. "Basically she said, 'Yeah, so?' She had always known, and in fact she'd been really thrown when I got married! If only I could have heard something like this when I was thirteen."

Ellen's casual "So?" disguised a whole stew of mixed feelings that would eventually surface. "I was relieved – through his teens he kept slipping away, and I was afraid I'd lose him," she says. "Of course I was afraid, after what happened to Bobby. But I was also proud of Patrick for having the courage to come out. I was ashamed, because I hadn't been there for him when he was so isolated and he had no one to turn to. And I was grateful – when Patrick came out, he gave me the courage to look at my own life in ways that I had never done before."

Sitting at her kitchen table, I notice that her fingernails are painted a startling sky blue. "Oh that," she laughs. "When I go down to Halifax, Patrick's friends do my hair and my nails. They even get me into makeup, which normally I'd never dream of wearing."

Finding Patrick Patrick West lives in a decaying high-rise in downtown Toronto. He's twenty-nine, the same age as Patrick Ryan. On a hot mid-summer day an electric fan shoves muggy air around his bachelor apartment. Patrick's mother, Catherine, is an occupational health nurse, and his stepfather, Charles Bergey, is an industrial designer for an aircraft company. They live in the suburbs west of Toronto, but today they've come into town to talk with me, and to make signs for Pride Day. We only have a couple of hours before Patrick has to go to work, making salads at a restaurant in the gay village.

Catherine Bergey's journey is remarkably similar to Ellen Ryan's. Twice in primary school Patrick suffered from depression, and in both cases child psychologists suggested that he might be homosexual. The second psychologist also told Catherine that her son had a gender identity disorder. "It scared me so much I just ignored the whole thing and hoped it would go away," says Catherine. In 1966, five years before her son was born, she had seen her landlords, two men in Syracuse, New York, taken from their home by police on a sodomy charge. "So I had a pretty good idea of what society can do to people simply because they're homosexual. It's sad to say, but because of that fear, when Patrick needed me the most, I wasn't there."

By his first year in high school he had become increasingly withdrawn, ate in his own bedroom, and for months wouldn't speak to Catherine or Charlie, nor to his father in Syracuse. "I built my own bubble," says Patrick, "and that's where I lived. I certainly knew by then that I was gay. A friend had even convinced me to join a gay youth group. I really wanted to tell my mother, but I guess I was too scared that I'd lose her approval."

Catherine had developed some fears of her own: had he got some girl pregnant, was he on drugs, was he in a cult? The day after she'd had surgery to remove a lump from her breast, she finally resorted to a twenty-questions approach. After crossing off her more lurid fears, she came down to the one she'd packed away most deeply: Are you a homosexual? Yes. They cried, they hugged, and Patrick gave her a book to read, *Now That You Know,* highly recommended at the youth group.

Catherine asked their family doctor, a woman she trusted and to whom Patrick had already come out, what she should do. You have two choices, the doctor replied: accept him or reject him. "I just started to bawl," says Catherine. "There was no way I could turn my back on my child." Well, said the doctor, there's your answer. Still, Catherine wasn't convinced; surely he was too young to be sure of such a momentous thing. She asked him to see a specialist in adolescent medicine. "I thought maybe they could give him some kind of a test, you know, like those career tests?"

Patrick laughs. "Yeah, multiple choice – mechanic, teacher, lawyer, or homo!"

"Well, what did I know?" says Catherine.

Catherine and Patrick both continued to struggle with their fears. After about a year a gay co-worker suggested that Catherine get in touch with a local organization, PFLAG, Parents, Families and Friends of Lesbians and Gays. (More recently they've officially embraced bisexuals and transgendered people too.) Within a few months Catherine was counselling other parents. One fear she kept encountering was that their gay and lesbian children would be beaten up or even killed by gay-bashers. It can happen, she would say, and ultimately you can't protect them from it. The best you can do is encourage them to be careful and street-smart. Then it happened to her Patrick.

He had been coming out, quietly, at the Etobicoke School for the Arts, and his schoolmates tended to be cool with it. But one day a couple of thugs from outside came looking for queers. Someone pointed at Patrick. The thugs taunted him. He mentioned it to his best friend, Jade. She confronted the thugs in a stairwell. One of them shoved Patrick, and Jade punched him back. The thug knocked Patrick to the floor and started kicking him in the head, stomach, any target he could reach. Jade dug her nails into the guy's scalp, lost four nails, managed to pull him off, and kicked him in the crotch with her steel-toed boot. It was over. Patrick recalls picking up his assailant's lighter and handing it to him. The school called Catherine for permission to take her son to the hospital. He had a black eye, bloody nose and ear, bruises, and whiplash.

A few nights later at the regular PFLAG meeting, Catherine described the attack. "The room was totally silent," she says. "Then people started to cry. Here was their worst fear, and suddenly they had to face it as something that really happened." For Catherine this was a defining moment. Her message didn't change: love your gay and lesbian kids, and help them to be out there as safely as they can. But now a new theme would emerge: work like hell to rid the world of homophobia.

Circles of safety When Ron Hay came out to his father in 1986, Eldon was surprised, fearful that he might lose his son to AIDS. He wondered if he should have been more supportive after separating from his first wife in 1976 and then remarrying four years later. But he wasn't entirely unprepared. Ordained in 1957 as a minister in the United Church of Canada, since 1962 he had taught religious studies, specializing in world religions, at Mount Allison University in Sackville, New Brunswick. (He still lives there after retiring in 1997.) Along the way he learned to question dogma and to listen carefully to people whose lives and beliefs differed from his own. Gradually he'd become accustomed to addressing bigotry in various forms, whether he encountered it in class, in church or in the press. At a theological conference in the late 1960s, he questioned the vile treatment of homosexuals by the churches and got a sharp taste of righteous Christian backlash.

Ron's brother Keith, a doctor in rural Ontario, told Ron that if he were to bring a partner home for Christmas in Sackville, he wouldn't be there. Eldon confronted Keith, gently but firmly. Keith asked him how he felt about Ron being with Alex and James, Eldon's three year-old twin boys from his second marriage. "I was able to say, I think with complete honesty, that it was wonderful for them to have Ron. I hoped they'd have openly gay teachers, ministers, and doctors, and one of the things that grieved me was that Ron had grown up without any such models."

And so it went for the next few years, with Eldon taking on homophobia whenever it crossed his path. He wrote letters to newspapers, recorded commentaries for CBC Radio, worked on United Church committees, and intervened in university politics. Then a PFLAG pioneer in Ontario, Mary Jones, urged him to become more active. Eldon calls Mary and her husband, Laurie, "the godparents of PFLAG in Canada." When parents of gays and lesbians were in distress, Mary argued, it couldn't fail to cost their children, who already had more than enough challenges to face in a homophobic world. In the early 1990s Eldon made tentative moves to start a PFLAG group in the region. The local United Church congregation wouldn't have it, but to his surprise, the Roman Catholic information centre in Moncton opened its doors for him to speak, along with a gay-positive priest from Halifax. That night PFLAG Moncton was born. Since then Eldon has launched a second group that meets in Amherst, just over the border in Nova Scotia.

Currently, Canada has about forty loosely affiliated PFLAG chapters in eight provinces. Though they range in membership from one to hundreds of people, all of them depend on activists to keep them going.

A few years ago I was invited to speak at the inaugural meeting of a new chapter in Saint John, organized by a woman whose son is gay. I came to it a little sceptical: surely it's we who need the support, not our parents and families, some of which are our first and most enduring problems! The meeting heard from both queerfolk and relatives telling stories of fear, isolation, and bigotry, but also of courage and love. I was moved by how similar "their" experiences are to ours, the fears, costs, and rewards of coming out into the larger world.

The two PFLAG chapters that Eldon Hay runs – "facilitates," he calls it, but basically he keeps them alive – generally draw four to twenty people to monthly meetings. Since neither Moncton nor Amherst has a gay-lesbian community organization, the groups also serve as a refuge for the likes of us. "The other night, two new lesbians showed up," Eldon says. "They were both having a tough time at their workplaces and were fearful of coming out, so we were able to offer them lots of useful support." People get Eldon's name from notices in the local papers or by word of mouth. Most make contact by phone, though some, especially gay and lesbian youth, increasingly get in touch by e-mail. If people want to talk in person but won't come to a meeting, he'll go to their homes – anything to break the isolation and open doors.

As we talk over lunch in his kitchen, now and then Eldon whacks the table for emphasis. It occurs to me that even when a teacher retires, especially after nearly four decades at it, the teaching impulse carries on. In response to the recurring fear that their kids may be attacked by gay-bashers, he tells parents, "What we are trying to do is create circles of safety where people can be who they are without fear of reprisal. The more of these circles we can create, the safer the world will become for all of us, and that's one way I can help my gay son in Toronto." One night the circle included a man who had already come to terms with his gay son but who finally found a place where he could admit, for the first time to anyone, that he was an atheist.

True to PFLAG tradition, Eldon listens, encourages, but resists prescribing, though sometimes he's moved to push a little. "An issue came up the other night that frustrates me no end: a young lesbian said, Oh, I can't tell my grandfather, he's too old. I replied that since I'm getting on too, I certainly hope my children never do that to me – bury me before I'm dead. She phoned her grandfather the next day."

The homosexualist agenda For Ellen Ryan, a defining moment came with the brief but sensational career of Roseanne Skoke, the Liberal MP for Pictou County. In the mid-1990s, when gay and lesbian Canadians were slowly gaining civil rights, Skoke used her parliamentary platform to rail against homosexuality. She called it immoral, unnatural, and a threat to the family, inextricably linked to pedophilia and bestiality and the "homosexualist agenda" that was corrupting the nation and its youth.

It's a small world, New Glasgow. Ellen often runs into Skoke at the Walmart, and her cousin is married to Skoke's brother. "I *voted* for her," says Ellen. "I was so happy that a woman was running. She seemed strong, and pretty good on the issues. When this awful stuff started spewing out of her, I could hardly believe it."

Over the next year a few brave queerfolk in the area launched a new action group, taking its name from Skoke's own rhetoric: the Homosexualist Agenda. When Skoke's federal riding was merged with the adjacent one, she had to compete for the nomination with the other Liberal incumbent, who was considerably less hostile to homos. The Homosexualist Agenda, which Ellen and Patrick had joined, set about recruiting new Liberal party members to dump Skoke at the convention. "We managed to sign up about 150 people," says Ellen. "I've never felt anything quite like I did when they announced that Roseanne had lost by 147 votes."

The New Glasgow PFLAG chapter has a membership of one. "People will talk to me on the phone, but so far I haven't got any of them to come out to a meeting," says Ellen. "They're not ready for that yet. That's all right, it'll come. Twenty years ago I started an Alanon group, and for the first two years it was just me and God, but now it's thriving. When people are ready for PFLAG, the group will be there." In the meantime, Ellen has been working with Catherine Hughes, a Homosexualist Agenda instigator, to develop an anti-homophobia workshop for schools in the region. "Most boards and principals still say they're not quite ready for it," says Ellen. "The policy says that if a gay or lesbian student requests something like that, it should be done, but how many students are able to be that out? It's up to us to make sure they have the kind of support they need to do that."

In Toronto, though Catherine Bergey speaks at schools and anti-homophobia workshops and writes for publications in the city and beyond, she considers it her most useful function to be a role model for other parents, open and accepting, with nothing to hide. She wears pink triangle pins and rainbow t-shirts, and her car has a PFLAG licence plate. "Look out," Patrick hoots, "it's the PFLAG-mobile!"

Says Catherine, "Being in their face like that lets people ask what it means, so I get to explain about Patrick and PFLAG. So many people will say, oh, I have a gay cousin, or my sister just came out. And it's hard for people to be as nasty as they might like to be when I tell them I've got a gay child."

Catherine also works on the Toronto Pride committee and belongs to the Metropolitan Community Church, another safe haven for queerfolk and their friends. She's well known in the gay village, usually from fund-raising for one cause or another. Recently she got talked into entering a best tattoo contest at one of the bars. "I was working up the street," says Patrick, "when some guy comes in and tells me my mom is *flashing* at Woody's!"

"No, I wasn't," Catherine scoffs. "Anyway, I lost to Marvin. I didn't stand a chance, he had all these flames shooting up from his butt."

"Oh my god," Patrick groans, rolling his eyes, "I have to move to a new city."

After the torture-murder of Matthew Shephard in Wyoming, Catherine was asked to speak at a Toronto vigil in his memory. Given the quiet solemnity of the evening, she feared she might sound too strident, but others encouraged her to speak from the heart. Her voice ringing over the hushed downtown park, she concluded, "Families must not turn away their gay, lesbian, bisexual, and transgender children. To do so is a crime of hate. The taunts and name calling, 'queer,' 'dyke,' 'faggot,' and worse that we hear every day in every schoolyard must not be tolerated. The fundamentalist right must stop spewing hatred for gays and encouraging criminal acts against gays. This is a crime of hate. There must be zero tolerance for any and all hate crimes perpetuated against homosexuals. Gay-bashers must become the pariahs of society."

People told her afterwards that, amidst the grief, she had helped them get in touch with their own rage.

I wonder about this passion of hers: what is its source? She pauses, looks at her son, at her husband, then at the window. The traffic drones out there, down on Jarvis Street. Finally she says, "My mother was very racist. Even though I got beaten for it, I'd always speak out when she used the N word." Nigger? Catherine nods. She grew up in the United States. "When I was in nursing school in the '60s, I wanted so much to go to the (civil rights) March on Washington, but I would have been kicked out of school. When my first husband got drafted, I enlisted in the nursing corps – I was a military brat, I'd always wanted to join up and serve my country. Some nights we'd get a hundred air-evacs in from Vietnam, they'd been stabilized over there and shipped to us. Suddenly I started to see the real cost of the war. But I was terrified that if I spoke out and my husband got killed over there, somehow I'd be responsible. And when he got back, it would have ruined his career in the military if his wife had been a protestor. So there was always some reason I had to be quiet and stay in the closet, as I did when Patrick first came out. It was like that right from the start – my mother, an alcoholic, used to beat us, but she always told us what happens in this house stays in this house, so you couldn't tell, not anyone. Once I finally came out and started to speak up, I guess it's not surprising that I did it with a BANG."

A certain amount of shit As Eldon Hay gradually assumed a higher public profile as the father of a gay son, he experienced reactions familiar to many of us who are out, including nasty mail and phone calls after speaking out in the media. "The ones that hurt most were from colleagues. One minister said to me, 'At least *my* congregation doesn't have any room for queers.' There's no way I'd take that now, but at the time I was so overwhelmed I couldn't speak." Most churches in the area, even United Church congregations, won't allow any mention of PFLAG meetings in their bulletins, and most ministers won't touch the subject of homosexuality, at least not in a positive way, in their sermons. Nor will they let Reverend Eldon Hay, professor emeritus in religious studies, anywhere near their pulpits. "That hurts too," he says. "I'm in the club, so to speak, but not quite equal as a member."

For Eldon, the cruelest cut is to his research. Fifteen years ago, in a rural New Brunswick cemetery, he began to recover the lost history of a small Maritime Christian sect, the Reform Presbyterians, that had disappeared long ago, or so it seemed. "I dug up all kinds of amazing stuff on them from people's basements and attics. If I hadn't done that, and then written a book about them, all that material would have been lost within a generation."

He learned that a tiny, very conservative remnant of the sect still survives in the United States. In 1998 he was invited to report his findings at a research convention in that country. Then, quite suddenly, he was disinvited. His involvement in a homosexual rights organization had come to the attention of the organizers. "I was weeping on the phone," he says. "I've done so much work on this, and I was afraid they'd shut me out, they wouldn't publish any of my research." His tiny office is crammed with books and files, floor to ceiling. Some of his research has since been published in the U.S., but from Ireland he got an icy rejection: We have learned via the Internet of your "interests," they wrote, and thus can have no further communication with you.

When he reported all this to an old friend, she reminded him gently that, as Jesus had learned, "If you're going to live on the margin, you may have to do without mainstream approval, and you may have to be prepared to put up with a certain amount of shit flying around."

There's no shortage of it. "When I see Christians causing kids to commit suicide and get murdered, that kind of self-righteous mob mentality really frightens me. They are so very sure that God is on their side and that all their hate is fully justified." He thought he'd got over his anger. "It seems to be coming back, but hopefully now with a little more balance," he says. "The challenge is not to see someone who has strongly opposed views as my enemy but to stay open to them and really listen. I do feel proud when I manage that."

Openness is an apt image for the PFLAG process. When Ellen Ryan's son came out, she says, he gave her the courage to open some tightly closed doors of her own. Her birth father died when she was five; two years later her mother married a military man who adopted Ellen and her siblings. After years of travelling from base to base, finally Ellen came home, to a house just up the road from where she was born, on a long, easy slope over New Glasgow. The interior, she's been told, is a mirror image of the house she lived in after she was born. "That started to stir the memories, which helped me to start healing, so I've actually come full circle to finally grow up back where I started."

Some of the stirred memories are of sexual abuse, by a relative, when she was a small child. Although the abuser admitted it, Ellen's mother still holds her daughter responsible. "In her eyes the real sin wasn't him abusing me, it was me talking about it. She doesn't want it to have happened, just as she still says my brother died of a brain tumour. Now all the secrets are out. Bobby couldn't live his own truth in life, but now at least I can honour him by refusing to carry on the lie. I won't tell lies any more, not about my brother, not about my son, and not about myself." After years of having nightmares where her brother burned in hell, last year in therapy Ellen finally found him a safer place, at least in her thoughts. "Bobby was a wonderful ballroom dancer," she says, a smile in her voice. "He just loved it and he was amazing to watch. That's probably where he is now, dancing."

PFLAG grandmas When their sons and daughters come out, a standard, mournful refrain for many moms is "But now I won't have grandchildren!" Not so for Ellen Ryan, nor for Catherine Bergey. Patrick's kids, Emily and Travis, are back in New Glasgow now with their mother, Susan. At first she wouldn't let them visit Ellen's house in case there might be perverts present, but with time she's mellowed. Ellen can't get enough of the kids, who are ten and eight; she sees them more often than Patrick does. Next Tuesday it's Emily's birthday. Since Patrick can't afford the bus fare, Ellen will go fetch him home, a two-hour drive, then return him in time for the afternoon shift next workday. "I can't have him missing her birthday," she says. "It wouldn't be right."

Catherine Bergey had to wait a little longer. Down for a visit with his father in Syracuse, Patrick West became friends with Nikki, a graphic designer. In due course she and her partner, Karen, told him they wanted to have a child. Would he supply the sperm? When he reported to Catherine that he'd agreed, she cried. "I was so afraid I'd never get to see the baby, which is what often happens with the donor. Of course I can see both sides on that." But Nikki and Karen did want Patrick to be involved, and though he would be called "Uncle," perhaps one day when the time and circumstances seemed right, the child would come to know him as her dad.

For convenience, the sperm transaction was conducted in Catherine's house, with Patrick upstairs and the would-be moms on the pull-out in the living room. "Talk about pressure!" says Patrick. The would-be grandmother, a nurse, bought the syringes. No turkey baster? She laughs. "No way anybody's going to use my baster for that!"

K.C. entered the world in July 1996. "We see her mostly on holidays," says Patrick. "I get to be the male version of Auntie Mame."

Catherine adds, with some delight, "She's a wild child, articulate way beyond her years, and so smart it scares me. They're going to have their hands full."

Why? When will their work be done, these PFLAG moms and dads? When the world changes, says Ellen. As program coordinator at the Kids First Family Resource Centre and a member of the People Opposing Poverty group, she works with kids and their parents, mostly single moms, trying to keep some doors open in an increasingly brutal social system. "It's horrendous in Nova Scotia," she says. "They keep taking more money away from people who hardly had any to start with. Sometimes we have to fight for women who've been charged with cheating on welfare – we're talking about a few bucks here, just so they could feed their kids. Who wouldn't cheat, in this awful system they've created where the only way you can survive is by cheating? All people need is a chance."

In Pictou County youth suicide is well above the national average, and here as elsewhere gay youth are three times more likely to attempt suicide than their peers. "A young man died here recently," says Ellen. "At first it looked like suicide, but now they're starting to think he was murdered, and it may have been gay-bashing. Either way it breaks my heart that such things can still happen. But people around here won't even talk about it. It's the ostrich syndrome – if you deny something long enough and hard enough, maybe it will go away." At a recent seminar on mental health, she asked what support services were available for gay youth in the area. There are none, she heard, they just have to grow up and move to the city. "There's no way I can accept that," says Ellen. "We just have to keep pushing, and pushing, and pushing."

Eldon Hay fears that if he stops pushing, the PFLAG chapters in Moncton and Amherst may fade away. He knows how risky it can be for groups to depend on one person, in this case one with prostate cancer who faces a future of uncertain capacities. He also wonders, if he dropped PFLAG, a guiding passion for almost a decade, what would take its place? But for now he's still very much in the fray. In July 2000 he marched in Moncton's first-ever Gay Pride Parade. "Though I know that ultimately it's only the oppressed who can throw off the oppressor," he says, "I also know I'm not as likely to get shot as my gay son might be. That gives me a freedom, and therefore a responsibility, to do some things that might cost him too dearly to do."

A few days before the march, Eldon wrote in the *Globe and Mail,* "It's almost a cinch to walk in Montreal or Toronto, there are so many people. Besides, I know so few individuals in either metropolis. In Moncton I'm much better known. No escape into anonymity, persons on the sidewalk can see me and be seen by me. I can easily read the faces – curiosity, disgust, encouragement, indifference, anger, contempt. Some of the faces I will recognize. I cringe inwardly at anger or contempt. Contempt is the reaction that transforms my spine into sap, my spirit into mush. But when I conjure in my mind and imagination the fear my son might feel and the physical danger he might experience on any street in Canada one night, faced by a menacing coterie of persons intent on beating up fags, my blushing embarrassment pales perceptibly. I expect I'll be embarrassed, and feel awkward; I don't like it. But at my best, I hope it happens. That's why I'm marching in Moncton's Gay Pride Parade."

In Toronto, Catherine and Charles Bergey are also gearing up for Pride Day. This one will draw close to a million people, in a spectacular show of diversity and bravado. Still, as parents do, these two worry. "I think some people have a false sense of security," says Charles. "History tells us how quickly things can change, given a poor economic situation, and how easily people can turn on the Jews, the gays, anyone they choose to blame."

Catherine nods. "As long as we've got the Jerry Falwells and Fred Phelps and Stockwell Days spewing hate and getting away with murder, our work isn't done. I've heard some of the older gay people say how easy the young ones have it now, with all the services, all the places to go. But if things are so great out there, why do so many of our kids still get kicked out of their homes, why are so many forced to live on the street, why do so many still commit suicide?"

This was to be the end of the chapter, Catherine's rhetorical questions left for others to answer. But then in late October 2000, she called. Patrick, her son, had come home to stay with them for a while, until he could find a job and afford to get his own place again. He was taking an antidepressant. When he tried to get himself admitted to hospital for depression, the psychiatrist in charge told him beds were in short supply and Patrick wasn't sufficiently depressed. He did, however, double the dosage of antidepressant. Three days later, on October 7, Patrick hung himself in the basement at his mother's home.

"It should never have come to this," says Catherine, her voice breaking. "I can't stop replaying all the should haves and what ifs."

A moment later she adds, "We did have a wonderful ceremony at MCC to honour Patrick's life. The outpouring of love was amazing."

She and Charles will continue to work in the gay village. "It's our community too," she says. "Especially now, we need them as much as they need us."

12 My Name in the Snow

"COLIN" AND "AMY" PILE UP OATMEAL DOUGH ON THE KITCHEN table, smush it flat, then cut it into cookie shapes. Flour everywhere. "Terry" stands by the sink, watching, smiling. In jeans and a shirt, with sleeves rolled up and short hair, she looks sturdy, even a little military. What shapes does Colin want to make, Amy asks. She's more ample, more the earth mother. Umm – a cat, he says. Live ones wander through the kitchen now and then. But cat ears are hard to shape and tend to break off. Colin pushes and prods at the dough, and the grownups try to guess what he's made. "It's our house," he says, "can't you tell?" Ah, now I see it.

Amy continues to cut cookies, but Colin wants to show me his Pokemons. They have names like Slowbro, Hitmonlee, and Likitung, and, I gather, magical powers. Terry asks him if there's anything he wants to tell me. They've already talked about my visit, and why I'm interested in their family. "No," he replies.

"What's it like having two moms?" she asks, prompting.

"It's okay," he says. In fact he has three, he tells me: his biological mom Terry, Amy, and his other step-mom "Stella," the current partner of Terry's ex-husband.

"Things certainly are changing," says Amy. "One of Colin's friends has three dads."

Colin turns his attention to my tape recorder. He speaks, I play it back, he laughs. He's seven, not old enough yet to dislike the sound of his own voice. Terry asks, "Do you tell other kids at school about your family?" Singing, she'd probably be a tenor, with traces of a Newfoundland lilt. Colin watches the needle bounce in the sound gauge.

"No."

"Why not?" Amy inquires. "Are you afraid of what they might say?"

"No. I'm having too much fun." Fair enough.

"Colin's friend 'Alec' has two moms," says Terry.

"They live in the Valley," Colin adds. "We go there, and they come here." The Annapolis Valley is about ninety minutes' drive west of Halifax.

"Do you feel weird sometimes, like, when the house is full of lesbians?" Terry asks.

Colin thinks a moment. "Only if they're people I don't know."

It's bedtime, tomorrow being a school day. One more oatcake and Terry swings Colin onto her back for "the Bedtime Express" – a piggyback ride upstairs and then a story in bed. He says goodnight to Mom (Terry), Momma (Amy), and me. Momma better suits the cookie-making Amy, who's thirty-three. Terry is thirty. They warned me in advance that while Colin knows they're both lesbians, of the rest he knows nothing, not yet.

A lowlife bottom-feeder When Terry and Amy met in a Halifax gay bar, neither was much impressed. Says Amy, "I thought she was immature and quite the show-off."

Terry says, "And I thought she was a snob. When I was drinking, I would play up to people a lot, give them a rose if they'd kiss me, that kind of thing – I really wanted everybody to like me. But Amy gave me the cold shoulder, so I figured, well, *she's* certainly not worth my time."

"Halifax is a small place, and I happened to know Terry's reputation," says Amy. "I knew that she wasn't good to the people around her. On the other hand, I was immediately attracted to her, which really pissed me off!"

By their second encounter Terry had quit drinking. "I really had turned into a lowlife bottom-feeder. I had a child, but he was with his dad five days at a time, and I'd just go out and drink my face off, with other people who did the same. Finally I thought, I can't live one more day like this, I'm going to end up in a dumpster. So at midnight, New Year's Eve, 1996, that was the end of it." One night she was telling friends at the bar that she'd been sober forty-six long, hard-won days. Amy leaned into their conversation to comment, "Well, that's not very long."

"Me and my friends, our mouths dropped," says Terry. "Who the hell did this woman think she *was*?"

On their third encounter, a quiet night at the bar, it was Amy who approached Terry. They talked. They flirted. Amy says, "I was starting to think maybe she's not so bad after all. Actually, she's kind of interesting. But I still didn't see her as relationship material. I had already been in relationships of various kinds, but I thought, why not try a one-night stand? Since I didn't really care that much about this person, it would be safe and easy. I told Terry that's all I wanted."

Terry was petrified. "I've had a really hard time being in this body. I could only function as a stone butch, where it's you who does all the doing and your partners don't even get to touch you. Being ashamed of my body, I wouldn't even take my clothes off. But that first night with Amy, don't ask me why, I threw caution to the winds and got very intimate with her. It was the first time I'd ever been naked with a woman."

Apparently she chose the right one. Says Amy, "It was pretty obvious how nervous she was, so I said, well then, why don't I just show you how this body of yours works, and how you can enjoy it. And that's exactly what we did."

"I felt so comfortable and safe with her that nothing else mattered," says Terry. "I could have had six legs and horns growing out of my shoulders, and it wouldn't have mattered a bit. I've never felt like that before, not with anyone. I suppose these are the kinds of feelings that people discover in adolescence, only I got around to it a little later than most."

Though Amy had only bargained for a one-night stand, Terry kept turning up. "I couldn't stay away. I was so amazed that someone could actually like me when I was sober, that they could like me for who I was. Of course I didn't believe it would last."

"My friends thought I was making a big mistake getting involved with Terry," says Amy. "But I just pretended it wasn't serious, and I wasn't really interested. Also I'm an experience junkie, so after a while I decided not to hold back but to go for it. Maybe I'd get burned, maybe not."

After they'd been dating for a month, Terry knew it was time to come out. "I figured that if this relationship had any chance of lasting, Amy had a right to know, so she could make her own decisions. And better now than later, or finding out by accident."

"We must've gone through six hours of agonizing," says Amy. "I didn't know *what* was going on with her."

"I was trying to figure out exactly the right way to say it, that's all. I didn't even have the language for it. And I'd already had some pretty bad reactions. One friend got up and ran right out of the room. She hasn't spoken to me since, she avoids me like the plague."

Eventually, with both of them exhausted, Terry blurted it out: she was, had always wanted to be, probably always had been, and at the core of her being always would be – a man.

Amy was in shock. "I didn't know what to say. I was very confused, and quite scared. I had no experience of this at all. What did it mean for Terry, and for us? It was pretty clear to me by now that I wasn't interested in being with a guy."

"She asked me all these questions," says Terry. "I answered as well as I could. Though I'd always known in some way, I'd never had anyone to talk to about it, no resources, no help-line, no support. So I had to figure out for myself what it all meant, and how I felt. Then I started thinking oh my God, now I've done it, I should never have told her, I've ruined everything. But by then of course it was too late."

The wrong body Terry grew up Theresa on the west coast of Newfoundland. She believed that she was a boy. "My uncles used to call me Terry, and my brother would pass me off as his little brother. I really wanted to pee standing up at the toilet like him, and I couldn't understand why that didn't work. I just thought someone must've screwed up putting me together. My brother kept telling me don't worry, it'll grow in. Well, at sixteen things certainly started growing in, but not the way I wanted them to. The way I saw it, these people had all been lying to me, and this was some huge, terrible joke. I almost lost my mind. I tried to commit suicide."

Her best friend saved her life. "After that I figured the only thing I could do was push all those feelings down into the depth of me somewhere and take the correct path, the one my mother had always wanted for me." Terry took to wearing dresses and dating young men, many of whom turned out later to be gay. She married a navy man, became pregnant, and gave birth to a son, Colin. "When my mom heard I was engaged, and then pregnant, it was the happiest she'd ever been with me, in my whole life. That was great, but of course the happier she got, the more miserable I was."

With her husband so often out to sea, Terry became involved with another woman. "That kind of thing happens a lot in the navy, a lot more than most people would ever imagine." Eventually the husband found out, and they fought their way through a messy divorce and custody battle that ended in joint custody for Colin. Trying to make sense of her tangled feelings, Terry decided to identify as a lesbian. "At least that way I could be accepted somewhere. I could date women, which is what I wanted, and then maybe I'd even be a little happier about myself." This was the stone butch phase. "I really hated to have anyone touch me. I didn't want them being attracted to this body. They could be attracted to me, but not to this body – it was the wrong one."

Terry's lover before Amy was deep in the closet and told her parents that she was dating a man. "I had to tape myself down, dress the part and play the role," says Terry. "It was incredible. They treated me like a son-in-law, they thought I was the best thing since sliced bread! My girlfriend's mother made me lunches to take to work, they helped set up my apartment, and I'd help the dad do things around the house. The way they accepted me for who I was – or at least for who I wanted to be – that was really good for me, I loved it." After the relationship ended, the parents discovered the ruse and threw their daughter out of the house.

Amy also knew how it felt to be a misfit. "I hated where I grew up." Her roots are in rural Nova Scotia. "I never really fit in, and I always felt like an outsider. I didn't fit at university either. But after I moved to Halifax I got involved in environmental issues, and finally I found people that I felt some sort of kinship with. And for the first time – this is in my mid-twenties – I started to figure out what it meant to be me, to be gay, and how I might make a place for myself in the world."

Amy's relationship with her mother evolved with her sense of self. "We were very close when I was a child, then we really battled through my teens. But when I'd finally figured out who I was, my mom was the first person I went to. She said she'd known for years, but now she could brag to everyone about her lesbian daughter! My mom is great, she's one of my heroes."

Terry's emergence as a man reopened doubts that Amy had thought were settled. "The biggest issue for me was that I had fought a long, long time to find me, and now this comes along to challenge all that," she says. "How would being with Terry change me, what would it do to this rather fragile sense of self that I'd just managed to pull together? That really threw me. Mostly I worked through it all in my head, that's what I do, I just keep at things until I sort them out. And really, who else could I talk to about this? I began to see that it didn't have to change me at all, not who I really am, at the core of me. And then I started to realize that Terry hadn't really changed either. This person that I was starting to care about just became a little clearer to me, more in focus."

As she had done after their first date, Amy saw two options: either she could take a chance on the relationship, or she could run away from it. "And what would I gain by running? I would never know what it was like to have this particular experience with this particular person. On the other hand, if things didn't work out, it might be a bumpy road, but it wouldn't be the end of the world."

How does she manage being a lesbian with a partner who defines as a man? "This was another challenge, but I think that working through it actually broadened me," Amy replies. "What it came down to was this: Am I going to follow 'the lesbian rules,' which if you think about it are really crap and bogus anyway – why would a group of people who've said to hell with the rules want to make up *more* rules, what the hell is *that* about? – or am I going to follow my heart?"

FTM Over the next few months the two of them talked, cried, talked, and talked. Some nights Terry would lie in Amy's arms and howl. "For a long time I couldn't be intimate with her without crying to break my heart," says Terry. "I'd had all these emotions building up in me for so many years. Now it all came pouring out – I was sad, happy, mad at what I'd been denied, scared of what lay ahead, elated – all these raw emotions just came pouring out of me."

A researcher by inclination and training, Amy located some resources and a few transgender contacts on the Internet. They joined a list for female-to-male transgendered people. "Getting onto that list was like a rebirth for me," says Terry. "We encountered guys like me from all over the place – suddenly I wasn't the only one in the world! This whole trans thing is still so new. It's where being gay was in the '60s. We're only just beginning to gain some recognition." Terry and Amy have begun to meet face to face with other FTMs in Halifax, one of whom now defines as a gay man, and a support group has started up for partners of FTMs.

Next challenge: the relatives. Terry held back on telling her mother. She had come out to her only recently as a lesbian, after Amy said she wouldn't visit Terry's mother again until she did. "I was damned if I'd go all that way and be forced back into the closet," Amy says. Terry's mother took it badly. She threatened to fight her daughter for custody of Colin, because how could a lesbian ever make a decent mother? After much talk and tears, she backed off, but then announced that the two women couldn't sleep together in her house, as this would have a terrible effect on Colin. Terry's grandmother had already told Terry that if her mother had a problem with their relationship, they could stay with her. "My mom was really pissed off that I told my grandmother before her. But Nan only asked me two questions: Are you happy, and does this person love you? I had the kind of conversation with her that I really wanted to have with my mother."

Over time, Terry and her mother are working things out. She comes to stay with them in Halifax and sends them materials on lesbian issues that she's picked up in her travels as a shop steward with the Nova Scotia nursing union. "Even so," says Terry, "she and I still haven't had a real conversation about the lesbian thing, much less the trans thing."

"But she'll talk to me," says Amy. "She asks me all kinds of questions, and I'm very blunt in my answers."

Rather than come out directly to her brother, the one who promised her a penis, Terry told his wife, a psychologist, and asked her to pass it on. Next time Terry visited them in Cornerbrook, Newfoundland, the brother suggested that the two of them take a drive up to Deer Lake. After they'd driven some distance in silence, a rather nervous silence for Terry, suddenly her brother said, "I know."

"My brother is a man of very few words," says Terry. "He and I will go fishing together and we'll hardly say a word to each other all day. Maybe he'll tell a few jokes, or we'll talk a little about sports. But mostly we just enjoy each other's company."

A few miles on he said, "I'm okay with it." They rode the rest of the way to Deer Lake in comfortable silence.

"He talks a lot more about these things to me," says Amy. "I think he sees me as safer to talk to, being a woman."

"And strangely enough I can talk more easily to his wife," Terry adds. "My brother doesn't like to stay with emotions any longer than he has to. But he and I are very close. I know that I could call him up any time I needed him, and he'd be there."

The spirit of life Amy's coming out to her mother, "Iris," was freighted with an unusual precedent. When Amy was still a child, her father informed Iris that he was homosexual. "He told me he had known before we married," says Iris, "and in fact marrying me was part of his treatment plan. This was the early '60s, and his psychiatrist believed he could be cured, but he was told not to say a word to me about any of that. Coming from a rural community, homosexuality was something entirely new to me. I didn't know what to make of it. All I knew was I still loved him as a person, and he was a good father to the kids."

The marriage would carry on for another ten years. "I did find it hard to understand why he needed to include other men in our home life," says Iris. "He'd go away for a few days, then he'd come home with a man he'd want to introduce to the family. I'd say fine, whatever. I don't know where I was. I suppose I must've been absorbed with being a mother, taking care of the kids, and trying to maintain some sort of status quo. Eventually I realized that I also needed and deserved some sense of dignity in my own life. Going through that process was very upsetting, but finally it became clear to me that I didn't want to stay in the marriage."

Years later, Iris happened to meet her former husband's psychiatrist. "By then I was so angry for what he'd done, I could hardly speak to him," she says. "Finally I told him I felt like pinning his skin to the wall – how could he have discounted me so completely as a human being? He said if he knew then what he knows now about homosexuality, he would never have done anything like that."

In the meantime, Iris, a teacher, had been reading, asking questions, doing her own learning. "All of that helped me to grow, to appreciate the dignity in all human beings – in all *beings* – and our connectedness to each other." By the time Amy came out to her, her only remnant of concern was whether her daughter's life might be harder as a lesbian. "After that, our relationship became much fuller, and more adult," says Iris. "We became more accepting of each other. I think we came to understood that each of us had done the best we could. It wasn't so much a mother-daughter thing anymore, but now finally we could talk as adults about what each of us had been through – her childhood, my marriage, and all of that."

Despite her newfound ease with Iris, Amy fretted for some time about sharing Terry's news with her and her second husband, "Marshall." When she finally did, Terry went for a walk, too terrified to see their reactions. But as Amy reports, "My mother's first question was 'How can we support Terry?' She was more concerned about how I might react and what the impact it might have on the relationship."

They waved at Terry to come join them. "I thought, oh boy, this is it," says Terry. "But all they wanted to know was what they should *call* me. And was it okay to tell people. I couldn't believe it, I thought, who the hell *are* these people? How can they be so supportive?"

Easy, says Iris. "Terry is a dear. We feel warm and protective of her, it's such a struggle to find her place in society. For us the issue isn't a person's sexuality or gender but the humanness in all of us, and how we treat each other."

Marshall, a former Anglican priest, adds, "It was a very destructive thing that Christianity did when it made such a radical split between natural and spiritual life, and then defined nature, which of course includes sexuality, as dirty, messy, and evil."

The faith that he and Iris share now is rooted in the abundance of nature that surrounds their home, by a lake in the woods of southern Nova Scotia. Says Iris, "An earth-based spirituality doesn't make that split between sexuality and the spirit. When we can express our sexual energy with joy, it can very well be a way of praising the spiritual energy. And when you can recognize the spirit of life in all things, and feel connected to that, then you can identify much more fully with other human beings. That's the only basis I know for sustaining a relationship."

Your mom is a boy Amy, Terry, and Colin have also built another family circle for themselves: two women and their son in the Annapolis Valley, a single lesbian, and their various dogs and cats. "All of us – the people, anyway – grew up outcasts in one way or another," says Terry. "We're the ones that the cool kids made fun of and called names. Well, what do you know – now I'm one of the cool kids!"

"We go back and forth, sometimes here, sometimes to the Valley," says Amy. "When we're together, everyone's responsible for taking care of the kids and the animals, making sure supper gets on the table and so on. Our single friend will play with the boys or take them out for a ride in her truck. She's like an aunt to them. And the other boy is like a half-brother to Colin. They're the same age, they're being raised pretty much the same, and they're often together on weekends. It's a whole other level of family."

Terry says, "My mom and dad always had friends popping in for a meal or coming along on a picnic, and as I got older, I wanted to have that too at some point. You know, where you have this whole circle of friends, they have the key to your house and they'll drop by for a meal or whatever? Well, now I've got that, and I love it."

"I couldn't imagine life without these folks," Amy says. "We've been through a fair bit of stuff together, some hard times – the custody battle, a bankruptcy – and the mother of one of us was just diagnosed with severe cancer, so now it's her turn. We'll rally round, and put her in the centre for a while, give her the support she needs."

Terry says her mother got tired of hearing talk of this other clan. "But now that she's been here with them, she sees how well and how easily it all works. Like at mealtime, everyone just pitches in, you do this, I take care of that, and all of it with no fuss. After seeing that, my mother said to me, 'Wow, what an amazing circle you have.'"

"She's right," says Amy. "It feels like a blessing to have all these layers around me – this little family unit of ours in our own space, my biological family, and then this community of good friends. Everyone should have this. I mean, everyone who wants it."

Earlier, Colin told me about the double staircase at school. "The kids say that one side of the stairs is for boys, the other side is for girls, and the railing in the middle, that's for the gays." He made no further comment. But after he went to bed Amy said, "We're pretty sure that he hears more stuff like that at school than he lets on. I wouldn't be surprised if he's trying to protect us. If he doesn't tell us, we don't have to feel bad. Colin has a very big heart."

They also feel compelled to protect him. "Kids can be so cruel," says Amy, "and we don't want him getting hurt on account of who we are. Of course we can't protect him from everything out there, but we'll do what we can."

"Of course he has to have more freedom as he gets older," Terry adds. "Part of me hates that. It's weird, my mother used to send my brother and me off to go fishing all day with nothing but our bikes and our lunch. But now that I'm the parent – "

Amy interrupts with a laugh, "Terry would be tailing him everywhere if she could."

Terry nods. "It's true, I would. We let him go by himself to the corner store, but beyond that, how do you know what's safe as a next step? Where he goes to school now, it's pretty safe, even though he has to cross a couple of streets. But the big junior highs around here, that's going to be a whole other way of life, where black kids or a kid with a dyke for a mom can be targets. It's bad enough having to listen to people say you live with two moms so you must be a little faggot. Who needs to be hearing that your mom is a *boy*!"

When Terry and Colin go out in public together, as they did yesterday to toss a football in the park, it's not uncommon for them to overhear people saying, with an eye on Terry, "What is that, a boy or a girl?" How do they respond?

"Well, to tell you the truth," Terry says, "secretly I like it. Anyway, I would never want to say anything that might put Colin on the spot. But he just comes out with something like, 'What, are you stupid? It's my mom.'"

Here is the heart of Terry's dilemma. Colin's mother defines as a male, is thrilled to be taken for a male, but as the song goes, still ain't satisfied. "When I go fishing with my brother," Terry says, "regardless of who I feel I am, or who I want to be, I still can't stand up and pee off the back of the boat like he can. I want to be able to do that. I want to be able to write my name in the snow."

When Terry came out to a lesbian friend, she responded that she didn't believe Terry or anyone else could really be transgendered, it was all in their heads. "She said the problem is that society tries to force us into these cookie-cutter gender roles, you have to be one or the other, male or female. But – this is what she says – we don't have to submit to that. Just because she dresses up in a suit and tie and cuts her hair short, that doesn't make her a man. She likes having the body of a woman, and she likes being with women. Fine, I have no problem with that. But that's her, it's not me. Even though I don't hate this body the way I used to, it's still not the body I want. I don't want breasts, and I do want a penis. That's how I see myself in my dreams. That's who I am."

Does Terry contemplate surgery to realize the dream? "That's a huge question. A huge question." Terry sighs. "I've tried to lay it all out for myself, and I've talked about it a lot with Amy – what do I have, what do I want, what do I need? What I want more than anything, and what I finally have for the first time in my life, is a happy, loving, supportive family. So I have to ask, how would the surgery affect that? Would it foster it or would it threaten it? Putting all that together, what I've decided is that I don't need to proceed with surgery right now. I may *want* it, but I don't actually need it. One day maybe, when Colin is older, but not right now."

Again it comes back to Colin – even this, the long search for Terry's manhood. "Absolutely, no question," says Terry. "If I were to come out as a guy, I mean really come out in a public way, Colin's dad would certainly use it against us." In their first custody battle the lawyer representing Colin's father argued that as a lesbian, Terry could not be a fit mother. "The judge was quite old, and I really expected the worst from him," Terry recalls. "But he amazed me, he said my sexual orientation wasn't admissible. Period."

In the first round Terry won joint custody, and in the second, primary caregiver status, the right to make all significant decisions on Colin's behalf. Terry's lawyer in the second round told her a favourable judgement would be more likely for a single lesbian than for a couple. "It's the sex thing," says Terry. "If you're single, they don't have to think about that, but if you're a couple – ugh! But then if you add on top of that the whole trans thing, there's no telling what a judge might do."

So this is how it will be, at least for now. In Colin's world, Amy will continue to be Momma and Terry will continue to be Mom. "When I go out with him, like to a school event," says Terry, "I don't dress as a woman, I don't dress as a man, I dress as Mom. There was this one time I had to wear a dress to a formal dinner – skirt, pantyhose, high heels, the whole deal. I felt like I was in drag. When Colin saw me, he laughed himself silly. He said, 'Mom looks like a boy in a dress!' That's all he sees, his mom. And that will never change. Even if I decide to have surgery later on, and I get the penis I've always wanted, I'll still be Mom."

Terry grins. "I'll just be Mom with a penis. Now won't that be something!"

13 Modern Parenting

Leah's family "GRETA" AND I CHAT ON THE FRONT VERANDAH of her house on a shaded street in east-end Toronto. Her daughter, "Leah," is spending the afternoon with her other mother, "Carrie." Before I came by, Greta asked Leah if it would be okay to use their full names in this book. Leah looked alarmed. "Oh, no," she said. "If my friends' parents ever read it, they'll know you're a lesbian, and I don't want them to know." Leah is eleven.

"When I use the L-word now, she gets embarrassed," says Greta. "She says, 'Mummy, shhh, somebody will hear!' She doesn't want to be singled out or for people to think she's weird by association because her mothers are lesbian. All right, then, whatever she needs to survive and feel okay in school, we'll support it." For Greta it's just another strand in the complex weave that constitutes gay family.

Until she emigrated from Germany twenty years ago, Greta considered herself to be straight. Though her relationships with women were strong and intimate, and her encounters with men neither of those, she had only heterosex. In Canada, on the other hand, her partners have been women. "If we must have labels, I guess you'd have to say I'm bisexual."

The determination to have a child has been a constant with her, as has the preference to conceive by intercourse. In 1988 she returned to Germany, recruited a former boyfriend for the project, and came back to Canada pregnant. "He didn't want any responsibility for the child, which was okay with me. But I insisted that at least she should know who her father was, if that's what she wanted, and that he not deny it." Leah knows; when her father visits Canada, or they go to Germany to see Greta's mother, the three of them spend time together. That's as far as it goes.

But Leah does have another parent. While Greta was pregnant, she became friends with Carrie, a black co-worker at the women's shelter where she worked. Carrie told her she'd had two children in her mid-teens, and though she couldn't afford to keep them, she'd kept in touch; they were with her in-laws. Now defining as lesbian, Carrie had been hoping to meet a woman who was pregnant, to go through the birth with her, and to raise the child together. Okay, said Greta, let's do it. They talked at length about how co-parenting might work. They agreed that the child would be central, the raison d'être for their friendship, and the rest they would figure out as they went.

"You know there's a good chance the water may be cold and wet," says Greta, "but that's life, either you jump in or you don't." They jumped. Carrie attended prenatal classes with her and was her labour coach through the home birth. "The birth was beautiful," says Greta. "Very fast for a firstborn, with lots of friends around. And Carrie was fabulous."

It turned out that the water wasn't so much cold as rocky. For a while the three of them lived together. Carrie was working, Greta at home caring for Leah; the co-parents were friends but not lovers. "If I ever wanted to bring anyone home, it immediately reinforced Carrie's fear that someone else would take over her role and relationship with Leah," says Greta. She decided to find her own place with Leah, who would continue to have her own room for regular overnights at Carrie's, her other home. In this way Leah and Carrie could develop a more independent relationship of their own.

Carrie's fear was well founded, on one hard fact. "Since I'm the biological mother, legally speaking Carrie doesn't have a leg to stand on," says Greta. "She was afraid that if something happened to me, my mother or Leah's biological father could come in and say, 'She's our child.' Now I've made it quite clear in my will that Carrie is the legal guardian." But the fact remains that, should Greta ever deny her access to Leah for any reason, Carrie would have no legal recourse.

Have they considered the option of Carrie adopting Leah? "Carrie is thinking about it," says Greta. "But it's very expensive, and I really don't think it's necessary. All my relatives and Leah's father know and accept the situation. Also, Leah is very Canadian, and anyone trying to take her from Canada, or from Carrie, for that matter, would have to fight her hands and feet. In any case, in five years she'll be able to make her own decisions. But all of that aside, if Carrie feels that adoption is the right way to go, I would certainly support her in that."

When it became clear that the two of them weren't hearing each other's concerns very well, they decided to see a counsellor. "At first I had some hesitation about it," says Greta, "having grown up with the idea that you don't do that unless there's something wrong with you. But the last thing we wanted was to fight our differences out through the child." According to Greta, it took about three years to work out a comfortable rhythm as co-parents. Along the way, each major decision, whether on housing, daycare, or school, took long, delicate negotiation.

Another issue loomed early on, with Leah being white and Carrie black. When they were out together, people would sometimes ask if Carrie was the nanny. Carrie is strong enough to confront racism of this sort, but each time it took its toll. "When Carrie goes to school with Leah, I'm sure it's more challenging for the other kids to slot her in relation to Leah than when I go, " says Greta. "That's too bad, but it does happen." By grade three Leah began to tell Greta, privately and with some trepidation, "I'm not saying I don't like black people, but . . ." "Of course she didn't feel she could say these things to Carrie," says Greta, "and she didn't even feel comfortable saying them to me, with my own strong views on racism, so who could she talk to?"

Leah was facing other pressures in her life. She wasn't happy at school; one day she came home crying that she'd been teased by bullies, and didn't know what to do. Greta, a community development worker in public housing, had just bought a house for them, jointly with a straight male friend, the only way she could afford it. "Istvan" the co-owner, has an apartment in the basement. Carrie had moved to another house with her new partner, and the partner's two kids, a further disruption for Leah. Finally Greta and Carrie decided that what she needed was an independent advocate. They found Bernice, a child counsellor. After Leah worked with her for a year, she told Greta she thought that was enough. "The change in her is amazing," says Greta. "She's a lot more confident, and not nearly so bothered by things at school. She knows she can return to see Bernice any time, and she knows that nothing she says will ever get back to either of us."

Leah goes to a relatively small, racially diverse school in downtown Toronto. It's a hike from the east end where they live and Greta works, but worth the trouble. Each September Greta and Carrie explain their situation as co-parents to Leah's new teacher. They need to know, they tell the teacher, that if Leah has any problems – for example, if she's teased about having two moms of different races – she can feel safe to approach the teacher. And she doesn't like being singled out, even positively, as a token example of "an alternate family."

"Of course we do all of this with Leah present," says Greta. "That way everything is out in the open, and very clear."

Greta and Istvan, the house's co-owner, have been friends since they met shortly after Greta landed in Canada. "I'm so glad he's here," says Greta. "I used to worry that if Leah was only around women all the time, how would she ever learn to relate to men, would she get into abusive relationships? Istvan is anything but your typical macho man. They play with Barbies, and he reads Archie comics to her. I don't like those Archies, I think they're so stupid. But if I go up there when they're playing, she says 'Go now, mummy, I'm playing.'" Greta laughs. "She knows she won't get a lecture from him, which she sometimes gets from me. I can't help it – you know, sexism and all that. But sometimes, especially when you're a kid, who needs it, right?"

When Greta started to date "Alison," it was another significant transition, for all concerned. Greta is 43, Alison 50. Says Alison, who works in computer graphics, "We talked a lot on the phone before we actually met. I know how people talk about being honest with each other, but we really did get into things, what we want, and don't want, what bothers us, how we handle things. We figured we had nothing to lose, and if we did get involved we'd know what we were getting into." Greta made it clear that she came complete with a child, a co-parent, a house, and one housemate, male. "That's what you get with me," says Greta, "the whole package."

Though they talked about it at length, Greta's role as a parent remained somewhat abstract for Alison until they started spending more time together. "I had no idea how much of her attention would be focused on Leah," she says. "For example, it's virtually impossible to have a conversation without interruption."

"It's true," Greta laughs. "As a parent your attention is so constantly divided that after a while you hardly even notice it anymore."

"At first that got on my nerves but I'm adapting to it," says Alison. "I take the opportunity to do things I enjoy doing on my own, like reading, listening to the CBC or working with my art." Friday nights, Leah's regular sleepover at her other home, Greta and Alison have a standing date; it's her day off, so she has time to prepare. And every couple of months the two of them try to get away for a weekend.

Alison is gradually moving into the house from her high-rise condominium downtown. This weekend they will move her drafting table. "It's challenging to move into someone else's home," she says, "but this is such a nice neighbourhood, you can step out into the garden, just like that, and you can talk to your neighbours." As if on cue, the single mom next door hands over a jar of rhubarb-strawberry jam she's just made.

Alison's relationship with Leah is ripening at its own pace. "Each of us would like the other to like her," says Alison. "And that doesn't seem difficult with Leah. She's a really intelligent child, and fun, we can make each other laugh. But I don't see myself as being her playmate. I will do art with her, or help with her math homework, things that seem productive and come easily to me. It's great to connect with a kid like her, it's like getting an energy boost. But I'd never put myself in a position of authority over her. She doesn't need one more mom. I had a very authoritarian childhood, but now it's part of my philosophy that for every right answer, there's always another right answer. So I'm not interested in imposing my views on Leah."

"I wouldn't allow any partner of mine to do that," Greta adds, "or to take an active discipline role with Leah, or make any major decisions about her life. That's my role, and Carrie's."

As Leah gets older, new questions and challenges arise continually. "Is a boy ever going to ask me out?" she asks her moms. "When am I going to get boobs? Will they be big or small?" Greta wonders, and talks with Carrie and other parents, about how to respond if Leah tells her she wants to smoke or drink: Is it better to let her do it at home, so at least you know what she's doing?

And how should they respond if Leah gets rude and snotty in the current teen mode, which she tries out rather tentatively now and then? Should they ignore it, hoping it will pass, or refuse to accept it? And then what? "If you're trying to create a democratic kind of relationship, sometimes it's not easy to find ways to negotiate these things," says Greta. "And I worry about all the pressures on her to conform, not to stand out in any way. Oh well, Carrie and I will just have to discuss each of these things as they come up, that's all. I'm sure we can figure something out."

"I think Leah is really lucky," says Alison. "Who would ever have thought there could be so many different kinds of relationships, and families, and openings to life? What a great way to grow up!"

Skyla's family On their first date, a Bryan Adams concert, Natanya Mullen asked Paulla Meneses, "So, do you want to have kids?" Natanya, a lifeguard and swimming instructor, had wanted a child since she was one herself growing up in Alberta.

Paulla, an assembly worker making phones in Calgary, hadn't thought about it, not directly, but had always enjoyed kids.

Natanya also wanted to get married. "I didn't think you need a piece of paper to prove your love," says Paulla, "but if that's what she wanted, it was okay with me. In the end I'm glad we did it, it was a nice experience." Natanya's father walked her down the aisle. The best man was a friend, Russell Crowhurst, who had emigrated from Britain a few years before and met Paulla at a Lesbian and Gay Youth meeting in Calgary. The boys wore tuxes, the girls dresses.

Given their backgrounds, it's something of a role reversal for Natanya to be the more traditional of the two. Though her father is a minister, he's in the relatively liberal United Church of Canada, and in Natanya's upbringing there was ample room for choice. Paulla was born to a conservative Catholic family in the Portuguese Azores. Her mother died when she was two, and her father remarried, taking the family to Canada when Paulla was five.

"My father never hit us, but my stepmother certainly did," she says. "That was her specialty, yelling and hitting." When Paulla came out to her father a few years ago, she was disowned, her name never to be spoken again in their house. She had no contact with her parents for a year. "Finally, my uncle [her stepmother's brother] told her [stepmother] to wake up and get her *kaka* together. 'She's your daughter,' he said, 'and she's not the only who's gay, even here on the island' [the Azores]." Paulla is no longer disowned, and her father admits that he loves her. But they still won't allow Natanya into their home just a few miles across Calgary.

As a wedding gift, Aaron Wilson, a friend, had given the couple a turkey baster. Now all they needed was a little sperm. Natanya says, "For the child's sake, we wanted at least to know who the father was, so that eliminated the sperm-bank route." They asked three men, including Russell, a teaching assistant for special needs children with the local board of education.

Russell had serious doubts. "I really like kids, I worked with them in the United States and Israel, and I came to Canada as a nanny," he says. "I'm also the product of a broken home. My parents split when I was five. I was quite torn – did I really want to take on what I regarded as this huge responsibility, and risk separation and having no say if the couple split up or moved away?" Over the next two years the three of them kept talking. Finally Russell agreed, on condition that he not be just a donor but actively involved in the child's life.

Skyla Mullen Crowhurst was born in 1996. When Natanya had to undergo a caesarian section, the doctor said only one person could be with her. She chose Paulla. "So there it was," says Russell: "Only day one and the big division I'd feared already came up." But a nurse persuaded the doctor to allow a second person into the room. "We're very grateful to her," says Paulla. "I certainly wouldn't have wanted to be left out either, so I can understand how Russell felt." As their daughter emerged, Russell cried, and briefly thought the placenta was a twin. Paulla was thrilled. "She was the purplest baby you've ever seen, and she just screamed for dear life!"

As for Natanya, "Well, mostly I was drugged, paralysed, and throwing up," she says with a merry laugh.

With the baby happily settled with her two moms in their compact suburban house, tensions in the three-way parenting arrangement grew. Natanya was at home nursing, Paulla away at work. "When Skyla came home, I was afraid she'd develop more of a bond with Natanya, and even with Russell," says Paulla. "After all, it was her egg and his sperm. Sometimes I couldn't even see a place for myself in there. For the first couple of years I resented Russell. I just wanted it to be Natanya, me, and the baby. But Natanya reminded me what it was like not knowing my mother when I was growing up, and how would Skyla feel if she didn't know her father?"

Living across town, Russell was having similar anxieties. "Paulla and I both felt like the odd one out, for totally different reasons. The only person who seemed completely secure, aside from Skyla of course, was Natanya."

Natanya nods. "I kept having to be the go-between when the two of them weren't talking. Don't talk to me, I kept saying, talk to each other."

"It's taken us a couple of years," says Paulla, "but now we're much better at listening to each other and understanding how the other one feels."

Finding a couple of hours when all three parents could meet with me together took intricate planning. Russell works full time plus two evenings at the board and a part-time job on Saturdays. In addition, his mother emigrated recently from England to live with him, and won't go anywhere without him. Paulla worries that he won't have time to find a boyfriend and that having his mother in residence will only further cramp his style. "I don't *have* a style," says Russell. "That's the problem."

As for Natanya, she rarely knows more than a week or two in advance when she'll be required to work a shift at the local pool. And though Paulla has a new job where she works fewer hours and is closer to home, she also takes upgrading courses two evenings a week at the community college.

To care for Skyla, they've worked out a complicated schedule that flexes to accommodate all these comings and goings. After we finish talking tonight, Russell will take Skyla home with him. Tomorrow his mum will care for her while Russell is at work, and then he'll bring her back here, forty minutes' drive at the best of times, to coincide with Paulla's return from her job. And so it goes. When the two moms go to Portugal in the fall to visit Paulla's relatives, they can't afford to take Skyla, who will be nearly five and thus full fare – photos will have to do. For those two weeks Russell will take care of Skyla full time. School will just have opened, so it won't be easy, but his sister, who also lives in Calgary, will help out.

How does Skyla deal with all this traffic? "She's amazingly adaptable," says Natanya. "She seems perfectly happy wherever she is, with whoever, and in whatever combinations of us and whatever environment."

Watching the three of them watch Skyla, who's about to put a gluestick into her mouth, I ask if they have different parenting styles. They all burst out laughing. "Very different," says Natanya. Paulla nods. "Russell and I don't let her get away with as much as Natanya does. None of us would ever hit Skyla, but he and I will raise our voice more than Natanya."

"We don't raise our voice," Russell corrects, "so much as we change the tone to give it a little more gravity, to say this isn't funny more." I can hear the nanny in his tone.

"We were all brought up differently," says Paulla. "I'm learning how to do things without yelling. I'll sometimes watch what Russell or

Natanya do, or I'll call one of them up and say, 'Look, she's pushing my buttons here, what do I do?'"

"These guys are way more cautious with her than I am," says Natanya, "especially with outdoor stuff."

"It's true," says Paulla, "I had to take care of my younger sister, and if anything happened, it was me that got into trouble. So I'm always worrying, if we let her go into the backyard by herself, what if someone grabs her and we never see her again?"

"Whereas with me," says Natanya, "as long as I can see her it's okay."

Back to the gluestick. "It's non-toxic," says Natanya. "That's why we bought it."

"But that doesn't exactly mean it's edible," says Paulla.

"We aren't going to put that in our mouth, are we," says Russell. Skyla decides that she'd rather play the harmonica for us and does some bluesy runs. "My father used to play the harmonica for us when we were kids," says Paulla, "so I couldn't resist getting one for her." Her parents still won't let Skyla call them grandpa and grandma, only Martino and Lucie. "It's kind of crazy," she says. "How long will they keep shooting themselves in the foot?"

Natanya and Paulla plan to have another child. Says Natanya, "It was our idea all along that Skyla wouldn't be an only child." Paulla adds, "It's better when a kid has someone to play with that's closer to their own age and an ally." This time she'll be the one that gets pregnant.

"If possible," says Natanya, "we also want to have the same dad."

"If Russell can stand the stress," says Paulla with a laugh.

"Oh, not to worry," he replies, with an airy wave of the hand, "Easy come, easy go."

Jayka's family James Johnstone, one of Jayka's dads, is busy preparing a family dinner in the house he shares with his former partner, Keith Stuart, another of Jayka's dads. I'm assigned to chopping herbs from the lush garden behind their house in east Vancouver. As Jayka's family gathers, I have to make notes to sort them out: Laura, Linda, Jules, Tara, Rebecca, James, Keith, and Richard.

Jayka herself is a noisy, effervescent four-and-a-half year old who basks in the adoring attention she draws from all these adults, like a plant leaning to the light. At one point in the busy kitchen, with dinner almost ready, she demonstrates a dance move. Flailing behind her, one small hand lights on my thigh and grabs hold for balance. I'm a stranger. She didn't look, just assumed that someone would be there. As far back as I can remember, not once in my life have I ever felt such easy trust.

Laura Mayne, who's thirty-two now, loved to babysit as a young girl and always assumed that one day she would have children of her own. Through her early twenties she read anything she could find on lesbian parenting, grilled moms at the Michigan Women's Music Festival where she did childcare, and joined or facilitated support groups for lesbian moms. Working at a women's shelter, she saw how hard it can be to parent alone. Nor did the couple route seem quite right: it looked too isolating, too dependent on the quirky tides of relationship. At the shelter she met a co-worker, Cathy, who intended to move back to Ontario but who offered to support Laura as a mother in any way she could, for the long term. Linda Schulz, who had known Laura since 1990, working in women's shelters, also got drawn into the baby project. Jayka's family had begun to form.

Next on the agenda: sperm. "At first I thought a sperm bank would be easier, and safer in some way," says Laura. "But my former girlfriend, who was adopted, had recently found her birth mother, and that gave me a whole different perspective on the need for a child to at least know who the other biological parent is." Not knowing any men she wanted to ask, she cast a fairly wide net: Did anyone know anyone who might make good dad material? A friend who worked at Canada Post reported that a co-worker, Keith Stuart, had recommended his boyfriend, James Johnstone, a Japanese-language translator, tour escort, and freelance editor. Laura called him.

"It was pretty much out of the blue," says James. "Well, it was and it wasn't. In a spiritual development course I'd taken, three different psychics told me exactly the same thing, that I would have some sort of contract with a being who had a female body. I found this ridiculous, it seemed so improbable. Then Laura called." He was thirty-six.

On the balcony of the west-end Vancouver apartment he shared with Keith, James, Laura and Cathy talked sperm, babies, and the nature of family. "I still didn't know how it might work," says Laura. "But by then I did have some pretty clear ideas of what I did and didn't want."

Says James, "Though I like children, I had never given any thought to actually being a parent. I was surprised how comfortable it felt, talking about all that. Laura seemed to me a kind of fertility goddess, with all these eggs ready for the hatching."

"I liked that he said he wanted a connection to the child," says Laura. "And I liked the way he was connected to a wide community. That seemed healthy to me."

When James told Keith about the various options they'd discussed, Keith questioned whether being a donor would be enough for James. Mightn't he want more contact with the child? Deeply hurt when his homophobic brother and sister-in-law shut him out of their son's life, Keith had only begun to heal when a connection grew between him and one of James's nephews. Keith became the boy's favourite uncle.

After dinner Jayka goes upstairs with a rotating series of her people, so that each of them gets a chance to play with her while the others talk to me. We can hear them making energetic music up there on what sounds like an electric keyboard. Then Jayka pops back into the dining room. "I want *everybo*dy to come upstairs and play."

"How about I come up now, and then the others later?" Linda offers. "Okay?"

"Okay," says Jayka, and departs.

Talks on the baby project continued for another six months before Laura, Cathy, and James settled things. "We never wrote any legal documents," says James. "The whole thing was done on faith, and quite organically."

Shortly before Laura conceived, she met Jules Siebert at a music festival, and they became lovers. "Laura's plan to have a baby was something entirely new to me," says Jules, who was then twenty-seven. "I found it both scary and exciting, and wondered what kind of role there might be for me." She was there for Jayka's home birth, as was Linda Schulz, and another close friend, Sarah. "After that," says Jules, "it seemed quite natural to love and take care of Jayka. She became part of my life. Over the first year of her life, my relationship with Laura changed, but they remain family, and I don't think that will ever change. I love having a young person in my life."

Linda Schulz, who's thirty-two, lived with Laura and Jayka for a year and a half before going to study social work in Victoria. "But I still see my relationship to them and to this family around them as long term and very important to me. Not having a biological or a partner role, I do struggle sometimes to define what my role actually is, especially when others who don't know the situation find it hard to place me in relation to Jayka. We're still so tied up in the traditional roles." How does she describe her role? "Sometimes I'll say there's a little girl in my life that I love and to whom I'm committed. Sometimes I'll say I'm like an aunt. It really depends on what I think people can get their heads around."

With such a strong support network around them, Laura had thought she could live on her own with Jayka. But when Jules moved out, she had second thoughts. "I realized that quite often it was still just me and her, which put all kinds of pressure on both of us." She formed a new house with Linda and another friend. Then she met Tara, who was doing childcare for a queer moms group; Tara moved in, and joined the family. I didn't catch her age, but I'd guess she's in her mid to late twenties. "I've cared for young people in different ways for quite a while now," she says, "working at camps, teaching swimming and so on. Children are also quite an important part of my Jewish heritage."

When Jayka was seven months old, Laura resumed her job as a family support worker. On the days she works, various people have made regular commitments to be with Jayka, which requires a structured schedule and a fair amount of driving around. But last year they found a house that shares a back fence with James and Keith, and now Jayka can call out from her kitchen window to James, working in his garden. Says Laura, "My goal now is to bring everyone closer somehow, so we can have a looser schedule, and as Jayka gets older, she can have more say in where she wants to be and who she wants to hang out with. I'd like to find that kind of spontaneity for all of us."

Meanwhile, Jayka's family continues to grow. When Rebecca started to date Jules, it was clear that she would also be connecting to Jayka and her family. "It's a wonderful experience for me," says Rebecca. "I've thought about having kids myself, and since I'm bisexual, I suppose I could end up with a man someday. Unfortunately I don't like most straight men, but I do know some gay men who'd like to have kids too, so I'm really glad to see how well an alternative family like this can actually work."

When Richard started to date James, he wasn't sure what else he might be getting into, or how it would work. (In another strand of this remarkable web, he now lives in James's and Keith's old apartment in the west end.) "Somehow it all just melds together, and there's always somebody ready to be backup," he says. "I'm amazed by Jayka's flexibility. She just seems to go with whatever's happening, with no fuss at all."

"For Jayka it's really not that complicated," says Laura. "It just is. That's the beauty of it: this is her normal. It's only *our* stuff that makes it complicated."

Rebecca adds, "What I think most people don't notice is how much effort Laura puts into making it all work so smoothly."

I notice. When James calls Jayka the hub of this family wheel and the rest of them the spokes, in that analogy Laura strikes me as the outer rim, keeping the whole spinning enterprise intact and on course. But she refuses any such credit. "It's quite practical, really. I believe most people want what's best for their children, but it's so easy to get overwhelmed by circumstances, and the less support you have, the harder it is. I've seen how those pressures can wear people down, so I think everyone should have a set-up like this, even people in couples. It's a myth that if you're a couple, you can do it on your own. That's why I love talking about what we're doing, to anyone who'll listen."

As they prepare to walk home – it's well past Jayka's bedtime – Laura adds, "I think this is also a really good response to the gay oppression that tells us we pose a threat to children, and to a system that works to discourage any contact. Families like this let adults relate to a young person, and the young person relate to a variety of adults, with all that each of us has to offer. What can that possibly do but make the world a better place?"

Given how deep-seated that oppression is, and how tenuous the ground we've gained, I'm surprised to hear that only one official document supports this intricate, highly unorthodox, evolving family structure: Laura's will, naming Cathy as Jayka's legal guardian. "I don't have a lot of confidence that the legal system is going to look out for my best interests or Jayka's," says Laura. "To me it feels better and safer to build a community based on trust and good intentions. It's that community I count on, not the courts, to look out for us if things get hard, and the bigger that community is, the better. We're not extraordinary people. The reason this works is because we all have so much support."

In the midst of our good-nights, Jayka says, "My turn," pointing to the tape recorder on the table. "And so it is," says Laura. "You've been very patient while the rest of us had our turn. Do you want to say something about your family?"

A moment's hesitation, then Jayka says, loud and clear, "I like my mom. My big fat mommy. I like my Linda. My big fat Linda. My nice fat Tara. I like my big fat Jules. My big fat Rebecca. My big fat James. My big fat Keith. I like my big fat shaved Richard."

The adults explode with laughter. "That's not shaved," Richard says, patting his bald head. "That's *me*."

"There," says Jayka, as the laughter subsides. "Now it's someone else's turn."

Zacchary's family Aaron Wilson and his son, Zacchary, joined Jerry Walton for Gay Pride Day in Victoria, British Columbia, a year after the two men met. Following the street festival, the three were walking together hand in hand, the boy between the two men. "This is really neat," said Zacchary, who was seven at the time. "Now I have three dads." Later the same day, he said, "Dad, I hope you and Jerry stay gay forever." Aaron and Jerry were astonished, and greatly moved by both remarks.

Within a year this innocent encounter showed up in quite another form, as the final item on a list of charges that Aaron's wife submitted to an Alberta court. She was applying for divorce and for sole custody of Zacchary. Her trump card, as Aaron puts it, was to argue that by taking their son to a homosexual event, Aaron had proved he was not a responsible parent. "We'd had a clear but unspoken rule that neither of us would ever use the gay thing as a weapon," says Aaron. "Until then I had no idea how vicious she was prepared to be to get what she wanted."

Among the lessons that Aaron learned over the ensuing year, the fragility of trust and the hollowness of unspoken rules would leave an especially bitter taste.

He grew up in a working-class neighbourhood in Winnipeg. His parents' household, though ostensibly Christian, was torn by fierce battles, mostly due to his father's problems with drugs, alcohol, and anger. When his mother remarried, things didn't improve. By the time Aaron was thirteen, he knew that he wanted to be a father himself, and he knew that he would do it differently. Since he didn't see a woman in the picture, he assumed he would have to adopt.

Christianity remained a lifeline for him, or at least a thread. At Trinity Western, an evangelical university in Langeley, B.C., he met Deborah, the woman he would marry. He also had a conversion experience, the emotional jolt that's usually known as being born again. "I already knew I was attracted to men," says Aaron, "but I was wilfully determined to get over it. The thing I wanted most was to be accepted and loved by my fiancée and her family, who were Baptist fundamentalists. Being straight looked like the only way I could have that." The conversion experience didn't stick. "It felt like buckshot, it wasn't organic either to my being or my political evolution, which was something along the lines of liberation theology. I got called a commie pinko faggot by the upright Christians at Trinity."

When Aaron and Deborah married, he was nineteen. "Eventually I started to talk to her in a very tentative way about my sexuality," he says, "and how hard it was to cope with the tension of denying it. Then Deborah told me she was pregnant. She offered to separate, but instead I recommitted to the relationship, hoping that maybe the birth and raising a child would be all-consuming enough to sweep aside any problems I had with my identity." It worked for a while, but by the time Zacchary was four, Aaron's torment had become intolerable. "If Zacchary hadn't literally been in the next room, suicide would probably have been my choice. It was easier to feel responsible for him than for myself, and suicide would have been a terrible betrayal."

When I met Aaron in 1994, he had separated from Deborah and was living in a tiny basement apartment in Calgary, where he had come out as an increasingly confident and articulate gay activist. Apparently inspired by his example, Deborah had formed a relationship with another woman, Bonnie. Aaron and I drove up to Didsbury, a small town north of Calgary, to have dinner with the two women and Zacchary, a friendly, rambunctious kid. Deborah reported, with a mixture of chagrin and delight, that he had called over the back fence to a neighbour, "I've got two moms!"

Within a year Aaron had moved to Vancouver and found work. Deborah and Bonnie followed soon after with Zacchary, and enrolled him in a French immersion kindergarten. Weekends were Aaron's time with him. At one point Deborah persuaded Aaron to sign a child-custody agreement assigning her primary care of Zacchary. She said that social services wouldn't provide child support payments without it. Shortly after, she informed him that she and Zacchary were going back to Alberta. "She wasn't interested in talking about it, and it didn't even occur to me to contest it," says Aaron. "I just didn't think in those terms, and I still trusted her."

Aaron visited as often as he could, driving 1,500 kilometres each way, or flying when he could afford it. On one of these visits, just as he was leaving for the airport to return home, Deborah told him she intended to remarry and handed him the court papers. She had applied for a divorce, as well as sole custody of Zacchary, and full control as the primary parent. The child-custody agreement that Aaron had signed in Vancouver supported her case. He had ten days to find a lawyer and respond.

The lawyer he consulted in Vancouver told him he'd need one in Alberta, and he retained Sandra Sebree, a Calgary lawyer who has since come out as a lesbian and won a ground-breaking gay adoption case. Aaron's divorce-custody case took most of a year and thousands of dollars to settle. "In the end," say Aaron, "I got nothing I wanted, and Deborah got everything she wanted. I kept saying I ought to be something more than a wallet in Zacchary's life, but that was all she wanted, and that's what she got. The process was incredibly demeaning. I actually found myself questioning the validity of my role as Zacchary's dad." A year later, he's close to crying as he recalls it. "You hear all kinds of talk in the courts about protecting the best interests of the child, but it's bullshit. If they really meant it, they'd protect the relationships that are truly beneficial to the child. In our case the court didn't protect me or my relationship with my son. I have no say at all in any significant decisions regarding his life."

In addition to the monthly payments to Deborah that the court ordered, which Aaron manages by working two jobs in psychiatric rehabilitation, he flies to Calgary to see Zacchary when he can, or flies him out to Vancouver at his own expense. "So far she hasn't obstructed my access to him," says Aaron, "but I feel very much at her mercy." Zacchary will visit this summer and spend time with his two gay dads.

When Aaron and Jerry first met, they quickly identified a startling piece of common ground in their close encounters with the Christian right. Jerry was raised in a military environment. "It had two effects," he says. "I learned that all the important decisions are made by someone else, and if you follow orders, you'll belong. At the same time, I got taunted constantly because I failed to live up to the ideal that was supposed to constitute a boy or man in that obsessively male culture. So even though I was attracted to men, I was also quite alienated from them. By my late teens I was very isolated, and I had hardly any sense of self at all." Then Jesus, or rather, Another Chance Ministries, offered salvation.

At the Vancouver branch plant of the powerful U.S. fundamentalist "ex-gay movement," the deal was clear: since homosexuality resulted from early dysfunction, it could be corrected, but only with the help of God and Another Chance. "It had an immediate appeal for me," says Jerry. "They promised that God would take care of me, that he had something better in store for me – heterosexuality, marriage, the whole family values package. And they promised they could turn me into a real man, normal and natural." The recruit joined a "support" group – he gestures the quotation marks – and for nearly a decade worked and prayed hard with individual counsellors to clear up the childhood dysfunction that had turned him from God and manhood.

But as so many ex-ex-gays have reported, though it cost him some years, it didn't work. His faith began to show cracks, and he began to wonder whether Christianity, at least as practised by Another Chance ministers, could really be all that healthy. The battle of the Gay Games was a turning point for him. In 1994 one of Jerry's counsellors, Frank Sheers, a prominent ex-gay leader who was by then married with kids, led a ferocious campaign to keep the Games out of Vancouver, hurling the usual fire, brimstone, and lies: homosexuals molest children, corrupt the family, cause AIDS, and so on.

"At that point I was still prepared to believe that homosexuality wasn't supported by God," says Jerry. "But I was appalled by this awful, virulent hatred for gays and lesbians, especially from people who called themselves Christians, the models we were supposed to emulate." Meanwhile, though he had diligently tried dating women, his feelings for men hadn't changed, "not one iota. I got really tired of living with this continual conflict between attraction, and then guilt and shame – the same thing over and over." Finally he exited the ex-gay group and the church that harboured it. Frank Sheers left by another route. Discovering that he was HIV-positive, he went on a frantic sexual spree, came out tearfully to his family and congregation, and died of AIDS.

Aaron and Jerry were both amazed to find someone who could speak the same language and who had wrestled the same demons. They also found each other hot. With Jerry at school in Victoria, and Aaron working his two jobs in Vancouver, they spent as much time together as they could manage. When Aaron introduced Jerry to Zacchary, their own connection deepened markedly. Says Jerry, "I have tremendous respect for how Aaron and Zacchary are with each other, the way Aaron challenges and affirms Zacchary, the respect they have for each other, and just generally how well they connect. Over the years I've been quite close to nieces and nephews, but the quality of this relationship was something entirely new to me."

This is what Aaron had wanted since his own adolescence: to be a father, and to do it differently. "With Zacchary I'm trying to create the kind of bonds and emotional openings that were missing from my relationships with my own fathers." He noticed with relief how comfortably Jerry and his son connected. "That's always been a major concern for me," he says. "I couldn't be with anyone who didn't get along with Zacchary. For his part, Zacchary is a remarkably open, mature, and loving person. He accepts Jerry fully, just as he accepted Deborah's new husband. He does acknowledge me as number-one dad, and I'm really grateful for that since I'm so far away most of the time. But his heart is big enough to embrace the others too."

For reasons both practical and political, Jerry and Aaron have built a non-monogamous relationship for themselves. On the practical side, to see the other means five hours travel each way, and that's when the ferries are running on time and not being cancelled due to stormy weather. Jerry works part time and goes to school. Aaron may not know until Friday afternoon whether he has to work additional shifts on the weekend that he can't afford to refuse. When I met with them at Aaron's home in east Vancouver, it was the first time they'd seen each other in three weeks.

On the political side, when they met, both of them were busy shedding second-hand dogma and making up for lost time. "Having been schooled in heterosexuality, I learned to want one perfect lifelong relationship – in other words, a wife," says Aaron. "Even when I accepted that I was gay, that desire turned into wanting a male substitute, someone I could move in with and settle down. But since I've moved to Vancouver all I've run into are men who are quite happy having casual sex. So when Jerry came along, I thought, well, hallelujah, finally here he is!"

Jerry also came with baggage. "I used to feel I needed someone else, whether it was God or another person, to rescue me and make all the hard decisions. But now that I've seen how much that kind of dependency can cost, I know that I have to stand on my own two feet and be responsible for my own decisions. Now I'm my own rescuer."

Aaron nods agreement, and adds, "When I made my marriage vows at nineteen, I meant it, forever. When all of that dissolved, it profoundly shook my original beliefs, including my sense of 'forever.' And life continues to show me that nothing, absolutely nothing, is solid."

In their open relationship, each is free to have sex with other partners. They always talk about it, often in advance. Aaron explains, "If either of us is interested in someone, we'll say so. That tends to create a field of comfort. It's quite different from having to absorb the news after the fact. It really helps to know there are no secrets."

"We do make a clear separation between sexual and emotional monogamy," says Jerry. "To me, sex is for pleasure and fun. Other sex partners are not the people we go to for emotional support or to grapple with the issues that really matter to us. They're not part of our intimate circle."

Aaron adds, "I feel that my emotional bond with Jerry is unique, and that's partly due to the level of trust we've developed with each other. Having come out late, I'm so grateful to be able to explore like this and not to feel a sense of resentment or wounded entitlement from my partner."

As it happens, each of them has only had sex with two or three other partners since they met. "The critical thing," says Jerry, "is the freedom."

When I asked them to introduce themselves at the start of our conversation, Aaron said, with a little bow to Jerry, "Ladies first." Executing a sort of seated curtsy, Jerry replied, "Why, thank you." They're gay men, it's a joke, but I was startled enough for it to register. It turns out gender is one of the realms in which they've felt increasingly free to play. "I've never identified as particularly masculine," says Jerry. "I've always been more emotional than cerebral and more interested in skipping and artsy things than team sports. I used to hate the sissy in me, and certainly got lots of negative feedback for it, but there never seemed to be anything I could do to change it. Even in my jobs I've usually been surrounded by other women [he supported himself through university with secretarial work]. It's just more comfortable for me. Now I've come to accept that there's nothing wrong with this, it's just an aspect of who I am."

Aaron is heavier than Jerry, with a deeper voice and a stronger grip. But Jerry calls him Babyface. "We've reached the point where we can play with it," says Jerry. "He's the brutish man, I'm the little woman, that sort of thing. In fact I do see Aaron as the more masculine, and I the more feminine, and that's perfectly fine."

"Like most of our play," says Aaron, "this tends to be about things we're working through. And if you're both clear about what it is you're playing at, and you know the rules, and you're playing as equals, why the hell not?"

Zacchary arrives for a summer holiday in just over a month. They'll pack as much adventure as they can into the two weeks that Aaron can afford to take off from work. "As he gets older, he'll be able to make more of his own decisions," says Aaron. "If he said at twelve, 'I want to live with Dad,' we might still have to go to court, and it might cost a small fortune, but at least at that age his own wishes would have to carry more weight with any halfway reasonable judge, even in Alberta."

Still, Aaron isn't pushing. "That's the whole point, he needs to make his own decisions. And I have to admit, his life really isn't so bad where he is. He lives on a homestead in the country, quite idyllic country with access to the wilderness, and he has good connections to Deborah's extended family. Of course there are all kinds of opportunities here that aren't available to him there, but that's the way it goes. I'll just have to bide my time."

On the calendar by Aaron's phone, the date of Zacchary's arrival is circled, several times around, in a particularly vibrant red.

14 The Parental Urge

On the appointed day in March, Cathy and Grace set out from their isolated home in Prince Edward County. Grace drove, Cathy practised what she would say. "I was so nervous, I was actually shaking," Cathy recalls. "The way we saw it, our lives were in this woman's hands." Under a surly sky, the roads had a dark sheen – black ice.

Cathy went in to see the social worker by herself; Grace waited in the car. "We had no idea how she'd react to us being a couple," says Grace. "And since it would be Cathy's name on all the documents, we decided it would be safer, at least for the first time, if she went in alone."

An hour later, Cathy emerged. They would need several sessions with the social worker, police checks, medical and financial records, references, a home study. The process would be complex, demanding, unpredictable, and expensive. But it could work.

The second session the two of them went in as a couple. Says Grace, "We didn't want to get caught in a web of lies that could haunt us in the long run."

Cathy adds with a laugh, "If I have to invent, it can get *very* involved." In fact, the social worker told them she had spotted a certain evasiveness in Cathy's responses to her questions about living arrangements, and wondered if a partner of the same sex might turn up.

International adoptions test both the resources and endurance of any would-be parent. "You have to do all the research yourself," says Cathy, "and you have to find an agency that you can trust. In theory you could make your own contacts, but it makes a lot more sense to pay an intermediary who already has the contacts and knows the ins and outs of the particular country." At an information session given by the Ontario Adoption Council in Toronto, they were the only same-sex couple.

They learned about provincial procedures, the experiences of others who had adopted internationally, and the requirements of various countries. Guatemala and China seemed to be the adoption "hot spots." Systems were fairly well established there, and people had reported good experiences in both places. Peru was less accommodating, according to two women they met. "In their case the whole thing dragged on forever, and their expenses just kept going up and up and up," says Cathy. "Then suddenly at the last minute the Peruvians got suspicious that the woman who was adopting might be gay, so they interrogated her for hours before they'd let her leave with the child. It was a real horror story."

But Cathy had waited too long to be put off. "Even when I was a child I always took it for granted that one day I would have a big family and that I would live in the country. As I got older I wanted to be sure I had children before I turned forty, so I'd still have the energy, but there would also be time to put money in the bank so we could afford to spend more time with the child."

Grace had felt the parental urge too. "I just buried it," she says. "I wasn't prepared to be straight, and not knowing how else it could happen, I'd resigned myself to accepting that it never would."

By the time Cathy turned thirty in 1988, her drive to have a child was so compelling she told Grace that she had no choice, she had to find a man. "I really thought she didn't want me anymore," says Grace, "and though I could understand the pressure she was feeling, I thought I'd better get on with my own life." After seven years together they split.

Grace got involved with another woman and moved out. Realizing what she'd lost, Cathy asked her to come back. In 1997 the two of them moved to Prince Edward County, bought a house on a remote peninsula, and opened a bed and breakfast called Serendipity. Their guests would wake up to loons calling. Cathy was thirty-nine, Grace forty-one.

Another couple I met in Dieppe, New Brunswick, experienced a similar dilemma. Françoise and Louise met at university in 1982, and now they collaborate in Louise's chartered accountancy practice. Says Françoise, "When I was young, people would ask me what I wanted to be when I grew up, and I would always say I would never marry, but I would definitely have kids. Where we lived, we saw kids that were so poor they hardly had anything to eat. I wanted to take care of children like that, the ones who needed it. But eventually I stopped even thinking about it. I just assumed that if you're gay, that's it, you've made your choice, no kids."

Louise nods. "Early on, part of me wanted children so bad I would have married, but even then my only interest was the children. Then with Françoise I thought I would have to choose – either I could have the relationship with her but no kids, or I would have to go with men. I chose the relationship. It seemed more whole to me." In recent years other doors have opened. "Now for the first time we know a few people who've had kids by AI [artificial insemination]," says Françoise, "or from a previous relationship. That was a wake-up call for us that it could be done."

They decided to try AI and to look into adoption at the same time. "I want more than one child," says Louise. "I believe they shouldn't be raised alone if possible. And we're not getting any younger, so we thought we'd better try both routes." The AI didn't take, and they discovered that New Brunswick has a ten-year waiting list for domestic adoptions. "We'd be in our mid to late forties by then," says Françoise. "As it is, we feel like we're starting late." Françoise is thirty-five, Louise thirty-eight. A friend mentioned international adoptions. They did some research, found an agency, and looked into the criteria for various countries.

Some don't accept singles. Others require that adopters be under thirty-five. Guatemala has more flexible criteria and is easier to get to from New Brunswick than the other most frequent choice, China. "We feel it's important both for the child and for us to be able to visit the home country later on," Louise explains. "We've struggled a lot with this whole idea of cultural displacement – by bringing a child to Canada, would we give them a worse or a better life? From what we know of the situation in Guatemala, chances are it could be better here."

Françoise adds, "Certainly the child will be a little different from the mainstream around here, but then as lesbians we've had to make a place for ourselves in this community, so we hope that we can help our child to do the same."

A little sperm A few years ago, David, a litigation lawyer in Toronto, got a call from an old friend, Shelley. A lesbian friend of hers wanted to have a child: Would he be interested in providing a little sperm? She assured him the couple would make good parents; they already had a child. But David would not have any contact either with them or his offspring, unless the child happened to request it later on. Any communication would pass via Shelley or the couple's lawyers. David asked his partner, Paul, what he thought.

"Knowing how much David likes children, I was concerned about how he'd handle not knowing who the child was, or how the parents were doing," says Paul. After much discussion David consented and signed an agreement waiving all paternal rights. They named the mysterious lesbian moms "Wilma" and "Betty," after the Flintstone characters. Shelley reported back that the second sperm donation did the job, and eventually a daughter was born.

For as long as he can remember, David has wanted a child. "When I was fourteen my dad had the usual talk with me about the birds and the bees, the plumbing and all that. I remember telling him I would never marry but instead I would hire a woman to have a child for me." Later, a major criteria in his choice of partner would be a shared desire to parent. Paul likes children – "little people," he calls them – well enough to work full-time with them, teaching French and music at primary level. "I enjoy their energy, their freshness, and their sense of optimism."

Shelley, the go-between, also wanted a child of her own. Her mother claims that when she was ten, Shelley informed her she intended to have a baby one day, but no father would be required. "I wanted to do it by the time I was thirty," says Shelley. "That would give me time to settle into my career a little." A special-education teacher, she teaches a community living class for young people with mild to moderate intellectual disabilities. She and her partner, Shirley, live near Peterborough, in central Ontario.

Nearing thirty, Shelley signed up with an AI clinic in Toronto, got pregnant, but had a miscarriage. Then she called David: Would he do the same for her as he had for Wilma and Betty? He and Paul decided that this time Paul should be the donor. "I wanted a donor more than a dad, but part of me also wanted the child to know the father at some point," says Shelley. "My own father was adopted, and even now that he's fifty-five, he still regrets not knowing anything about his biological parents." Once again Shelley reported that the second donation took, and in due course her daughter was born. Though Paul had waived paternal rights, he and David were welcome to visit and see what might evolve.

Before long Wilma and Betty asked for contact with David. Their daughter looked so much like his photo that they were curious to meet. Daughter and dad connected, and so did the two couples. Meanwhile, perched on the toilet one day Shelley's daughter suddenly asked, "Who's my daddy?" Now she knows too. Paul and David visit every few months, and both girls have stayed over with them for weekends in Toronto. The two lesbian couples also exchange occasional visits, and the two daughters have become friends. "They're not related," says Shelley, "but to watch them together you'd almost think they were." Still, it remains quite clear that as this unusual triangle evolves, the mothers continue to make the crucial decisions.

"I guess we have the best of both worlds," says Paul: "two beautiful daughters, and virtually no responsibility! Sounds pretty much like the stereotypical idea of a male, doesn't it?"

But then these two males don't quite fit the stereotype. When I met them in their north Toronto townhouse, they were preparing for a home visit by their Children's Aid Society case worker – a final step in the approval process to adopt a child of their own. Their references include all the mothers of both girls.

A visa for Michelle Among other tests, prospective international adopters like Cathy and Grace have to convince federal immigration officials that they have sufficient income to support a child. "We could have lived quite nicely off the B&B and odd jobs, but it turned out that wasn't good enough for Immigration," says Grace. "And it doesn't matter what savings you have – you've got to have what they regard as a real job." By coincidence Cathy's former employer, a bank, had been hounding her to come back to her old job developing software, but this time in Vancouver. Says Cathy, "I knew it would be the same rat race I'd left behind in Toronto. But if I didn't go, there was no way we could have qualified to adopt."

Cathy headed west, found an apartment, and started work. Grace rented out Serendipity and followed in the car with Monty, their springer spaniel. "Our Prince Edward County neighbours must have thought us very fickle," says Grace. "We were only there a year, and then suddenly we were gone. But with so many uncertainties, we didn't want to tell anyone what we were doing, in case it didn't go through."

At one point it looked as if they'd have to move back to Ontario to complete the adoption process. But after six months of negotiation, they finally got their official go-ahead from the Ministry of Community and Social Services. Immigration approval followed soon after. At eight a.m. on July 28, 1998, the agency called from Toronto. They had found a Guatemalan child for them, a five-month-old girl named Michelle. Her only problem, they said, was a lazy eye. "They give you a little time to think before you have to make your final decision," says Cathy. "We asked a doctor about the lazy eye – it's not that uncommon, and not hard to fix, so we phoned the agency back the next day and told them to go ahead."

Then the other half of the process began in Guatemala City. "There was tons more paperwork," says Cathy. "Affidavits, more references, my birth certificate, photos of the house and even my church. We got a friend in Prince Edward County to photograph the biggest one in Picton." The wheels turned, slowly. An envelope of photos arrived. Grace waited to open it until she could meet Cathy in a park near her office. They tore open the envelope and fell in love with their soon-to-be daughter. Finally, on February 2, by chance Michelle's first birthday, they were told they had two weeks to get to Guatemala and bring her home. They booked a flight for the first day Cathy could get off work, Saturday, February 6.

Since no same-sex couple stands the faintest chance of getting adoption approval in Guatemala, their social worker had concluded it would be safer to write up the application for Cathy alone, as a single parent. Meanwhile, the social worker who handled Louise and Françoise's case in New Brunswick insisted that they apply as a couple. It was normal now, she argued. Gay couples were accepted. But not in Guatemala, they countered. Friends of theirs, a gay couple, had been turned down for exactly that reason. The social worker felt she couldn't do a proper home study without acknowledging their relationship. Louise argued that in legal terms they were still considered single adults, as in the income tax forms that she prepared for many of her clients, and if the social worker wrote them up as a couple, she would effectively block their chances of adopting. Finally the social worker gave way. Françoise would be the sole applicant.

On Sunday, February 7, Cathy was ushered into a room at the foster home to meet Michelle and a startling number of her relatives. This would be their first chance to meet the *gringa* who would become Michelle's *madre,* and it could be the last time they would ever see the child. Grace went in as Cathy's *amiga.* "Being on display like that, I was quite nervous," says Cathy. "But there was this amazing, beautiful child. The foster mother who'd taken care of her for the past ten months handed her to me, and the relatives gave me some sort of cereal for her to eat on the trip. And that was that."

"None of it seemed real to me," Grace adds. "I remember experiencing the whole thing more like a dream."

Since foreigners coming to adopt Guatemalan children had been attacked as kidnappers, the agency warned Cathy and Grace to leave the country as soon as possible and to stay in their hotel until they did. Their return flight was booked for Monday morning. Suddenly someone realized that the Canadian Embassy had neglected to issue a visa for Michelle. A last-minute scramble, and it came through an hour before they had to leave for the airport.

The family bed We're sitting down to supper in their Vancouver apartment on a warm afternoon in early May. Grace is grilling chicken on the barbecue up on the roof. Michelle has already eaten. Cathy wipes remnants of carrot from her tiny hands, her face, her glossy black hair, the highchair, the wall beside her, the floor below. Monty growls when Michelle tries to retrieve a toy that he's claimed. She backs off but doesn't look alarmed. She has two teeth on the bottom, four on the top, including three new ones that have bloomed since she landed in Canada.

Grace arrives with the chicken, and Cathy's nephew shows up to take Monty for a much-needed walk. Cooing happily, Michelle tries several times to pull my tape recorder off the table. We string the cord high over a picture hook on the wall. A book they've bought on parenting, *The Family Bed,* advises parents to let their infants sleep with them. The agency agrees, saying it's particularly important with adopted children. "At some point they want their own bed," says Grace, "but in the meantime it's supposed to solve all sorts of problems." Grace is relegated to the guest-room, and Monty splits his time between the two.

"Sometimes Michelle is so wound up and excited it's really hard to get her to sleep," Cathy says. "She just wants to shriek and play. If she's not asleep by the end of her bottle, you know you're in trouble."

Cathy's job is their main source of income and Grace stays with Michelle during the day. "When she comes home from work, I say please talk to me, I've been doing nothing but baby talk all day," says Grace. An evening job providing care for an elderly man gets her out of the house for a few hours and gives Cathy time alone with Michelle. "Otherwise Grace would always be telling me what to do!" Cathy says, with a laugh.

Both moms have had to learn on the run. "You should have seen us trying to put on the first Pamper!" says Grace. "It's strange – you go through that long, complicated process to get approved, and then someone hands you the child and suddenly you're on your own. No one checks up afterwards to see how you're doing. The agency just moves on to the next case."

Michelle points at my chin, and says, "Bob! Bob!" Grace's brother Bob also has a beard. "Isn't she amazing?" says Cathy. Clearly it's a rhetorical question. "This is all so new to us. We're endlessly fascinated by everything she does and every sound she makes."

"The social worker insisted that we hire a babysitter and go out at least once a week," says Grace. "But we can't bear to leave her!"

Applicants 1 & 2 As the others did, David and Paul faced the question of whether to adopt as a couple or as individuals. Says David, "After M&H [the Supreme Court decision that redefined spouse to include people of the same sex], we could probably have done it as a couple, but we decided it would still be simpler to do it in two steps." Paul will adopt the child, and then as his partner, David will adopt Paul's child in a separate procedure.

In the past few years the adoption system in Ontario, or at least in Toronto, has opened markedly to gay and lesbian applicants. In law school David wrote a research paper on adoption and found that Ontario and British Columbia were the only jurisdictions *in the world* where the right to adopt has been won by gay and lesbian people. "Most countries won't even let single heterosexuals adopt. So we're really quite lucky to be in Ontario." He adds, "Despite the present government."

Though they were the only same-sex couple in their adoption course, Paul and David detected no bias either in the Children's Aid Society workers or their procedures. The application forms use outdated language – "How long have you been married?" and questions directed to "the man"/"the woman" – but no one objected when David and Paul simply rewrote the terms to read "Applicants 1 & 2."

From the beginning the CAS wants a sense of the would-be adopters' preferences, the characteristics they hope for in a child. "We said we'd prefer not to adopt a child with severe mental or physical handicaps," says Paul. "A child with two dads will probably have quite enough challenges to handle already."

David adds, "For the same reason we said it might be easier if the child was Caucasian. And since a boy could get teased more about his family situation, it might be easier for a girl."

"But we'd welcome either," says Paul.

"We'd prefer the child to be as young as possible, to start with a relatively clean slate in terms of the stereotypes that might have been learned," says David.

Paul adds, "The other thing we said was that we'd be willing to adopt more than one child, preferably siblings."

Once their home study is complete, Paul's name will be included in the CAS list as ready to adopt. Then they'll wait.

Half the package When Shirley and Shelley began their relationship in 1993, the first for Shirley with another woman, Shelley made it clear that she intended to have a child – in fact, she was already pregnant via the AI clinic in Toronto (although the pregnancy would later miscarry). Shirley, on the other hand, had already been a mother for some time. From her first marriage she had two children (and now has a grandchild), and from her second, which had just dissolved, a daughter and two stepsons. The daughter, fourteen, lives two weeks with her mother, two with her father. "After I had my last baby at thirty-one, I said that's it, no more," says Shirley. "I really didn't want to be doing the daily bath routine and all that again, certainly not at forty-six. The whole thing was very difficult for me to work through. Finally I told Shelley that I would be a supportive partner to her, but not a parent."

"While I was pregnant she was kind and caring," says Shelley. "And when the baby was born, she was quite loving with her. But it was clear that I'd be the one up at night changing the diapers and so on. Basically I had to meet all the needs of the child, and I had a partner who was a separate entity with her own needs. At the same time I'd gone back to teaching and was trying to make that work too. I couldn't balance anything."

Shelley worked days, and Shirley stayed home with the baby. "Having already experienced the insecurity of being a non-custodial parent, I didn't want to get attached to someone else that I might lose at some point," says Shirley. "So without realizing it I built a wall between me and the child. Of course that gets in the way of everything."

"The situation became more and more painful," says Shelley. "I felt really alone." In 1998 the two women separated.

Three months later they decided to give it another try. "If there hadn't been a child involved, we might not have found our way back," says Shirley.

"I don't know if that's true," Shelley replies.

Shirley explains, "I'm not saying that it's because of the child that we're back together. Both of us wanted to work things out, that's why we're here. But if we didn't have to communicate about issues regarding her, we mightn't have talked at all. She kept the doors open."

I asked Shirley how she distinguished between being a supportive partner and being a parent. "That was the problem," she says. "I never could. It's not something your heart can do, not when you have this child right there in your life. During the separation I was surprised at how painful it was, the thought of losing her. You can't take half the package. Somehow through all of that I've come to a place where I'm actually ready to parent again." She's decided to adopt her partner's daughter. "It's a big step for me to say, yes, I'll be formally, permanently responsible for her. But I also wanted to make that statement to her, especially after the way we started, so she knows that this is what I want."

Well-built walls don't come down easily. "It was hard for me to believe when Shirley changed around on this," says Shelley. "For the first three years of her life, this was my child. Now it's not easy for me to shift to saying *our* child. It's a struggle."

"We're working on it," says Shirley. "In gay relationships you have to spend so much more time and energy figuring these things out. There are so many hurdles, and no rules for these new forms of family. I can say from experience that most heterosexuals don't give nearly this much thought to such things."

When Shelley told her dad she was going to have a baby by artificial insemination, he said he couldn't be happy about it because "the child wouldn't have been conceived in love." Shelley's mother retorted, "How can you say that? A lot more love and thought has gone into this baby than any that you ever tried to bring in!"

The last time I checked with David and Paul, finally they were dads. Ten-month-old Jared joined them in March 2000. In the photo David sent, he and Paul look very proud, while their son is busy discovering his toes.

As for Grace and Cathy, both say they'd prefer to be back at Serendipity, in Prince Edward County, but now that they're parents, they need the income from Cathy's job. And Cathy worries, how would a child with Mayan ancestors and two moms be received in a rural school? Grace argues that they could count on support from a growing number of gay and lesbian residents in the area. And their straight neighbours on Point Traverse have urged them to come back, saying they'd be delighted to help out with childcare. On the other hand their social worker told them of a black child adopted into rural eastern Ontario; on the first day of school his adoptive mother overheard another say, "Will you look at what's moving in. A nigger."

As ex-urbanites move into Prince Edward County its face becomes less homogenous, but still it remains strikingly white. Says Grace, "Prejudice can happen anywhere. It happens here in Vancouver."

"But here I'm sure the kids in school would be a lot more varied," Cathy replies. "You wouldn't be the only one."

Grace holds her ground. "I don't doubt there'd be problems, but I think we could deal with them." This conversation will go on.

When Grace and Cathy first approached the social worker, they said they might want to adopt siblings. She argued that it would be wiser to apply for only one child. She also warned them that it could be considerably more challenging to adopt an older child, one with a history, which is why it's so much harder to find homes for older children. Everyone wants a bouncing baby. But shortly after their bouncing Michelle settled in, her new mothers got a frantic phone call from the agency: Would they consider adopting her sister, who would soon be six? They had met Alicia briefly with the other relatives at the foster home and noticed that she was quiet and rather withdrawn. The agency explained that Alicia's life so far had not been easy. In fact, rather than going home with her mother, she had asked to stay at the foster home. Of course they would adopt her, said Grace and Cathy. It was simple: they wanted children, Alicia needed parents.

They still had to obtain the usual approvals in Canada and Guatemala, but this time the wheels turned much faster. On the last day of July 1999, Cathy flew to Guatemala City, memorizing a few Spanish phrases on the way. Two days later she brought Alicia back to her new home. A gay male nurse in their building has found a Spanish tutor for Cathy and Grace, a Mexican woman who lives nearby. In the autumn Alicia went off to school just down the street with a rainbow of kids and family arrangements.

Last time I checked, Grace reported that Alicia was fluent in English and loving school. The moms were struggling heroically with their Spanish. Michelle was making quantum leaps in eye-hand coordination, puzzling her way through buckles, doorknobs, latches. Nothing, apparently, can stop her.

15 One of the Family

EIGHTEEN YEARS AGO DANIEL McKAY HITCHHIKED FROM THE SOUTH shore of Nova Scotia to attend university in Halifax. Though he lived on campus, he was quickly drawn into the orbit of a unique downtown housing service for young men, at the spacious apartment of an "older man" in his thirties.

"Jim's place was amazing," says Daniel. "Nothing like that could ever happen now, you'd never get away with it. There was always sex going on, and there was always high drama, twenty-four hours a day. It was like being in an opera. You could easily meet more than a hundred people there in a week. Sunday mornings everyone who was there and functional went trooping out to some restaurant for brunch, half of them in drag. This was my first experience of any kind of gay lifestyle, and I had no idea how bizarre and out there it really was. I wouldn't have missed it for anything."

In 1983 Norval Collins, a transplant from Regina, was sharing a house on a quiet street in the north end of Halifax. One night in January he threw an orgy for his house-mate. Jim of the housing service brought along a few of his current favourites, including Daniel. "He had the most amazing blue eyes I had ever seen," says Norval. They chatted for a few minutes, went upstairs, and surfaced again the next day.

Since Daniel didn't have a phone, they pursued each other on the information highway. Daniel runs the Internet service at Dalhousie University and the feed to other universities in the area. "Neither of us can remember what date we met, so we mark our anniversary from the first e-mail, which I still have," he says. He moved in with Norval at the end of the school year.

Shortly after, they invited Daniel's brother Gary to supper. For Norval's first encounter with a McKay relative, they prepared a spectacular meal with candles, fine china, and flowers everywhere, thanks to their house-mate, a florist. "We had a nice time," says Norval. "It was easy and friendly." An hour after Gary left, Daniel's mother called to speak with him urgently. Is it true that you're living in a house full of homosexuals? she asked. "I guess there are worse ways to come out," says Daniel. "Basically I told them either you have a gay son or no son."

"They're great," says Norval. "Couldn't ask for better."

Early in their relationship Norval and Daniel worked out rules of the game: monogamy would prevail, unless either of them was out of town, in which case the field opened for both. So it was a bit of a shock, says Norval, with a laugh, "the first time we ran into each other cruising the same washroom." The rules had to be adjusted.

Says Daniel, "We worked out a structure where neither of us would be left at home alone while the other was out screwing around in the same city. That way you don't feel left out, and jealousy is kept to a minimum."

Norval adds, "Also we agreed not to bring anyone back to the house, so that the other doesn't come home and find some stranger here."

"We made that deal after one of us came home earlier than expected and found the house full of guys," says Daniel. "One of us was not amused. Basically we try not to do anything that might threaten our own relationship."

Says Norval, "More often now, it'll be another person who's involved with both of us."

"Another one or two," Daniel amends.

Daniel is thirty-seven, Norval fifty-one. Their household has evolved. The house-mate is gone, but now they rent out the basement apartment. The tenants, drag queens, run on a slightly different clock: they arise in the early afternoon, start dressing around twilight, go out on the town by ten or so, and return home a little before dawn. "You never know what you're going to see coming out of there," says Norval. "Usually they're rather sparkly, and often they're quite beautiful."

When the ancient stove in the apartment finally expired and Norval couldn't find a suitable replacement in town, Daniel called his father. He called back to say he'd found the perfect stove for $50, and he'd drive up that same night with a friend to install it. "The guys were just getting ready to go out," says Daniel. "I had no idea what would happen when these two worlds collided, so I just crossed my fingers. When I looked in on them to see how they were doing, my dad had just asked Mike, in full drag, to come sit on his lap and give him a kiss. Turns out my dad saw them as minor celebrities. He figured he was in the presence of some weird kind of majesty. I was so freaked out I backed right out of the room!"

Norval and Daniel have a Volvo station wagon, but when weather permits, they ride motorcycles. One morning Daniel delivered me to an interview in another part of the city. I attached myself like a limpet to his leather back, my teeth chattering in terror and an April wind off the Atlantic. As we roared through downtown Halifax, I imagined my head snapping off neatly at the neck in its helmet, bouncing downhill into the harbour, and the rest of me a long, unidentifiable smear on Barrington Street. Norval had already warned me that Daniel likes to tilt his machine deep enough into curves that the footrest sets off sparks on the pavement. I would have sold my soul to be coddled in the Volvo.

In the early 1990s, returning from a trip to Prince Edward Island on their bikes, they stopped off at a friend's house in Truro where a party was heating up. "There were some seriously unsavoury types there, punks showing off their weapons and such," says Daniel. "We also met this one kid who was really bright and charismatic. The next day I told our friend that if this kid continued to hang out here, he was going to get himself into some deep trouble." A week later, at another party, he did. The kid, Joe Gower, was fifteen.

"Because of that incident," says Joe, "I had to go away for a while. But Dan and Norval were there right through it, with the phone calls and the letters. It was like having parents to care for you." When he came back, they offered to be his guardians. He could come to Halifax and live in their house.

It's what they do. I had intended to stay at a B&B for the few days I'd be in Halifax for interviews, but Daniel, whom I'd never met, said, of course not, you'll stay here. "That was my parents' philosophy. If someone needs help, you give it, and ask questions later. If they hang around long enough, they become one of the family."

Norval and Daniel had already worked with a couple of young men; Jamie lived with them for six months. Daniel explains, "The deal was, no matter how well or how badly he did at school, at least he had to work at it. One day he came to us and said, 'I can't do it, so I have to leave.' You had to admire his honesty."

Says Norval, "He also said he had to change schools because some kids from his school had seen him cruising – and knowing him, hustling – on the Hill." Citadel Hill is a popular historic site and cruising ground in downtown Halifax.

For Joe the rules were tougher and included a curfew, 6 p.m. to 6 a.m. "That wasn't our condition," says Norval. "It was the court's. And it wasn't easy for us to be that strict. But the deal was very clear: no excuses. If he showed up one minute after six, we had to report him."

"Once we got used to it, it really wasn't that big a deal," says Daniel. "But gay or straight, living with a kid certainly changes your life. When it's just the two of us, if there's nothing in the fridge, no problem, we go out. When you're a family, you're always home by six, and there's always food in the fridge."

"It was good for me," says Joe. "If I'd been out on my own in the evenings, there's a good chance I would have got into trouble. I had enough problems during the day!"

His two guardians had to be alert. "I tried hard to play them off against each other," says Joe, with a charming grin that suggests he's no amateur. "But they always seemed to be one up on me."

"If the two of you are going to disagree on some policy, you do not do it in front of the kid," says Daniel. "Of course they'll figure out that different people have different approaches, and that's as it should be. But what you don't want is a situation where the kid can take advantage of that."

Toilet paper was a particularly sensitive issue, says Norval. "The deal was, the last person to use it when it runs out replaces it. Well, Joe would see how close he could get to the end without actually running out. One time he got down to two squares. Dan really raked him over the coals for that!"

For Joe this household was the first solid, supportive structure he had known. "Besides a home, they also provided good role models, friendship, and the chance to go to school. They made me think about things, like, what are my options here? No one had ever done that for me before. It wasn't a sexual thing with them, they're just loving people. I consider them my second parents – probably because they make me do things I don't want to!" He glances at Daniel. "That is what parents do, isn't it?"

When they bought him a second-hand motorcycle, there were conditions. Before he could ride it, he had to take a safety course, and for his first week on the road he had to ride with Norval. On a quick trip up to New Glasgow, Norval and Daniel went off to visit a friend. "After I had done whatever I was doing, I went looking for them, which means I was riding alone, without Norval," says Joe. "As a penalty he made me wait another week before he'd let me drive by myself. I really hated that. I'm not used to taking authority from anybody, and I've never had to take responsibility for my actions. They really did put up with a lot of shit from me."

Norval and Daniel are well known as surrogate parents in Halifax gay circles. As Joe is handsome, with that fetching smile and a hairy chest, he tends to get a variety of proposals from people of various genders. But rather than approach him directly, some of his suitors asked Daniel or Norval first, to get their permission. Even now that Joe's twenty-four, it still happens occasionally. "One guy wanted me to move into his house," says Joe. "It was close to the university, so I said sure. But then the guy asked if he could meet Dan and Norval to see if it would be okay."

Daniel laughs. "You'd think we lived in the sixteenth century! Or that we had any say in the matter." I suggested that they demand some land as a dowry, or at least a few good cows.

Six years ago Joe got into another legal tangle. "By the time he got back, he was an adult, and that changed the whole dynamic," says Daniel. "We couldn't really control what he did anymore, not unless we worked out a whole new set of rules."

But the door is open, and the kid still comes by. "When I have any difficulty with my life or at school, or when I just need a quiet place to be, Dan and Norval are the first people who come to mind."

"Especially Dan," says Norval. "More often than not I tend to give Joe a hard time or a kick in the ass."

Joe shakes his head. "Not true," he says. "The two of them have different ways of seeing things, and they give different advice, like any two parents."

"Actually, I try not to give advice," says Dan. "I don't remember my parents giving me a lot of direction, and I didn't ask for much. Mostly they would ask questions, and lead me to think about things for myself. That's the harder road, helping someone to work out their own solutions. Harder for me anyway – it's almost impossible to resist giving advice!"

When I leave, Norval is playing Ketelby's "In a Monastery Garden" on the piano in the living room, his bass chords booming through the house. Dan is talking intensely with Joe in the driveway, giving him advice on how to repair the valve seals on his bike – or, I expect, helping him to work out his own solution.

16 Bumps and Bruises

In the early 1980s Brenda Murphy became lovers with "Jackie," a client at the family services agency where she worked in Saint John, New Brunswick. Brenda had no experience in such things, this being her first sexual relationship with a person of either gender. "A relationship like ours would certainly be outside the acceptable client-counsellor boundaries now," says Brenda. "I also have a thing about rescuing people, so the whole setup was pretty unhealthy right from the start."

While serving time in prison, Jackie discovered that she was pregnant. On release she had nowhere to go, no relatives nearby, so Brenda's parents took her in, and after baby "Lisa" was born, they found a place for the three of them.

As a child, Brenda had learned from her parents that it's only right to rescue your neighbour. But from her church she had also learned that homosexuality is a deadly sin. She tried to convince herself that one relationship could hardly make her homosexual; Jackie was, after all, rather mannish. "Even so," she says, "for four of our eight years together I was sure I'd end up in hell, and I prayed really hard to be changed. Since I also came to feel that Lisa was my daughter as much as Jackie's, this was just one more reason not to come out, in case I ever had to fight for custody."

By the mid-1980s Brenda was working in community development for the United Church of Canada. She met a gay minister who pointed out that since God had created her a lesbian, how could it be a sin? He took her to a gay bar in Toronto, an experience as revelatory for Brenda as Saul's on the road to Damascus. "I know it's a little corny to say this, but I really felt as if I'd come home, " says Brenda. "Looking around at all the women, I started to think for the first time, maybe I *am* interested in other women!"

This revelation occurred in the midst of ferocious battles in the United Church over the suitability of gay and lesbian folk for ministry. "I heard awful things in some of the meetings," says Brenda, "such bigotry, such hatred, I could hardly believe it. The only positive effect is that finally I had to tell my mother. We'd always been close – I would tell her everything the second I got home from school. But this time it was very hard. She said she had known for years, and it didn't change a thing."

For Brenda it would change everything. In 1994 the church-based national urban action network she worked with held its annual conference in St John's, Newfoundland. One of the organizers was Jo Lang. Jo recalls, "At the closing dance, there was this whole table of lesbians, but none of them were up dancing. I asked them why not. With all those straight people, no one wanted to be first up. 'We'll dance if you do,' one of them said, so I said, 'I will if Brenda will.' It happened to be a waltz. Now this was a social justice group, but they certainly weren't used to seeing anything like *that*." Jo laughs. "So that was our first encounter – breaking new ground on the dance floor." However, both of them were partnered, so they left it at that.

By this time Brenda's relationship with Jackie had deteriorated to the point where they could no longer share a house. Brenda moved out of town to live with her brother. Devastated by the split, seven-year-old Lisa told Jackie she wanted to go live with Brenda. Jackie agreed to let her go, but only for a year.

When Brenda found it hard to combine a full-time job with parenting, her parents added a self-contained wing to their house where she and Lisa could live. This was the modest house where Brenda grew up, overlooking Grand Bay on a broad curve in the Saint John River. Moving there made life easier for them both. "But I think it was harder on Lisa, because I didn't have the language to explain who I really was in relation to her," Brenda says. "One day I went to meet her at the school bus [driven by Brenda's mother], and another kid said to Lisa, 'Who's she?' My mother told me afterwards that Lisa had this look of panic on her face. She didn't know what to say. My mother jumped in and said, 'Oh, that's her friend Brenda.' None of us was very helpful with the language."

Three years after their first ground-breaking dance, Brenda and Jo ran into each other again, this time in Edmonton, at another annual meeting of the same organization. Jo was out of her relationship by then and had concluded she would be better off on her own, at least for a while. "I wasn't going to have my head turned," she says, "not even by this cute woman from New Brunswick who was toying with me."

"I wasn't *toying* with you," Brenda protests.

"Oh, weren't you now?" says Jo.

Both heads turned, and the phone lines hummed between Saint John and St John's. For Brenda the calls had both a romantic and a therapeutic side. "After the split-up there was a lot of hostility between me and Jackie. I found it very hard to be patient with her. But Jo was really good with me on the phone. I'd sound off to her about Jackie's addictions, the bad effects they had on Lisa and so on. Then I could feel calmer when I had to talk to Jackie in person."

Jo had grown up in Newfoundland as a practising heterosexual with a childhood sweetheart and then a live-in boyfriend. But at twenty-one she met a woman, they kissed and she liked it. She started going to Cats, the gay and lesbian bar in St John's. "I felt very comfortable there," she says. "It was like finding my own skin." She continued to connect now and then with the boyfriend, which did not sit well with her lesbian friends. "I think of my sexual orientation as bisexual and my emotional identity as lesbian. I still find men sexually attractive, I enjoy looking at them, and sometimes I enjoy their passion. But my connection to women feels more natural in some way. It tends to be more serious, more intimate, and more committed."

In late September Brenda flew to St John's for the weekend. In less than a week Jo was in Saint John to see her receive a community service award. She came again for the Christmas holidays, arriving on Boxing Day so as not to impose on Lisa's Christmas with Brenda, though Brenda made sure that they met. In February Brenda celebrated Valentine's Day at Jo's house in Pooch Cove, a little up the coast from St John's.

A month later Jo moved to New Brunswick. "It was the logical choice. I was quite happy with my house and my kitchen garden at Pooch Cove. But now that I'd finished my degree in social work, it made me a lot more portable than Brenda, whose work with the church was pretty much rooted where she was. And goodness knows, moving to Newfoundland to look for work isn't a great idea at the best of times."

Brenda adds, "To Lisa it was unthinkable that I might leave the province. I've made a commitment to her that I'll be available at least until she's eighteen."

By the time Jo moved, Lisa was living most of the time with Jackie again. But Brenda had introduced Lisa to Jo, and they had talked several times on the phone. A week after Jo moved in with Brenda at Grand Bay, so did Lisa. She stayed a week, then went back to her biological mom. "I guess she was staking a claim," says Jo. "Just checking to see that her room was still *her* room."

A little later, when Brenda called the three of them "family," Lisa retorted, "Then how come she gets to decide things around here and I don't?" Brenda responded that in fact it was usually Jo who pushed her to ease up on Lisa, who was sixteen by then.

"It seemed to me Brenda sometimes treated her as if she was still twelve," says Jo. "I really couldn't see how it would do any harm to cut her a little slack now and then."

At the same time Brenda was facing pressure on another front. For eleven years she had been working for the United Church, coordinating social-justice outreach work in the Saint John area. After the 1988 battle on sexual orientation and ministry, many conservative church members withheld their donations in protest. As budgets shrank, Brenda felt increasingly vulnerable in her job. "Looking back, I think it gave them an excuse to withdraw support from the social justice ministry, something most of them had never really wanted to engage in anyway. I suspect my orientation was a factor too, though they were too underhanded ever to say so."

Eventually her position was merged with another, and Brenda was told she'd be welcome to apply. "I actually intended to. But Jo was very supportive of my coming out. And once I got out of the situation, suddenly it started to hit me that any support I'd had came from the community and hardly any from inside the church. When I finally realized that I didn't have to go back there, suddenly I felt so free, as if I'd just got out of an abusive relationship. The church does terrible things to people, it really does."

Brenda still works in community development but now with a local agency in Saint John, exploring how to undo barriers that keep women and children in poverty. Jo does individual counselling and group work with women in conflict with the law, and survivors of childhood sexual abuse.

The long haul Jo and Brenda have a nice, easy way with each other. When we settle in the living room after dinner, they are rarely out of contact, eyes connecting, a touch on an arm, a hand on a knee that comes within reach. "I consider Brenda my life partner," says Jo. "We seem to be exploring emotional and spiritual depths that are quite new to me." Spiritual? "It's hard to define, but there's a sense of peace and home here that I've never experienced with anyone before."

Home is the add-on wing they share in the house on Grand Bay. Sometimes Lisa stays with them, sometimes with Jackie. When I came to visit, she was at Jackie's, so I didn't get to meet her.

In the afternoon we climbed with the dogs up through the sand quarry behind the house, under an osprey nest in the hydro tower, up to the creek where Brenda used to come for picnics as a child. Now and then the two of them – three when Lisa's around – will dabble in the cedar-shaded pools or race plastic fish through rocks and reeds. "Even though it's not cool, once in a while Lisa will goof around with us too, if she's quite sure no one's watching," Jo says.

Coming back to the house in the late afternoon, Jo and Brenda bounded down the sandbanks hand in hand, shrieking. "Jo brought play into my life," says Brenda. "Or rather she brought it out – it was always there, but it needed a little coaxing to come out."

As their own relationship evolves, so does the family triangle. For Jo, dropping into a teenager's life turned out to be easier than she had expected. "It didn't take me long to like Lisa," she says. "She's a fine character, she's bright, and I enjoy her company – when she's not being an obstinate teenager. She and I have some good conversations. Also, not surprising given her background, she had a really hard time playing, so that lets me be the bringer of play with her too. Basically you could say I've acquired a family in a pretty lazy way."

In speaking on behalf of the absent Lisa, as I asked them to do, Brenda and Jo are careful and respectful. Says Jo, "It couldn't have been easy for her to figure out how I fit in here. Since I wasn't around for her first fourteen years, I can't really be called a parent, and I'm not a friend, not in the usual sense. But we seem to be finding our own way through that."

Two days after Jo moved in, Lisa skipped school for a couple of days. Since Brenda was away at work and Jo hadn't started her new job yet, Jo dropped by the school. "I told them Lisa lived with me and my partner Brenda, and would they please tell me what work she was missing so we could catch up on it at home. They didn't ask any questions, just told me what I needed to know and sent me on my way. I suspect most people get the idea pretty quick, and beyond that they really don't want to know too much."

For Brenda and Lisa, finding a comfortable label for their relationship hasn't come easily. When Lisa was away for a time at school in Nova Scotia, Brenda phoned one day to see how she was doing. "Are you her mother?" the official asked. "I'm her non-biological mother," Brenda replied. Lisa had insisted that she identify herself only as "a friend": If people knew she had two moms, they'd know they were lesbians, and then they'd think she was one too. But the school wouldn't give out information to "a friend," and to say "non-biological mother" seemed quite reasonable to Brenda, who was present at Lisa's birth and had always cared for her as a daughter. The official gave her an update.

When Lisa found out, she furiously denied that Brenda was her mother. The official, convinced that she'd broken a strict rule, called

Brenda back in a panic. They sorted it out, but Lisa wouldn't speak to Brenda for a month.

Jo has tried to help with the two-moms dilemma, and Lisa's additional fear that if she calls Brenda "Mom," it will mean she's being disloyal to Jackie. Jo told her that in her own childhood she had chosen to live for several years with another relative, whom she regarded as a second mom. Not long after, Lisa handed Brenda and Jo a Mother's Day card. Lisa still hasn't reached the point of actually calling Brenda "Mom," but now when Brenda introduces her as her daughter, Lisa seems to be at peace with it.

A stable relationship is a novelty to Lisa. Even though Brenda's and Jackie's endured for eight years, it never had the steadiness that children crave. "So initially she was pretty pessimistic about us," says Jo. "But now I think she sees us as pretty solid and in it for the long haul."

Brenda adds, "We're openly affectionate with each other, and Lisa seems to be comfortable with that. She just wants to be sure she's not left out. If we're in the bedroom with the door closed, sometimes she'll call out, 'Get some clothes on, I'm coming in!'"

"On the other hand," says Jo, "as she's got older we've tried to let her see more of the emotional range in our relationship. For instance, if the two of us have some conflict or a little spat, she sees that these things can be resolved and everyone comes out of it in one piece."

Their evolving triangle has had other benefits. "Jo is a good buffer between Lisa and me," says Brenda. "I've always been very careful not to say anything about Jackie that she could take as negative. But now we can have conversations where both of us are much more honest – for example, about her mom's addictions. That's something I never thought we would be able to do."

Jo adds, "If things get bad and Lisa wants to come up here, now she can tell us that without feeling she's being a traitor."

Says Brenda, "Often with her mom she's the one who has to be the adult and take care of her. When she's here for the weekend, it's rare for her not to call her mom, sometimes two or three times a day, to check on how she's doing. On the other hand she can go two or three weeks without calling here, I suppose because she knows we're okay."

When Lisa came home one weekend to find they'd hung a new picture in the living room, she was quite upset by the change. "That's life, we told her," says Jo. "Things change, and it doesn't always have to be for the worse. Of course, when you've had as much upheaval in your life as Lisa has, it's only natural that once you've got a little bit of your world close to the way you want it, the last thing you want is for somebody else to go changing it on you. But whether we like it or not, these things do happen."

A few years ago Brenda's parents separated. Her father still lives in the family house, but her mother moved to a mobile home not far up the road. Though in the past she tended to be closer with her grandma, Lisa now prefers to hang out with her grandpa next door – it's handy, and with him she can smoke.

Traditional notions of family die hard, particularly for one of Brenda's brothers. "Because I'm in a so-called helping profession," says Brenda, "right from the beginning they got stuck on seeing Jackie as one of my cases, and Lisa too, as if I were doing good works. They'll say she's *like* my daughter, but they can't quite bring themselves to say she *is* my daughter, or to acknowledge her as their niece or as a cousin to their kids."

Jo adds, "People seem to have so much trouble making that simple leap. If there's a problem with Lisa, as there's bound to be with any kid, what I hear from them is, 'Poor Brenda, after all she's done for that girl.' They would never say that about their own kids."

As most mothers do, Brenda has worked hard to build a level of trust that would encourage Lisa to approach her unafraid with any question, any problem. Brenda smiles. "You get what you asked for. Suddenly she wanted to talk about sex. Oh, my. I still see her as this vulnerable little girl that I want to protect. Of course you can't go through life without bumps and bruises, I know that, but I don't want her getting any more bumps than she's already had. Anyway, I didn't freak out. I just took a breath, and we talked about sex."

After their chat, Brenda bought Lisa her first package of condoms. "I don't know which of us was more surprised, me or her!"

17 youth.org

Down at the general store AT 9:18 A.M. LELIO'S COMPUTER loads the Internet Relay Chat software, and he jumps into the Gay Halifax channel. He types, *Good morning all.* Sandy MacDonald's online nickname is taken from an Anne Rice novel, *The Vampire Lestat,* in which the title character plays the trickster god of love, Lelio, in a sixteenth-century drama.

Lola is online but not active at the moment. I ask, "Lola as in the song, 'Whatever Lola wants, Lola gets?'"

"That's her, pretty much," says Sandy. "When you piss her off, she calls herself Bitch, and when Bitch comes on, everyone runs for cover." Lola and Bitch are the online nicknames of Sandy's friend and fellow bot-master, Betty. Probably she's occupied just now – she has three children and another on the way. Or she could be off gabbing in a private chat room or on another channel.

"Betty and I met on line, and now we're really good friends," says Sandy. "I'll go over there and visit, play with her kids. They call me Uncle Sandy."

In the tiny apartment he shares with his partner, Jerry, Lelio enters his password and asks the bot for ops. All this is way over my head. Bots, Sandy explains, is short for robots, programs that run the affairs of the channel. "In the past we had serious problems with gay-bashers coming in and kicking everybody off the channel. So now we have bots to control that sort of thing."

Sandy is one of three bot-masters who control the bot programs and function as referees on the channel. *Howard sets mode,* it says on the screen. Howard, one of four bots, has just granted operator status to Sandy. Apparently Howard keeps busy running seven different channels, but most of them are fairly quiet this time of day.

Gay Halifax is an online, real-time chat group, now in its sixth year. All you need to participate is a computer with Internet access and IRC software, which can be downloaded free from the Internet. It also helps to have an unlimited-hours deal with your server. Some months Sandy, Jerry, and a couple of friends have racked up over 240 hours. "It's like talking on the phone, except that you don't have to deal with answering machines," says Sandy. "It's also like the post office or general store in a small town, where everybody goes to pick up their mail, their milk, or whatever. You stop in for a bit of a chat with whoever happens to be there." In this case the people who stop by are mostly gay men, mostly young, and mostly local, though visitors drop in from as far away as Sidney, Australia. Or the Yukon – "There's a guy from Halifax who's working up there now. It's a good resource for people who've moved away."

The word seems to have spread that I'm gathering material for a book. *What's it about?* Scrappy 2 wants to know. *Gay relationships,* Sandy types. A moment later the reply comes back, *Relationships bite.*

Oooh, types Sandy, *so young and yet so bitter.* Someone else jumps in: *In this town, the book could be a sequel to Peyton Place.*

Sandy grew up in Glace Bay, an industrial town in Cape Breton. "I was the quiet shy fat kid," he says. At university in Sackville, New Brunswick, he majored in religious studies. One day he was idling at the computer, killing time. "Suddenly something clicked with me," he says, "and I knew I wanted to have more of a life." He started going out, and coming out, to the gay and lesbian group on campus. A friend told him about Gay Halifax, brought him online, and introduced him to some of the regulars at the general store. "By the time I got to the city in 1996, it was like home to me already. People I'd met online gave me a place to stay, they helped me find an apartment, and they threw a big welcome party for me."

After the online gay-bashings, some of the people who launched Gay Halifax started talking about the need for bots. "Some argued against them," says Sandy. "They didn't want anything to interfere with their right to free speech. But sometimes you have to balance one freedom against another." Once the decision was made to install the bots, bot-masters had to be selected. At twenty-six, Sandy is one of the elders on the channel and well suited for the task. "I'm known to be fair. People seem to come to me in everyday life with their problems, and I'm not inclined to take sides. Now if someone is harassing someone else, that's a different story. A few weeks ago one guy was hitting on another, and when the second guy said he wasn't interested, the first one said, fine, then you're not welcome, and kicked him off. That person has lost his ops rights." No one gets or loses operator status on Gay Halifax unless the three bot-masters concur.

In the beginning the two other bot-masters didn't want their identities known. Gay Halifax is a small town, and you never know who you might run into at the general store. "So I ended up the fall guy," says Sandy. "I had to put up with a lot of rude people for a while. But I'm the one who talks everybody down anyway, so I can deal with that." In time, the other bot-masters gradually came out too.

Like any general store, the channel has its pros and cons. First pro: it's an easy way for people to connect. "Most of the people I know in Halifax I met online," says Sandy. "When you've been on for any length of time, you start to run into each other in person when you go out Friday or Saturday night." Until then, many people know each other only by their nicks, unless they've moved on to more intimate contact in a private chat room. Some people at the bar still call Sandy "Lelio." The channel also serves as a community billboard. "The other night we had a rally in memory of Matthew Shepherd, and most of the people who came heard about it on Gay Halifax," says Sandy.

The channel also offers a safe place to come out, or at least to start the process. "We get lots of people from the more rural areas, especially the south shore and Cape Breton, where it's very hard to come out. One friend of mine, who'll soon be eighteen, first got to know people online, and then gradually he came out to us. Then his mother came on a few times. She had all kinds of questions that she didn't feel she could ask anyone else. Now she's writing pamphlets for PFLAG!" That's another advantage to the channel, says Sandy. "You can throw out any kind of problem, and in no time you'll get back a wide range of advice, most of it friendly."

Never having been very effective at the bars – my small talk never seemed quite small enough – I can imagine the appeal that this virtual meeting place might have. For example, a person might not be dismissed quite so quickly on looks alone. Sandy shakes his head. "There's a lot of people out there who are very shallow," he says. "You could have the best personality in the world, but if it doesn't come wrapped up in exactly the right package, and you don't have photos to prove it, they won't even bother to open it."

At the same time, both the medium and the market tend to foster illusion. "Online you can say anything you want about yourself," says Sandy, "and you can easily find a picture to support it. One fellow was all high and mighty, he said he was a doctor at Dalhousie, and he'd have people drop over at night for a quick affair in his office. But when someone called him on it, it turned out he's a cleaner up there. He has keys to all the offices, so he'd just throw on a lab coat and play doctor."

When a relationship is in trouble, Sandy discovered, things can get rather tense at the general store. Though a friend had advised him never to date anyone he met on the channel or at the bar, Sandy got involved with Patrick Ryan online. "Unfortunately our relationship was public right from the start," says Sandy. "People knew what was going on with us all the time, sometimes before we did, and they would immediately take sides. When we broke up, everyone knew within an hour. Instead of our working it out between the two of us, it ended up being fought out between my camp and his. Everyone had an opinion one way or another, and it turned into the most godawful mess." They survived and remain good friends, online and off.

Patrick's mother, Ellen, is a Gay Halifax regular and a friend of Sandy's. (For more on Ellen and Patrick, see chapter 11.) "It made me sad when Patrick broke up with Sandy," she says. "Patrick wasn't ready for a relationship. I think he's had regrets about it since. Sandy is such a great guy."

Online, Ellen Ryan is Momma E. She connected to the channel while I visited with her in New Glasgow. Channel Slut is online. "He used to come on as Marsha Mallow," says Ellen. "That's his drag name, and I liked it better." And here's Quique. Though she's never met him and doesn't know his real name, they often talk online, and she can tell from his server name that he lives in the area. She types in that I'm writing a book, why doesn't he come over for a chat? *Why me?* Quique replies. *What does he want?* Ellen sends back, *Come over and find out.*

Got any cookies? he asks. "That's not the computer-type cookies," Ellen explains, "it's the real ones. I'm famous for my cookies." *No cookies,* she replies, *but a cake, just baked.*

Ellen is a den mother on Gay Halifax. "I've never met most of them in person," she says, "but even so, I had no idea how close you can get to people by talking back and forth like this. There's one guy, he's only seventeen, but he has more on the ball than just about anyone I know. You'd think you were talking to someone who's forty." Another young drag queen adopted Ellen as a surrogate mom after his own mother died.

As she's watching chats develop on the screen, Ellen says, "There are lots of new people on here tonight that I don't know yet." When the boys get too trashy and gross with each other, she says, Patrick will scold them, *Be careful, my mom's on.* "But I'm in their space," she says, "so I'll take what comes."

Quique shows up in person, drawn by cake and curiosity. He doesn't offer his name and Ellen doesn't ask. Turns out he lives about ten minutes up the road. He's thirty-two, a computer programmer, and not out to anyone in his family in this notoriously conservative part of Nova Scotia.

The IRC offers him an opening to the larger world outside. "It brings down the barriers," he says. "It lets you say and do things that you probably would never do in person. You can be really trashy if you want. It lets you be yourself for a change." Occasionally he will meet in person someone he's come to know online. "I have to talk to them long enough to feel secure, and then we might meet for coffee," he says. "I've met a few nice people that way, but nothing came of it." Soon he will move on, probably to the U.S. "I don't much care where I go," he says. "I'll just follow the money."

As I prepare to leave, Ellen is chatting online with someone called Redkin, a gymnast who promises he'll do her hair next time she's in Halifax.

Queer as Fuck The words are stencilled over and over on the sidewalk that leads to the LGBTOut office: "Queer as Fuck." Over each of these pungent messages another stencil has been superimposed with meticulous care: "Degrade." I asked Bonte who's responsible for the Queer as Fucks. "A group of students we know nothing about," he says with a wide grin. And the Degrades?

The grin vanishes. "A group of assholes we know nothing about."

Welcome to Bonte Minnema's world.

In 1999, after a survey at the University of Toronto revealed alarming levels of homophobia among first-year students, Bonte and other activists launched a campus-wide referendum to win support for a "lesbian, gay, bisexual and transgendered positive space." Basically the funding would cover an office and a staff person. The need isn't hard to see. Their current space, where we are talking, is a dark hole in the wall of an arched walkway. Bonte says it's double the size of their previous one. But for me to sit, wedged between the desk and a file cabinet, he has to move a bicycle, a carton of file folders, and a pile of posters for the upcoming Homo Hop. My tape recorder teeters on a stack of documents for a new campaign, Queers in History. Bonte, who's quite tall, folds himself into another gap in the mayhem.

The positive space referendum drew exactly the kind of hostility that the campaign hopes to counter. Hundreds of ballots were spoiled with scrawled messages, "Die fags die," and the like. At Hart House, a campus fitness and cultural centre, fundamentalists put up rows of posters: "Homosexuals don't need positive space, they need Christ."

With help from the progressive Student Christian Movement, positive space campaigners took down the posters. But instead of throwing them away, they transformed them into a life-size papier mâché sculpture of Jesus on the cross, with a banner quoting from the sermon at the Last Supper: "As you did to the least of my brothers, you did to me." They carried the crucifix in a solemn procession through St Michael's, the Roman Catholic college at the university, and the identified source of many spoiled ballots.

A few weeks later, at twenty-two, Bonte ran as an NDP candidate in the Ontario provincial election. Canvassing in his west Toronto riding, he and his campaign workers stopped one evening to talk with a group of young people hanging out in a parking lot. One of them identified Bonte from the crucifix procession at St Michael's and told him to fuck off. "I was amazed that she recognized me," he says. Bonte, I suspect, is not unaccustomed to being recognized.

His university career began at Trinity College. "It's an awful place," he says. "In every class, I kept asking, what about the queers? The answers I got were pathetic. One professor actually told me there weren't any in Europe before World War II! And the only thing most of the students want to know is what private school you came from. Well, honey, I grew up on a pig farm."

Bonte went to the Catholic school in Glencoe, a small town in rural southwest Ontario. By grade five he was telling anyone who would listen that he wanted to be a dancer, singer, actor and/or director. "I was an artsy-fartsy little flamer," he says, with a giggle. "When women teachers took up wearing pantsuits, I tried to dress the same. Even when I had leadership positions in the scouts and the 4H, I was always queer, and the fag jokes always made me flinch."

In his last year at high school he came out, to say the least, by organizing a public protest against Roseanne Skoke, the former federal MP. A right-wing Catholic, Skoke made her name attacking the "homosexualist agenda" which she claimed was corrupting the nation and its youth. "In one moment I went from being every mother's favourite kid to their worst nightmare," says Bonte. "The principal, who had written these glowing reports for my scholarship applications, actually spat at me."

A couple of years ago Bonte went back to Glencoe for his grandmother's eightieth birthday. The celebration included a service at the Catholic church. "At the end of it they did that sign of peace thing, where you're all supposed to shake hands with each other. People I went to school with, including my teacher for five of my eight years in elementary school, they wouldn't look me in the eye. Nothing has changed there. This is a sickening little town."

Along with a certain fire, Bonte Minnema took to university a lesson he'd picked up from his Fresian (a region of Holland) parents: if you work long enough and hard enough, you can accomplish anything. "Part of me knows that's bullshit," he says. "If you didn't go to Upper Canada College it's not likely you're ever going to be CEO of the Bank of Montreal. That's simply not within your range of options. On the other hand, I know these are all man-made barriers – I do mean *man*-made: Upper Canada College, for example, is an all-boys school – and I know these barriers can be fought."

His parents, especially his mother, hoped that Bonte would emerge from university a lawyer. Instead, he chose to pursue a liberal arts degree, with a dual major in women's studies and sociology. "I love it," he says, "at least the women's studies part, it's exactly where I belong." Bonte's journey over the past four years has been driven much more by political than academic forces. In his first year he joined the lesbian, gay, bisexual and transgendered student organization, LGBTOut, mostly "because I didn't know where else to meet other guys." The group had recently split into social and political factions and had run up some heavy debts. "I really wanted to pull the social and political together again, and get more people involved. It's the only way we could pay off the debts and grow."

Their first event, a Carole Pope concert, was a disaster. Bonte had to inform the singer that somehow they had neglected to promote the event and only two tickets had been sold. "Now we produce the best parties in town for queer youth," he says. "We get *twelve* year olds!" As if on cue, a young man stops by the office. He looks about sixteen. His name is Juan and he just heard about the Homo Hop. Can he have a few posters to put up in his residence? "Are you kidding?" says Bonte, and hands him a stack.

Bonte got a part-time job at the student career centre, to figure out how to make its programs more inclusive of lesbian and gay issues. He helped write a brief to the Sex Education Centre, addressing complaints of sexist and homophobic attitudes at Health Services. In another summer job he produced a queer resources directory for students, and now he's developing a related web page.

LGBTOut sent a survey to all department heads at the university, exploring the relevance of their curricula and resources to queer students. "Some of them wrote back, 'Dear Ms Minnema' – that happens all the time – 'We have no time for your survey, it's not within our mandate.' We wrote back, 'You have queer students, so either it does fit, or perhaps you need to revisit your mandate.'"

The engineering department has been notoriously slow to revisit its mandate. "Queer positive graffiti gets cleaned up over there before the paint is dry, but the homophobic graffiti isn't touched," says Bonte. When Homo Hop posters were removed from engineering bulletin boards, LGBTOut replaced them with City of Toronto posters that declared, "Being lesbian or gay isn't a crime. Bashing is." Vandals crossed out words and letters to leave the message: "Being lesbian or gay is a crime. Bash."

The LGBTOut social coordinator, a close friend of Bonte's, was an engineering student at the time. "We were really pissed off," says Bonte. "We borrowed a megaphone – my favourite toy – and a bunch of us marched through the building. All the marches, all the rallies, National Coming Out day, Pink Triangle day, all of it is designed to raise queer-positive visibility. I knew a guy who killed himself last year on campus. At his memorial no one said a word about the fact that he was gay. Not a word. That's what killed him, that silence! Of course everything we do for queer visibility leads to more anti-queer reaction. It pisses me off that we still have to do these things. It's straight people who have the problem, not us. I'd be happy to point it out to them, but I don't see why we should have to fix that too."

Aside from his work with LGBTOut, which at the moment includes organizing a queer youth talent showcase, Bonte also serves on various campus advisory committees, as well as the advisory board of the national Foundation for Equal Families, and the board of the province-wide queer youth phone line. Earlier in the summer he and a few friends hit seven northern and eastern Ontario cities on their Priscilla, Queers of the North tour, to promote the youth line. "We made lots of good connections," says Bonte, "and we got the message out – it's okay to be who you are, and if you need to talk, we'll be there."

Bonte also teaches Sunday school at the mostly gay and lesbian Metropolitan Community Church, where he's helping to organize a queer youth spirituality conference. He is lesbian/gay/bisexual director of Ontario New Democrat Youth and its federal equivalent. The night before I met him, he camped out with about thirty other students at Allen Gardens to protest against a brutal police campaign against homeless people who sleep in the downtown park. "People ought to try it sometime," he says. "You wouldn't believe how cold fourteen degrees can feel when you're trying to sleep out in the open and on the ground."

One of the things that drew me to Bonte was the fact that his passion for justice doesn't begin and end with queer issues. For him, everything connects. "I've been kicked off computer lists because they've said this is about poverty, it's not queer stuff. But people who work at some of the downtown health clinics say 30 per cent of youth on the street are there because of sexual orientation and gender issues, because their families won't accept who they are. At the same time it makes me mad as hell that so many gay people don't give a shit what happens outside the bar. That's a very small world, honey. Right outside on Church Street there are lots of squeegee kids, kids hustling and panhandling. Well, don't go after them, go after the homophobic families that kicked them out."

Given his in-your-face approach to politics, I'm surprised at his continuing loyalty to the NDP, which keeps veering further towards the right and into irrelevance. He nods, and sighs. "I'm very ambivalent about the party. They keep doing things that really piss me off, like those three NDP MPs voting for that stupid 'defence of marriage' amendment." (Under right-wing pressure, the federal Liberals tacked it onto their 1999 same-sex equity legislation.) "We had huge e-mail wars over that, I mean, what the hell is this crap? On the other hand, in terms of the legislatures where you can actually make and change the laws, the NDP is the best hope we've got right now. When they were in power in Ontario, they provided funding for the youth phone line. Now we have to put huge amounts of energy into fund-raising. I just wish more people on the left would get involved with the NDP and turn it into the kind of party we really need."

His commitment to the church also surprises me, given the background he describes. "I'm a little surprised by it myself," he says. "I thought I'd had it with religion. But when a friend took me to the MCC, I couldn't believe how friendly everyone was, all these aunt and uncle types with grey hair. Up to then my only experience was at Colby's [a gay bar], where everyone wants you to think they're somebody famous, and they get off on not talking to anyone. At MCC I feel fully accepted for who I am. It's like a community centre. I also like the message I hear there. It's really quite simple – it's okay to be who you are, you *can* be free, and you *can* be happy."

Since this book is about relationships, what about his? "You can put me down as single and available," he says, with a smile. Available to whom? "For one thing, I'd like to date someone with similar values. I'm lucky enough to have seen how things connect, and how much they matter. But there's not too many people at Woody's [another bar] interested in having that kind of conversation. Mostly what you hear is who's bought which designer item. Are we trying to buy equality, or what? And homophobia's still such a huge problem. Even on Church

Street it's rare to see gay and lesbian couples even holding hands, they've learned so well not to do that. I want someone who's not afraid to touch me. I'm not an untouchable, I want to hold and be held."

I imagine that, not unlike myself, Bonte could sometimes be a little prickly to hold. "It really makes me mad that some people I wouldn't mind dating won't even talk to me because I'm out," he says. "Being out, being an activist, being a Sunday school teacher, all of these seem to be barriers to relationship. Why? It's depressing. I've written poetry about it, but I don't want to show it to people, it's so full of frustration. Sometimes I wonder what's the point of being out if you can't date anybody because they're not." It's been a while, he says, since he dated anyone. "But there are times I see the potential for it, the sparks, in some of the talented, creative people I meet. I think what good times could be had, and what really hot passionate sex. I want those sparks to turn into fires."

What about family, chosen or otherwise – how do they connect? "I love my parents," he says. "But I've changed so much since I've been away, I don't know any more how to tell them who I am. The Bonte they see in the paper doing a polygamous wedding on Parliament Hill [to protest the 'defence of marriage' amendment] is so far from the Bonte they knew." His brother has threatened more than once to shoot his "Paki boyfriends." Bonte's chosen family includes two close friends who live across the street, a few people at MCC, and people he works with in various struggles for change. "You can end up spending a lot of time together, and in some fairly tense situations. Some of those people have come to fill familial roles for me, though I may not have said that to them as much as I could have."

Bonte's father called early this morning to remind him that the time was coming, not too far off, when he'd have to start paying his own way. A career counsellor asked him recently what he thought would be his ideal job. Homosexualist philanthropist, he said. "I see so many great projects, and they could go a lot further if they just had some decent funding behind them."

How might he fund his philanthropy? "Yeah, that's the problem, isn't it?" he says. "With a liberal arts degree, I guess I'll have to sell myself to the highest bidder. I'm interested in journalism, TV, radio. Do you think they have openings for an activist? I've learned all kinds of skills that could be useful in a whole range of jobs. Apparently human-resource people identify thinking outside the box as a marketable skill. That's good, because being queer, that's where I live, outside the box."

Bonte has to leave, he's due at another meeting. This time he's chairing a committee to organize the first-ever lesbian, gay, bisexual and transgendered scout troop in North America. He calls over his shoulder, "It's about time, don't you think?" and flashes a grin, and speeds away on his bicycle.

A party at my Aunty Kevin's Helen was a tomboy and the son her father never had. "We worked on his car, I helped him build speaker boxes – he was a DJ – I played soccer, he coached. Like him, I would work in aviation." At high school people often spoke of her as "he." Women stared at her and sometimes challenged her in washrooms: What are *you* doing in here?

As punks, she and her sister didn't blend well among the preppies and football players in Belleville, a small, white, conservative city in eastern Ontario. Helen became friends with two women at school, a couple, and by association also got labelled a dyke. When the friends moved to Toronto, Helen was left on her own, to be verbally assaulted, threatened, and chased. "My sister was the only person who protected me. She's a big girl, and she'd go right after anyone that dared to mess with me."

At a party her sister's boyfriend, a skinhead, assaulted a gay friend of Helen's. She got him to safety, then sat in a corner, drunk, and crying. Her sister asked, "What's wrong?" Helen told her she was a dyke. "Then you're not my sister," her sister replied, "and you deserve everything you get at school."

"That threw me right back into the closet," says Helen. "I became a skinhead too. It's the only way I could have her protection again."

When she went up to North Bay to train as an aviation mechanic, Helen met another skinhead. "As people we were pretty well matched, but I kept wishing he had breasts!" she says. She put up a notice to start a gay group at the college, but only got one call. "There were about two hundred guys and maybe six women [on campus]. Most of the women were fine with me, but most of the guys had never met a gay person before, and some of them wouldn't talk to me for a whole year. They would ask stupid questions like, how can two women do it, can I watch? But once you got through the bullshit, then they started asking some real questions that I was more comfortable answering." Still, the isolation and exposure took their toll, as did the suicide of one of her few friends at the college. Helen failed her exams, returned to Belleville, and let her hair grow.

Before the North Bay expedition she had attended a few meetings and dances of the Quinte Lesbian & Gay Group, but by the time she got home, it had collapsed. So had three other groups that followed. Even so, said Reverend Diane Fisher, the Belleville MCC minister, a young gay man wanted to get a new youth group going. She asked if Helen would lend a hand. For the next few months, Helen, Sean, and Shari met every Tuesday evening, just the three of them, at Helen's apartment in downtown Belleville.

Then Sean Keegan moved away to Toronto. Under constant threat at school, he had quit grade nine, and by the time he was sixteen, Belleville had grown too small for him and too dangerous. In Toronto he intended to be a star, a great drag queen. For a year he supplemented his welfare cheques by turning tricks, always practising safe sex with johns. But he and his boyfriends regarded condoms as barriers to love. At seventeen, Sean tested positive for HIV. Less than a year later his body was found in the stairwell of a downtown parking lot. He and two other prostitutes, one pre-op transsexual, the other a woman, had been shot in the back of the head. Thirty-year-old Marcello Palma, married with a young child, was charged with the three murders.

To Helen, Shari, and others back home, his life and death reinforced the crying need to create a refuge for gay youth in Belleville. They called their group Free to Be Me. As a co-founding veteran of the group and the closest thing it has to a coordinator, Helen agreed to round up some of the crew for a chat with me. We get together on a hot summer evening in a small room upstairs at St Thomas Anglican Church in Belleville. The local PFLAG group also meets here. A women's group is busy preparing food in the big hall below.

Shari is twenty-six. Like most of her peers, she grew up believing what she absorbed from her parents and schoolmates, that homosexuals were freaks and child molesters. Her father told her that if any of his three girls ever told him she was gay, he'd take her out back and shoot her. "My drinking and drug use compounded about tenfold at the time," says Shari. "But I didn't put that together until later, in treatment."

During the summer she lived in the family trailer parked in the driveway. One night in her late teens she was rolling her own cigarettes and listening to Melissa Etheridge's fourth album, *Yes I Am.* "That was an incredibly powerful experience for me," says Shari. "Until then I had no idea Melissa was gay, I just liked her music. But now suddenly I was thinking, well, maybe there's a whole other side to this gay thing. I guess you could say at that moment a dyke was born."

Now twenty-two, Darren grew up in Stirling, a smaller and even more conservative town north of Belleville. As a kid he liked playing with dolls and skipping rope with the girls. When he was about ten, he read a book on sex that informed him homosexuals were dysfunctional (he had to look up the word) and inevitably came to a bad end. "I decided that if I wasn't straight by the time puberty hit, I would kill myself," he says. But by the time puberty hit, his mother was ill and Darren had to help out at home. Instead of suicide, he buried himself in schoolwork for the next few years.

On a school trip to Toronto he invented an excuse to escape the group and went looking for Church Street. "Holy shit!" he says, "there were all these rainbows! And gay people, all kinds of them, all over the place! I went into a store and found the Pink Pages [a gay directory], and there was a listing for MCC in Belleville. When I called, Diane told me about this youth group. I couldn't believe it, I freaked."

Kim, who's twenty-five, was also a loner at school. When others paired off into standard couples, she told herself she had no time for such things. She would go to university, and she would make something of herself. At Baptist summer camp she finally consented to date a boy. "I wanted to have kids, so if I couldn't find somebody to make me happy, at least they could make a family happen," she says. At about the same time she became friends with "Andrea," who admitted that she might be a lesbian. One day the two of them had a tickle fight that ended in a long kiss. "I'd been taught that gay people are the Anti-Christ, and they're all going to hell," says Kim. "But kissing her made me so happy,

I thought, well, now what do I do?" She moved in with Andrea. Kim was sixteen.

Their relationship lasted seven years. "She was quite abusive, but I didn't realize it until I was much too involved to walk away," Kim says. They have a five-year-old son, "Tyler." Andrea is the biological mother, but for the first two years Kim was the primary caregiver. She had just begun the legal process to adopt Tyler when she and Andrea split up, and Andrea assumed sole custody. Kim had to sue for shared custody. "I want him to grow up with both parents," she says. "He has that right, and so do I."

Kim was recruited briefly by the local branch of Youth for Christ, an international right-wing evangelical organization. "I overheard one of them say, there is a church where *those people* go. I thought, cool, I better have a look." Through MCC she discovered Free to Be Me. The group has been a great support system, she says. "With these guys I found out there's a lighter side to life, and I could actually laugh. If we're going to hell, I couldn't ask for better company."

Twenty-four now, Calvin grew up in Campbellford, another small town not far from Belleville. "By the time I was eight or so, I'd figured out that I was liking the little boys who were liking the little girls," he says. "But I couldn't be gay, not me, because gays were guys who dressed in women's clothes and tried to get down little kids' pants, and I wasn't like that. It took me a while to realize what bullshit all of that was." A decade later, in his graduating year, Calvin finally informed a few friends on the school bus that he was gay. "By Monday the whole school knew," he says. "A lot of people were freaked out and disgusted. I got some nasty e-mails and people would yell at me in the corridor, but my friends protected me pretty well from most of it."

One night he was walking with two women friends in the Campbellford park. Another group moved closer, and one young man, quite drunk, asked Calvin if he was a fag. I'm gay, said Calvin. "He started to ask me all kinds of stupid questions, and then he got two of his buddies to beat me up." Calvin's friends intervened, and the three of them ran to their car. They drove directly to the police station, where they laid assault charges against the two attackers. "One guy pleaded guilty," says Calvin, "but he was a minor so he just got a slap on the wrist. The other guy we couldn't identify. The thing that really surprised me was how cooperative the police were. I thought they'd tell me I got what I deserved."

Another night in Campbellford, Calvin and a friend wanted something to eat so they took a drive down to Taco Bell on the fast food strip in Belleville. Calvin noticed a particular group of young people there, mixed, but in his eyes, surely gay. And some of them noticed him. Says Kim, "I saw this guy and I thought, that has to be the tallest fag I've ever seen." Calvin stands 6'3". Others noticed his multicoloured pride rings strung on a necklace. And Free to Be Me added another recruit to its growing list.

Also at Taco Bell that night were Sarah and Stephanie, FTBM regulars. Stephanie was never happy dating boys but assumed that it was her own fault and if she just kept trying, eventually she'd get over it. Then one night, rather drunk, she tumbled into bed with a woman. "At that point," she says, "I finally started to clue in."

As young queer lives go, Sarah's sounds a lot smoother than most. Because her mother wasn't well, for her first eight years she spent weekends and summers with her aunt and her wife in Toronto. "They considered themselves married," says Sarah. The couple had two sons, and two close friends that Sarah still calls "my Aunty Kevin and my Aunty Paul." Until she got to high school she assumed that everyone would consider these arrangements as commonplace as she did. She moved to Belleville with a boyfriend and happened to come out to Stephanie's roommate, "a fanatic matchmaker." He introduced her to Stephanie, and now the two of them are engaged to be married. Sarah is twenty-three, Stephanie twenty-eight.

Looking round the table, it occurs to me that the *parents* of most of the people gathered in this room could be younger than me. Given societal changes in the more than two decades since I came out, I wonder out loud if it's got any easier to break The News to parents. A brief silence, then Calvin groans, and everyone laughs.

When Calvin told his mother, she was half asleep watching TV. At the end of it, she woke up and said, "Pardon?" "She doesn't like to talk about it," says Calvin, "but at least she knows I'm not going to change." His father wanted to send him to a psychiatrist. "We can beat this thing," he said, and asked if anyone had abused Calvin as a child. "We haven't spoken more than five words since," says Calvin. "We never did get along, but now we hardly even look at each other." Calvin left home a month ago and now has an apartment on "the gay corner" in downtown Belleville, same floor as Kim, upstairs from Stephanie, across the street from Helen.

Setting off to her first Toronto Pride parade in 1995, Helen worried that her mother might see her on television and "fall dead of a heart attack." So she took her out to lunch, said she had something to tell her, and told her. "Well," said her mother, "at least you're not pregnant." And that was that. "We don't talk about it," says Helen. "She worries, what if the neighbours find out, what if your younger brother turns out gay too? So that's her wish – it's not to be spoken about." When Helen told her father, he replied, simply, "You'll always be my daughter."

Three years ago Darren's mom found a steamy gay love letter he'd received and left, apparently by mistake, on the couch. "The next morning she was crying so hard, I thought somebody must have died. She asked me, 'Are you really this way?' It was hard for her. She has a gay cousin who has AIDS and who's been beaten up, so she was afraid for me. But now she totally accepts it. She's ready to march in the Pride parade, but she doesn't want to be on TV, not yet."

Sarah's mother and step-dad are comfortable with her sexuality and relationship. "My mom saw what her favourite sister went through being a lesbian, and her parents not speaking to her for years. I think that's why she made it so easy for me." Her father, on the other hand, still insists he'll find a husband for her through the want ads. "He was raised Irish Catholic, which is even worse than normal Catholic. If I mention Stephanie's name, he just goes silent. A couple of months ago we had a big fight. I told him don't call again until you can accept that she's part of my life."

For Stephanie, the parental roles are reversed. Her dad and step-mom accept her fully. Her father went to Toronto last year for the Pride parade. "But my mom, who's *very* Roman Catholic, thinks I'm her punishment from God for something she did wrong. She's convinced that me and my friends are going to burn in hell. But then, she likes Sarah. Things are a little better now – we've come to a kind of truce."

Kim's Baptist parents also wondered what they'd done wrong. "My mother would just look at me, shake her head, and walk away." Finally they told her she would have to move out while her sister "still had a chance to turn out normal." Yet they would invite Andrea for holidays, and they enjoy their grandson. "When I needed to come home after the relationship with Andrea broke up, they found a place for me. It was in the garage, but still. . . . And they love Shari. I guess you could say we're at a maintenance level."

Since her father had threatened to shoot any daughter of his who turned gay, Shari came out to her mother first. "I figured I'd just move to some place like Siberia, call him up, and work it into the conversation somehow." She's been negotiating with her mother for a couple of years now. "At first she'd say gay people have a mental disease. We worked on that. Then she decided it was a phase, a way of avoiding the responsibilities of adult life. I've got a job, I pay my bills, I'm in a relationship, and we're raising a kid: how is that not responsible? Now she's says I'm not a traditional female, because I don't pick up after myself! Anyway, we're working on it."

For Shari, Kim turned out to be a major asset in dealing with her father. "When he told me off, she would take his side, so of course he liked her right from day one. So I thought, okay, maybe I can work with this." When Kim stayed over, Shari would sneak downstairs from her own room for an hour or two, terrified that she'd be caught. One Christmas she came downstairs, and stayed. "Just so long as the two of you don't sleep in the same bed," said her father. Eventually Shari got up the nerve to have "the big lesbian conversation" with him. "He told me he thought lesbians were women who carried big rubber dicks in their purses."

The rest of the Free to Be Me gang roar with laughter. "Really," says Shari, "that's what the man said. I told him I don't carry a purse. There was a lot of yelling and crying, then three days of total silence. After that he started talking again, and he hasn't shut up since. He keeps asking me all these questions, like, What's that rainbow flag on your t-shirt, what country is that? I guess it's turned out pretty good – he didn't kill me."

Most of the people here tonight are gearing up for the big Pride weekend in Toronto. It will be Calvin's first. "I'm really excited," he says, and sounds it. "It's one day when you don't have to worry, you don't have to guard your words, and you don't have to feel that you're alone out there."

Helen, the veteran, nods. "I couldn't believe how safe I felt the first time I went."

Sarah adds, "This will be my first Pride, and our first vacation together. Stephanie and I are invited to a party at my Aunty Kevin's. I can't wait. Around here you have to watch yourself all the time. I choose my words carefully, and I play the pronoun game very well. I can't wait to drop all that and surround myself with gayness!"

The lure of the big city is strong. Darren studies journalism at Ryerson Polytechnic University in downtown Toronto. "A person can gain so much confidence by experiencing big time gay life in the city. Hopefully you'll meet someone special there, and then you might want to come back to Belleville, or some place like it, to help younger people come out."

Why do the others stay, what keeps them here? "Both my parents are here," says Stephanie, "and I have a good job." She manages a restaurant.

"I stay here because Stephie's here," says Sarah.

"All my friends are here, either here or in Kingston," says Calvin, "and I have a full-time job that pays decently." He cooks in a restaurant.

"My family's all here," says Kim, "my parents and two sisters. I do intend to go to school, though, either in Kingston or Toronto." She plans to be a lawyer.

As for Free to Be Me, says Helen, "It's not easy to keep the numbers up. People leave, or they get into a relationship, or develop their own circle of friends, and then they don't need the group. And Belleville's not that big, there's only so many people you can drag out of the closet." But for her, the work of sustaining the group has had an unexpected reward. "It got me involved in the church, and that helped me to realize what I want to do with my life. Aircraft engineering is what others wanted me to do. Ministering to gay and lesbian youth is what I want to do."

Her current job in a local bakery is helping to finance her studies for ministry in the Metropolitan Community Church. "This church has the potential of reaching out to youth in so many small towns. It's a place where young people can come to heal the wounds that society and especially religious groups put on them." Her studies will take her to New York and then to Los Angeles, MCC headquarters.

I have one more question. Last year a CBC host asked me why we gay people continue to agitate. "Haven't you got pretty much everything you want?" My response started with the suicide statistics, still shockingly high among queer youth. But now I want to know what these folks, the oldest of them half my age, have to say on the subject: Haven't we got pretty much everything we want?

"Nowhere near," says Sarah. "There are still so many walls that need to come down."

"You can still be arrested for sodomy in lots of states," says Helen, "and you can still be executed in some countries for being gay."

"It's still hard for most people to come out," says Shari. "We need more local heroes, more role models. Melissa Etheridge is fine, but she's so far away. We need more visible local heroes."

"When we don't have any more ministers like Fred Phelps and Jerry Falwell preaching hatred, then we'll be free," says Darren.

"We still lose so many young people to suicide and substance abuse," says Kim. "As long as people are dying because they don't know where to turn, we still have work to do."

18 Some Kindred Spirits

Chris Bearchell composes her e-mail bulletin by candle-light, a softer glow than the white glare of the propane that has to be hauled from the mainland. She uses a lot of propane in the fall, putting up harvest pickles: two kinds of carrots, spiced Vietnamese and Indian, also mustard cauliflower and sweet beets. She'll get to the marmalade, chutney, and apple butter after she's hauled her firewood.

Until work is finished on her one-room house, she's living in an unheated trailer, on twenty acres next to a swamp up a mile-long road into the woods. She moved to the trailer after a storm flooded her tent and a wind-snapped tree just missed flattening it. Though winter temperatures rarely drop far below freezing here, fierce autumn and winter storms come roaring up the Georgia Straits to batter the little island.

Since her electricity comes from two car batteries that she charges up with a small gasoline-powered generator, only essential functions get juice: a water heater for washing dishes, clothes, and bodies, and at least as critical, power for the computer. E-mail is Chris Bearchell's lifeline to the rest of her clan, the other Walnuts, scattered across the wide world out there.

I met Chris in 1974, at the Gay Alliance Toward Equality in Toronto. It was a heady time; we were bursting from our various closets, propelled by a passion to remake the world. I remember Chris as a nineteen-year-old lesbian and socialist from Alberta, with a searchlight intelligence and a ready laugh. For a while we did a performing homo duet, a sensible chat – don't be afraid, we're just like you – at schools where teachers were brave enough to invite us. I remember Chris's calm, sometimes sardonic responses to the usual stupid questions – but you do molest children, don't you? – and my own desire to smack the weedy boys snickering at the back. On one of these excursions she told me that one day she would return to the West and settle where she belonged, in some wild back-country place.

In the meantime she worked in a tangle of gay-lesbian organizations that sprang up through those fervent years. At *The Body Politic,* the now-legendary Toronto gay journal, she joined the collective and became one of several paid workers. By the mid-1970s, apparently we had gained enough ground to alarm the authorities. One night in December 1977 police raided *The Body Politic,* seized crates of material, and arrested three collective members. Their crime: publishing an article, "Men Loving Boys Loving Men," in which one of them, Gerald Hannon, had argued for a fresh look at the complexities of intergenerational sex.

Over the next six years the Conservative government appealed one acquittal after another at taxpayers' expense, while the paper and its supporters had to raise almost $100,000 in court costs. Overwhelmed, some collective members were tempted to accept a deal, a manageable fine in return for a guilty plea. Others, especially Chris Bearchell, argued that pleading guilty would only encourage the authorities to further repression. On that ground there could be no retreat. This view prevailed, and eventually the Ontario Tories quit trying to silence T*he Body Politic*. "That was my early education as a free-speech activist," says Chris.

But they weren't done with us yet. Late one night in mid-winter 1981, 150 armed policemen stormed four steambaths in downtown Toronto. They searched, fingerprinted, harassed and jailed 309 men, the largest mass arrest in Canada since the War Measures Act was imposed on Quebec in 1970. At around ten the next night, outraged protesters started gathering at a downtown intersection, and by midnight more than a thousand of us had spilled off the sidewalks into the street. Police ordered us to make way for traffic, but we were in no mood to obey. I remember the icy night, and waves of white heat in the belly, a potent mix of fury, terror, and joy. I remember Chris Bearchell standing on a mailbox, her voice ringing through the canyon, "NO MORE SHIT!"

In the early 1980s Chris met Danny Cockerline at *The Body Politic*. On the Walnut website she describes him as "brilliant and reckless, a queer queer, an outsider among outsiders." The two of them clicked, and in 1983 somehow they gathered the down payment on a narrow three-storey house, 97 Walnut Avenue. It's a short street, only four blocks, set oddly askew in the King-Queen-Bathurst grid. Now the whole area has gone upscale, with factory shells transformed into condos, corporate temples, and smart restaurants. But twenty years ago it was still a working-class neighbourhood, a region of outsiders and home to a queer refuge called Walnut.

Says Chris, "The people who lived there or who were drawn to the house shared commitments to particular struggles for justice. That was our common ground. We wanted others to know about these situations, and to help us transform them." Having met people who made their livings as performers in pornography, Chris and Danny both developed an interest in the well-being and rights of sex workers in general. "For Danny it started as an intellectual thing," says Chris, "but then he got into doing sex-work himself. He became quite renowned as a prostitutes' rights activist and did a lot of work organizing sex workers in response to AIDS." Danny and Chris helped found Maggie's, the Toronto Prostitutes' Community Services Project, a drop-in and advocacy centre in downtown Toronto. When Danny left his job there, Chris took it on.

The Canadian Organization for the Rights of Prostitutes was hatched at 97 Walnut, as was the Canadian Committee against Customs Censorship and a host of other such initiatives. When Irit Shimrat and Chris became lovers in 1984, Irit moved into the house, where she edited and published *Phoenix Rising* out of the basement. It was a national magazine for former psychiatric inmates; Chris handled layout and design. Irit says, "It was a really powerful experience for me to hear the stories of other people who'd also learned the hard way how dangerous psychiatry can be."

In the late '70s, facing bouts of depression, Irit had been locked up and forcibly drugged by psychiatrists. She had lost several friends, imprisoned, tortured with electroshock and drugs, even killed in psychiatric institutions. In 1990 she was elected the first coordinator of the newly formed Ontario Psychiatric Survivor's Alliance. "I was very moved to find people at Walnut who understood the anti-psychiatric cause, even though they had no direct experience of it themselves. Before I got there I was lonely and isolated, I didn't fit in anywhere, but at Walnut I finally found some kindred spirits."

Says Chris, "The support wasn't abstract or theoretical. I already had serious doubts about psychiatry, probably first sparked by your writing in *The Body Politic*." (In 1974 I wrote a long article on my year of electric shock "aversion therapy," meant to stamp out my homosexuality, and another article the next year when I discovered that the shrink who administered this torture was himself a homo.) She continues, "But when your lover or friend or house-mate is a psychiatric survivor, or a prostitute, suddenly the issue becomes quite real and compelling." In 1991 Irit created two radio documentaries challenging psychiatry for *Ideas*, the CBC radio show. The producer was another Walnut.

After making a ruckus for fifteen years and becoming what activists in several countries considered the finest gay journal in the world, suddenly in February 1987 *The Body Politic* died. I asked Chris why. "It was a victim of its own success," she responded in an e-mail. "Gay liberation brought more people out of the closet, swelling our ranks and giving us more credibility, just as we'd hoped. Our movement evolved from 'gay liberation' to 'gay rights' to no movement at all, but instead became this much more amorphous thing, the 'gay community.' In this tidy, respectable 'community' there was very little room for a principled defence of sexual freedom."

To fill the void, Chris, Irit, and others launched a new magazine, *Epicene,* which the dictionary defines as "a person with characteristics of both sexes." As usual with such ventures, funding was a major challenge. "Most of us had experienced the compromises that come with being dependent on funding from official sources," says Chris. "So we've learned to do as much as we can on the smallest budget we can. That was the *Body Politic* model, where you had a handful of modestly paid staff and a vast network of committed volunteers. And that's pretty much how we did most things around Walnut – we relied on each other's skills and passion." *Epicene* folded after five issues. But the second-hand equipment that Will Pritchard had gathered to produce it would now serve *Phoenix Rising,* until it too folded in 1990.

Will Pritchard's story is classic Walnut material. He designed *Epicene* and lived for a while at the house. Through Walnut connections he became immersed in prostitute activism and eventually decided to turn tricks himself. Then he got a job at Maggie's, doing outreach work to male sex workers. "He did an amazing job there in a very short period of time," says Chris. "He designed our materials, our 'look' on paper, he made signs, he did all kinds of wonderful things to fix up the space, and at the same time he also managed to do more street outreach than anyone else on staff." Burned out, he headed west to Vancouver, and there established the first Walnut outpost.

Life at 97 Walnut reflected its shifting constellation of inhabitants. Shortly after Danny bought the house with Chris in 1983, he went to England for six months and sublet his room. Bruce Martin responded to the ad. In Berlin where he'd worked as a nanny, Bruce had encountered *The Body Politic* at a gay bookstore and became a devoted fan. Returning to Canada, he was determined to live where the paper lived, in Toronto. He called Walnut, and Chris invited him to dinner; he would meet everyone, then they could all decide if they wanted to live together. "The conversation was amazing," says Bruce. "Peggy Miller was there that night, and Gwendolyn, they were getting the Prostitutes' Rights Organization started. I just sat quietly and listened. I knew I wanted to live there, but I didn't think I had a chance. I was so out of their league, being a boy from the suburbs and quite naive politically." When Chris called to say they wanted him to move in, he asked why. What really did it, she said, was his red pants and yellow shoes.

Bruce settled happily into the hum and throb of the house. "Dinner was always a big event, with wonderful conversation and always more people at the table than lived in the house. My contribution was being an eager cook. Walnut had fewer rules than other co-op houses. Everyone just seemed to end up doing the chores they liked to do. So they fed my mind, and I fed their bellies. I loved being there, it was the perfect place for me." When Danny came back, Bruce was prepared to leave, but instead Chris offered to tame part of the basement for herself and left her room to him. After a year or so Bruce became lovers with one of his house-mates, David.

One of the things Bruce liked best about Walnut was the continuous flow of people. "Where I'd been raised, in suburbia, everyone has their own quiet little house with the curtains drawn. There were always more people staying at Walnut than ever paid rent – people in trouble, people who'd lost their housing, people passing through Toronto. I loved living in a place where the door was always open for people to come and go, or come and stay. After all, that's how I got to be there."

The idea of Walnut as a refuge had been clear to Chris from the beginning. "Most of us Walnuts don't have kids of our own, but we do have a history of taking in people who've been spurned by others. I'd been on my own from a very early age, a runaway without many resources, and often without a place to live. A lot of people helped me out, and that left a strong impression with me. When you've been a hitchhiker and then you get a car, you stop for hitchhikers. Now that I finally had a place where anyone, even people I didn't know, could take refuge, it was a good way to pass on some of that support I'd got. And if someone shows up in the middle of the night, in desperate straits, what are you going to do?"

People did arrive in the middle of the night, and in desperate straits – for example, three young men who'd made a video of their three-way sexual encounter and got entangled in a huge child pornography investigation by the Toronto police. Though they had no intention of selling the video and all three had taken part with evident gusto, the two younger men were labelled victims, and the older one, who was only twenty-one, a child pornographer. "All three of them passed through Maggie's or Walnut," says Chris. "With us they got the shelter and support they couldn't find anywhere else. They also divulged a lot of information you'll never find in the official police reports – the actual circumstances before the bust, the appalling treatment they got from the system, and how little chance they had to defend themselves. It was a real education in what goes on behind the headlines, and it was partly the grounds on which we criticized the new porn legislation that criminalized consensual youth sex."

Bruce attributes his own political evolution to the support he got from Chris and other Walnuts. As he listened and learned, he became more confident and more actively involved. "Chris was always prepared to listen," he says, "and to share whatever information she had. Unlike some activists I've encountered, she never made me feel unworthy, like these were things I should already have known." In the early days of HIV and AIDS, Bruce wanted to confront the alarming, widespread notion that safe sex was boring. "Chris encouraged me not just to talk about it but to actually *do* something. She said if I didn't get the word out, she would." He wrote an article on hot safe sex, Irit edited it, and they published it in *Epicene*. Bruce and Chris also co-wrote and narrated three safe-sex radio ads for university stations across the country.

Chris rejects the idea of herself as primary author of the Walnut experiment or even uniquely central to it. "Walnuts recruit other Walnuts. I'm sure there are Walnuts I've never even met."

Bruce laughs. "Don't listen to her. We all added our various colours to the house but the shape it took depended very much on who she is."

The first five years were the best, he says, at least for him. Then rifts deepened, and tension mounted between the original co-owners, Danny and Chris. Danny sold his share to her. Others moved on, and new people arrived who were less inclined to live as a community and much less tolerant of the always-open door. After Bruce broke up with David, he stayed on another year, then got an apartment with a friend who, like him, worked at This Ain't the Rosedale Library, a lively, near-queer independent bookstore in the gay village.

By January 1995 a mix of internal and external pressures had brought Maggie's close to collapse. Chris and her young friend

Andrew Sorfleet, a former hustler who had also worked the last frantic year at Maggie's, both quit their jobs. They stuffed their worldly goods into an $800 van and rented trailer, and headed west in a snowstorm with Chris's ancient cat, Micah, in her lap. Andrew had his own reasons for making the move; on a previous jaunt to Vancouver with Chris and another Walnut, he'd fallen in love with Will Pritchard. After a week-long, perilous journey, Chris landed in the wild place where, as she told me a quarter century before, she belonged. She sold the Walnut house to another activist.

Chris asked me not to identify her island off the coast of British Columbia. "Given the kind of crazy over-development that's happened to other Gulf islands, the less attention we get the better." It's a small island, with a very small year-round population that doubles in summer, phone service but no hydro, mail three times a week, no cops, and a periodic ferry.

To Chris, it's paradise. She gets by with occasional freelance writing, part-time work at a small business that makes buttons and souvenirs of local woods, and odd jobs that come her way – recently she was hired to cook a Thai birthday dinner for twenty. She also counts on a little help from her friends on the island and, as always, the Walnuts.

A Walnut found the land that Chris co-owns here with another Walnut. Another Walnut delivered her here, another provides occasional work or covers her rent when her own funds run out, and others are helping to clear the land and build her house. Irit Shimrat worked most of the past summer with Chris, living in a tent and hauling hundreds of wheelbarrows of rock, gravel, building materials, drinking water, propane tanks, generator fuel, and groceries up the long driveway. In 1993 when Irit moved to Vancouver, where affordable housing is harder to find than winter sun, a well-connected friend found her a tiny but pleasant apartment in an old building in the west end. Irit put in a good word for another migrant Walnut to get an apartment in the same building, and he's done the same for two more, as well as helping Irit out for a while with her rent. This is what Walnuts do.

Chris explains, "We've come together around complex, controversial political beliefs, most of which aren't exactly popular in the general culture. Since it's only a small minority of the planet's population who seem prepared to do that kind of thinking, you can easily get to feel very isolated. So when you do meet people who share these perspectives, or who are at least willing to grapple with them, you definitely don't want to let those people go."

The Walnut building In the mid-1990s Deborah McIntosh was coasting through a fairly comfortable life in Ottawa. She was thirty, a lawyer and land-claims analyst with the federal Department of Indian Affairs, and in a long-term relationship. But there were things that didn't sit well with her: aspects of her job, a clear, steady drift to the right in national gay politics, a huge silence on sexual politics in general, and in her neighbourhood, a righteous citizens' committee that had sprung up to drive out the prostitutes. "In the rather stifling climate of Ottawa I felt quite nervous about raising serious questions about these things," she says, "so to avoid being too isolated, I started a web page to open up some dialogue." She also searched the Internet for related sites and found two of Andrew Sorfleet's: the Sex Workers' Alliance of Vancouver, and the Commercial Sex Information Services, "a clearinghouse of information about laws, sexual health, commerce, and culture as these topics relate to sex work." Deborah says, "It was such a relief to find people who were taking a less conservative path, and supporting a more radical sexual politic."

Andrew connected her with Chris. The two corresponded by e-mail, then Chris invited Deborah out for a visit. They've been friends and lovers ever since. In Vancouver Deborah also met other Walnuts, including Irit, Andrew, and Will. "When my relationship broke up in 1996, I really couldn't see any good reason not to move here," she says. "There was a lot more going on here in native politics and land claims, and now I had this extended family here too." And an apartment in the Walnut building.

It's in her apartment where we're chatting over breakfast – Deborah, Irit, Chris, and I, on a wet Sunday morning in early May. It took Chris most of a day to get here, hitchhiking to the dock on her island, then two ferries and a bus. The apartment is tiny, tidy, and tastefully furnished. "Deb has the fanciest furniture of any of us," says Chris.

Deborah nods. "I do inhabit a more mainstream version of the world than these guys. I grew up in a middle class suburb, I'm a lawyer, I go to work in a big office tower. That's partly why I value my association with the Walnuts so much. They give me the energy to keep looking critically at the world. I also like their sense of community, the ways they've developed of being family to one another that seem to avoid the pitfalls of more traditional family structures."

Irit adds, "I've had someone just out of the psych ward come stay at my apartment, which is no bigger than this one, and someone who was trying to avoid getting locked up stayed with me for over a month. Before I got involved with the Walnuts I would never have done anything like that. I would have been too afraid of the unknown. It's really about learning to be responsible for each other instead of leaving it to the official structures that can end up doing so much damage to us."

How does a person qualify for Walnutship? "Well," says Chris, "I suppose you'd just have to hang out with one or more Walnuts, either in meatspace or cyberspace, and then if you discovered a shared passion or two, maybe you'd decide to maintain contact with some or all of us. The rest of us would have no say in the matter. There are no tests, no rites, no secret oaths. And we don't all have to like each other. As with biological clans you don't get to choose your in-laws."

The Walnuts are only human. "Like most conventional families, we have our share of dysfunction," says Chris. "We've been together, some of us, for a long time. We've lost people, sometimes through rifts, sometimes they just drift away. It's hard when people who matter to you don't stick around. But these are the same things that make you sad in any kind of family."

"Generally I find these guys pretty tolerant of each other," says Deborah. "But if someone is acting out, or in trouble, they have a remarkable way of policing each other's conduct. It doesn't strike me as malicious, it's just that they're all accustomed to thinking critically. Then they'll go around lobbying each other to build support for their particular case."

Chris laughs. "You can easily gang up on someone, and of course everyone says it's for their own good. If they don't agree, then you've got a fight on your hands. We all do that to each other."

With the Toronto house long gone, Walnuts scattered across the country, and Chris an expensive daylong journey from the nearest branch, the lifeline function of her car-battery-driven computer becomes clear. "I was quite torn about leaving other Walnuts behind in Toronto, but with the Internet I can be on my little island in the middle of nowhere and still have regular contact. We've become a cyberclan," she says. She composes richly detailed bulletins on island events, visitors, the change of seasons, pickles she's prepared. "I think that started at *The Body Politic*. We were obsessed with writing each other memos all the time, to stay connected and keep each other informed, that's mostly how the collective process worked there. It translates wonderfully to e-mail."

Deborah adds, "Any difficult conversation I've had with any Walnut has been by e-mail. It's a really good way to focus your thoughts. In person it's so easy to get distracted by nature, or pot, or sex. . . ."

The Internet is also a great way to carry on political work, says Chris, on a minimal budget. "The Lunatics Liberation Front web page reaches far more people – 93,000 hits so far, actually – for a lot less work and money than *Phoenix Rising* ever could." Irit runs the page, listing herself as "an escaped lunatic," and she credits Andrew and Will for design and resources. Her intent is "to promote the liberation of people who have been or are in danger of being labelled mentally ill – those who go nuts or get too angry, too 'high' or too miserable for their own and/or other people's comfort."

The page is one of several that share the Walnet website which Andrew designed and manages. The site includes a page from a Montreal prostitutes' rights organization, a page called "Jane Doe" that documents the struggles of several Toronto prostitutes to confront police abuse, and "Trailboys," a webzine about gay sex outdoors and in other public places, which offers practical advice on "how to stay healthy and avoid unwanted attention."

In the first months of 1999 the tone of Chris's e-mail bulletins suddenly darkened. "In early December," she wrote, "I discovered a lump in my left breast. In early January, I finally confirmed that it was cancer." At the same time, she'd been laid off at work, she'd injured her knee, she wasn't registered for provincial medical insurance, her water supply had frozen, and one of her cats was seriously ill. She concluded, with characteristic understatement, "It's been a complicated winter."

Not being a Walnut, I had missed a whole earlier chapter in which Chris grappled with her options, and sought input from the extended family. E-mails and phone calls flew across the country. "It was very family-like," says Bruce Martin. "Suddenly people who hadn't had much contact for a while were talking back and forth, what's to be done, how will she manage, how can we support her? It was like a body springing into action, the adrenalin pumping, and all systems going on high alert."

In Chris's first messages about the diagnosis, Bruce had read an unfamiliar fatalism. "Chris always seems so strong, so unstoppable in any external crisis, but now suddenly she was saying this is how my mother died, this is what happens in my family, and there's nothing to be done. She didn't even seem interested in getting any information, which is what she normally would do in taking on any other issue. That was very upsetting. I didn't want her to lie down and die without putting up a real Chris Bearchell fight. Having lived with her, I knew how crucial it was that she find the grounds to fight. When Chris gets angry, it stirs her, she goes into action. Well, finally she did, she got angry, really furious with this doctor and she started railing about the information she was and wasn't getting, and I thought, great, that's it, that's the turning point."

Much of the debate on Chris's situation turned on people's attitudes to conventional medicine. Some Walnuts, including Chris, had been sharply critical of the role that corporate science played in defining HIV/AIDS research and treatment. On the other hand, Bruce Martin's partner is an oncological nurse, which made Bruce more amenable, as Chris puts it, to trusting the medical system. "Probably most of us would admit that medicine is a weird mix of art and science," she says, "but how do you distinguish which is which, and what or who can you trust? It's such a complicated, emotionally wrought area, particularly with something as loaded as cancer."

Says Deborah, "One time I just wailed at Chris, 'Your position is too cynical, I can't stand it!' At the same time, of course I recognized that finally it was Chris herself who had to make these incredibly hard decisions about her own health."

"I actually got less input than I expected," says Chris. "As I discovered later, several people withheld the opinion that I shouldn't get involved with conventional medicine at all. But that's not so surprising. I suspect that most of us are quite reticent about influencing someone else on such a critical matter, even when they've asked for input. I mean, what if they take your advice and it turns out you're wrong?"

Chris did what Bruce had seen her do on many other fronts. She gathered all the information she could find, in print and on the Internet, and worked her way through the available options, statistics, pros and cons, to reach her decision: surgery to remove the lump, which turned out to be malignant, and several lymph nodes, which did not. A month of radiation treatment in Vancouver followed.

And life goes on. Work proceeds on the island house, 16 by 20 feet, one storey with a root cellar below, a vaulted ceiling, bay window and skylight, a chimney for the woodstove, salvaged windows, and covered porches. Last time Chris wrote, the outhouse was ready and the water reservoir under construction. With luck and fair weather, she hoped to move into the house by the end of the year.

In the meantime, she writes, "Strange things do happen to people who live alone in the woods. I, for instance, have become fascinated by birds." She describes these neighbours in some detail, from tiny wrens and thrushes to eagles, a great horned owl ("heard often but seen only once, from behind, under pursuit by a flock of robins"), and a family of six majestic trumpeter swans.

"Still," she continues, "I'm only just learning to recognize many of the birds' songs and the pattern of their comings and goings. This year, I know to expect the rufous-sided towhee back for the winter, but I'm not sure I'll recognize its call until I see one chirp. This May I'll be waiting to hear the first solitary vireos sing their greetings to the dawn and the dusk. And I'm sure that next fall I'll be craning my neck and stretching my ears for any sign of those amazing swans."

Her e-mail concludes, "More later."

19 The Burden of Gravity

On Saturday night a bland voice from the nursing home informs me that my mother's bowels have stopped working. She's been sent to hospital for assessment.

When I was a child, I used to imagine her in an elegant Viennese café, dancing to her favourite Strauss waltz, "The Blue Danube." Ringed by handsome admirers, she's a little drunk, a widow on a buying trip for the antique gallery. She has two children back home in Canada, but she's still young, still an object of desire, and, at least for the moment, she's free. Dance did that for Mollie. It freed her from the burden of gravity and all things not beautiful.

Sunday morning a surgeon slices into her and finds the lower intestine kinked like a garden hose. A section of it is dead, beyond salvage. If she were younger, they might have fitted her with a bag. Instead the surgeon stitches her up and washes his hands. Her own wastes, fermenting, will kill her within a day.

The young Mollie danced in the manner of Isadora Duncan, barefoot, interpreting the seasons, ancient legends, the wind and waves. Grace embodied, said the Montreal papers. She married an artist, another lover of beauty, and thereafter would dance only for him. She bore two sons, Eric and Michael. A daughter died one day old. Then her husband died of cancer, the day before Christmas 1948. Her sun and her moon, she called him, suddenly extinguished, leaving her with the boys, seven and four, like freshly hatched chicks all mouth and noisy demand. Later my mother would recall of those grim days only grief and terror. I wonder where the rage went.

Her boys get to the hospital mid-afternoon Sunday, Eric from Prince Edward Island with his wife, Jean, I from eastern Ontario with Brian. Mollie has managed to keep the morphine at bay long enough to greet each of us in turn. She's a little woozy but still present, still gracious. Then her eyes close, and she slides into fog.

In 1949 she found work at Ogilvy's, a posh Montreal department store, for $35 a week. In no time she was managing the antique gallery, flying off to Europe in a roaring pot-bellied Stratocruiser to find indulgences for her wealthy clients. She assigned our care to her mother, Isabel, a powerful, dangerous woman who should have been running an army, not a household with small children in it. At the end of the day Mollie came home on the bus wilted from her labours but forced to administer domestic justice, a role she hated and for which she was manifestly unsuited. Every night she went to sleep with a pill or two.

Together the three of us might have been a match for Isabel, but my brother learned early how to disappear, and only once can I remember Mollie taking my side in battle. Christmas was the darkest time of year in our house. On this particular morning my grandmother and I were fighting over my attire, which she deemed inadequate to hear Her Majesty's annual address to the Commonwealth. "I try so hard to make Christmas nice," she wailed, "not for myself, but for all of you. If no one cares, I might as well throw myself under a truck." This was not a new threat, but as predictable, in one form or another, as the Queen's performance.

Suddenly my mother appeared, barefoot, from the safety of her room. She glared at her mother with a molten fury I'd never seen before. "Do you know what you are?" she asked. I held my breath. "You are a *tyrant*." Then she turned and was gone. My grandmother retired to her room in a stony silence nearly as rare as Mollie's rage. Eric and I exchanged wide-eyed looks. I was terrified, and thrilled. This was a first in the whole history of the world. My mother had stood up for me.

In a little while she came downstairs again, no longer steaming. I heard her say she had been wrong. For the next hour she grovelled, begging forgiveness from Isabel. In due course the two of them emerged, my grandmother glowing with righteousness, my mother blank, ghost-grey. We all sat quietly to watch the Queen.

At sixty-five Mollie retired from Ogilvy's a vice-president, and turned her skills to volunteer work – not seeking it out, but, as always, doing what was asked of her. A series of mishaps, a twisted ankle, odd failures of balance, all were easily explained: "You know how it is with me, I was looking at the moon." Then one day she told me she'd been diagnosed with Parkinson's disease. I imagined nothing more serious than a Katherine Hepburn twitch that would simply heighten her effect. From birth Mollie had been taught to see herself only as reflected in others' eyes. Beauty, poise, and graciousness had constituted her passport through life, a radiant smile her currency. If a quirk in her brain was now to threaten these, she would simply have to work that much harder to keep up appearances.

The beginning of freedom Her sons and their partners take turns holding her hand, stroking her head and feet. Not much is left of my mother, skin stretched over bones, transparent and laced with blue veins. For a while I think I can read a slight response from her hand, but as night falls, it softens to nothing. Does she want her hand held, I wonder, or do we do it for our sake, so we can feel useful and connected? She's so helpless, I hate to impose. Still, I won't let go, not yet.

Through the long night, nurses glide by on soft soles. I hear muted cries from other rooms. No one belongs in this twilight domain. When two nurses come in to turn her, my mother's face contorts. Pain, or the indignity of being handled? They ask us to leave the room so they can change her gown. We shuffle obediently out. But a fresh gown, *now*? We should be in there defending her. Later, one of the nurses whispers to me, "Shall I increase the morphine a little in her drip?" Why didn't they ask sooner? Why didn't we?

Towards the end of her previous hospital ordeal, my mother asked Brian and me to help her sit up. He handled the IV tubes, I eased her legs around to dangle off the bed. Her bones were so bare of flesh, surely something would break. We moved her, inch by inch. Suddenly she snapped at me, "You really are utterly useless!" Brian glanced at me, shocked. I was embarrassed that he'd heard it but not greatly surprised. It used to be that my mother would slash at me like this only when her tongue was loosened by the third vodka martini. Here it was pain that freed her from good manners.

"Shamelessness is the beginning of freedom," Simone de Beauvoir wrote in *Aging*.

Now I talk to Mollie, but without sound, our joined hands the medium, I hope. *Let go, dear soul, let go* – I would never talk to her like this aloud – *there's nothing more you have to do here. Finally you can be free.* A few years before, when my mother and I were struggling to connect as adults, we got to talking about sex. She told me that her father, Andrew, had sexually molested her through her mid-teens. Mollie delivered this in the same smooth tone she would use to report a chat she'd had with a neighbour.

Of course I was stunned. "But it can't have been all that bad," she said. "He did teach me to have orgasms." Apparently he also chided her for being less accommodating than her younger sister.

Mollie was involved with a religious youth group at the time. Since one of its rules was absolute honesty, she told her mother what her father had been doing. Isabel ordered Andrew to leave. A few months later he was hit by a car. Nearly three decades after his death, Mollie's brother, Ernest, shouted in a drunken rage that it had not been an accident at all but deliberate, a suicide, and it was Mollie's fault.

In her last apartment before the nursing home, my mother told Brian and me that she no longer wanted to live. Her religious beliefs would never permit her to take her own life, but she would let go of it gladly when the time came and that couldn't be soon enough. Living had become too much work. It took an hour to put on her make-up, without which she would not consider facing the outside world, another hour to dress herself, another to manage the few steps from bed to kitchen or bathroom. She'd fallen more than once. She knew she needed help but couldn't face sharing a room with a stranger. Mollie's apartment was her sanctuary, her dressing room, the one place where she didn't have to perform.

Let go, let go.

It occurs to me that I'm doing a lot of talking, but no listening. So I ask her, soul to soul, "Is there anything you want to say to me?"

I hear, faintly, "I'm afraid. I'm so afraid." Her voice, or one of mine?

I can only think to reply, "And why not? What could be more frightening than what you face? But never in your life have you known what the future held, never for one moment. And whatever sustained you through all of that, surely it will sustain you now." It sounds too studied, like something a social worker or a minister might say, but I can't bring myself to say anything comforting to her about God – it's her God, not mine. If pushed, I suppose I could lie out loud, but not in the silence, surely she would know. Instead I say, "I'm sure the universe will receive you gently." Where did that come from? Does the universe really give a shit?

Then I hear, or imagine I hear, "I'm afraid of the devil." Damn the church. In middle age Mollie converted to Roman Catholicism, beguiled by incense and Gregorian chants at a Benedictine monastery. What on earth can I say? If the devil is evil embodied, I see it in dictators, in generals and CEOs who eat the world, in false prophets who curse us with shame and guilt. "As far as I know the devil belongs only to this world, in which case you have little to fear in the next." So inadequate.

Then I hear, "Water. Water." She has changed the subject. She would. But of course she's right, intravenous hydration could never replace a good drink. I let a few drops fall from a straw onto the desert of her lips. Holy water. After that, I hear nothing more from her.

God's will A year ago my mother told me that for the first time in her life she doubted her faith. She had always believed that God's will was her guide, but in the face of death she'd lost her way. Why did she confess to me, of all people? As I see it, God is an idol, and far too many zealots would still happily burn anyone who won't bow down to it. A few years ago I would have said all this to my mother. I would have hurled it at her. But now she had confessed to me that she was afraid. She had trusted me that far.

I'd been searching too, for some life-resource deeper and more enduring than my own intellect. She and I, we were both hungry. I proposed to her another way of looking at sin: What if the purpose of life is not to atone for the original sin, as we've been taught, but to become as wholly as possible the blessed person that each of us is meant to be? In which case we sin only to the extent that we fail to heal divisions within and between ourselves, between us and the universe. All of this came to me second hand, but it made more sense than anything I had ever heard at Sunday school.

Mollie was intrigued by this more forgiving vision – or was she just being gracious again? Or perhaps, like me, she was making an eleventh-hour grab at what might turn out even now to be some little strand of common ground. But we had too little time left to learn each other's language. Mollie asked what I thought of the Holy Trinity. An exercise in marketing, I wanted to say. Instead I found a surrogate, Nora, a Presbyterian minister, closer to Mollie in age and worldview, to provide counsel. Should I have wrestled her myself, like Jacob with his angel? But we'd done so much of that, the two of us, we were tired.

Now Nora has arrived with her travelling communion kit, an ecclesiastical picnic basket. Mollie can no longer speak for herself, so Nora asks, do we feel she'd want communion? "The communion of saints, the forgiveness of sins" rings in my head, echoes of Sunday school, long ago in another life. Yes, we believe she would. Being a Catholic, would she mind if it were conducted by a Presbyterian? Not at all – brand loyalty never ranked that high with Mollie. Who else wishes to take communion? Nora asks. My Presbyterian brother and sister-in-law consent, Brian and I do not. Would I be willing, Nora asks, to serve Mollie her communion? No more would I deny her this than a few drops of water.

Nora dips a tiny lump of bread in a miniature goblet of red wine and hands it to me. I touch it softly to my mother's parted lips. A red drop slides down her chin. I think of the soldier at the foot of the cross – but wasn't that vinegar? What if the bread slips, goes down her throat, choking her – "This is my Body, which is broken for you," Nora says. "This is my Blood. . . ." Does Mollie know what's happening? Or does it really matter with communion, isn't it the gesture that counts? But counts for what, air miles? "Amen," says Nora.

Mollie's last residence, the nursing home, had a cloistered court for safe outings. The spring flowers were nearly done, irises drooping, tulips bare of petals. The sun warmed us, me on a wooden bench, my mother folded into her wheelchair, a bright scarf, carefully chosen, at her neck. An ancient woman tottered over to us, murmuring vaguely of a real or fancied past. We sent her gently away. Mollie told me that strangers blundered into her room late at night; they'd turn on the light, then wander out again. She couldn't reach the switch without getting out of bed, a painful and perilous undertaking. One lost crone even clambered into bed with her. My mother laughed in recounting it, but I knew her worst nightmares about privacy had come true in this sadly public place.

In the pale sun Mollie began to slide into one of her freezes. Who knows whether the Parkinson's caused it or the medication, but in a short while she couldn't speak. I did what she and I were both trained to do in awkward situations – I kept right on talking. She struggled mightily to do the same. Her tongue pushed out of her mouth, doubling on itself, plump and pink. Her eyes nearly popped with the effort. Too slow, the cruel irony dawned on me: the harder she tried, the more she froze. I asked her simply to nod or shake her head in response to my questions. Was it getting worse? Nod. Did she want to be left alone? Shake. Did she want to go inside? Nod. As the door slid shut behind us, her tongue relaxed, and just like that, she could speak. In this moment, paralysis looked to me like the price of a gracious life.

How people show their love The light in her dims so subtly, we can't tell when it actually goes out. Around nine in the morning we're debating among ourselves: Is there still a ghost of a pulse, and is it hers or the echo of our own? Finally we call a nurse. She stands a long while holding my mother's wrist, then says, "She's gone." 9:43 a.m.

The noisiest baby in the nursery: this was my mother's first and most enduring memory of her second son, and the primary image by which she would define me for the rest of her life: a pest, a crank, always at her, challenging, provoking, badgering, never giving her a moment's rest. For my part, I have four indelible images of Mollie. In the first, which she described but I never saw, she is dancing in Vienna, unencumbered by care, free of us. In the second, she takes my side against Isabel, only for a moment, but long enough for me to know how it might feel to have an ally.

The third image is a scene, most of it played off-stage. I'm about seven. "Tonight your mother will be working late," says Isabel. I know the drill, it happens about once a month: turn on lights in the basement playroom, close the curtains, tidy the daybed, set out two glasses on a tray with the ice bucket and tongs, rye, gin, tonic and ginger ale, crackers and cheese. Then I go to bed, but stay awake until the Jaguar pulls up, purring. The two of them come inside, I hear whispers, they hang up their coats. I watch from the landing upstairs, mesmerized. Out of the big lynx coat he's suddenly smaller than my mother, portly and balding: Brigadier J Aird Nesbitt, president of Ogilvy's, equerry to Her Majesty Queen Elizabeth II. In another age the equerry would have been charged with caring for the royal horses, but now it's a title that can be got like a Jaguar. I don't know this man, but I do know that I hate him. They slip off to the basement, to work late.

After some months or a year of this arrangement, my mother receives an anonymous letter. Its author threatens to inform the brigadier's wife. Mollie tells me later, much later, that she had good reason to believe it was written by my grandmother's sister. The Jaguar stops coming, and my mother stops working late.

In the fourth image, early one morning in my thirties, I happened to see Mollie before she'd had time to apply her make-up, "put on her face," as she said. I was amazed. This was the only time in my adult life that I can remember seeing her so starkly exposed. I was struck less by how she looked than by the simple fact that suddenly she was unmasked. I had a fleeting glimpse of someone I'd always wanted to know.

So there we were, year after year, Michael clawing at Mollie's artful masks, Mollie marshalling her resources to keep her shaky self intact. Once in an unguarded moment she told me that she feared me. She said that sometimes with me she felt like a mouse being watched by a hawk. We must have wanted the same thing all along, each from the other: Love me as I am, make me believe that I'm worthy. She had learned as young as I did, and from the same source – her mother, my grandmother – that love is never given freely but must always be earned, in direct proportion to the quality of one's performance. Isabel must have had her teachers too. Mollie was a virtuoso, and I her star pupil.

Take the matter of compliments. Mollie reported that some stranger on a train told her she was beautiful, wasn't that nice? I knew exactly what she wanted from me. Like someone with an eating disorder, she couldn't digest the compliment on her own. She was begging me to confirm it, to prove that it was true. And I demanded the same of her. Both of us were skilled enough to give the required assent, smiling but with a shading of tone that ensured the other understood it had been extracted under duress and was therefore not entirely to be trusted. I came to believe this is how people show their love.

Aside from the psychiatrist who tried to shock me straight, my mother was the first person I told that I was gay. I had embarked on an Italian ship bound for North Africa, with no return ticket and no plan except to find or lose myself, whichever came first. I wandered among imperial ruins and managed to elude countless opportunities for sex with stunningly sculpted young men who expected little more in return than conversation and a meal. After brewing up a pot of sweet mint tea, a handsome Libyan truck driver took my hand and kissed me. Mortified that he thought me queer, I fled to my shuttered room in a cheap hotel that smelled of couscous and piss. A few days later, I wrote to Mollie that I might be – still hedging – *might* be homosexual. They handed me her response at the American Express in Cairo: "Whatever you are, I still love you," she wrote, then chatted on about this and that, as Mollie did.

My mother never liked to be caught uncomposed. Faced with any remark or situation that threatened to upset her, she would simply say, "How interesting." Pleasant but opaque, it gave her a moment to gather herself. To me it was another mask; I imagined if the world were to end, these would be the last words to pass Mollie's lips: How interesting. In my mid-thirties I wrote to tell her I'd taken up erotic wrestling – a brief romp that started with a classified ad and ended on a chiropractor's table. Horrified friends asked how could I throw such a thing in my poor mother's face. That's me, the noisiest baby in the nursery. In her next letter Mollie commented, "How interesting. I can imagine how you might enjoy that."

When she stayed overnight in my Toronto apartment, she would take the only bedroom; Brian and I would sleep on the living room floor. In the morning she had to step over us on her way to the bathroom. I watched her closely, looking for a reaction, as always. Barely awake, she trilled a bright "Good morning!" and managed to clear our two bodies, tangled naked under a sheet, without ever looking directly at us. As always, Mollie rose above. At Brian's first sight of her, floating across the kitchen in one of her gossamer gowns, he whispered to me, "I have seen an angel."

He and I sit with her body for a while. The nurses have tidied the bed. It looks like a display in a wax museum, not a bad version of Mollie but not the real thing either. I've never touched a corpse before, not a human one. I try to close her glassy eyes. It is what one does with the dead, isn't it? Brian, who has worked in hospitals, says it can't be done. The flesh is still warm, and very soft. He's right. The eyes re-open of their own accord. Only in the movies.

In the nursing home before I arrived for a visit, an attendant had helped Mollie to dress, put on her face, and settle herself in the wheelchair. We chatted, my mother and I, passing the time. Eventually she had to go to the toilet. No longer able to manage it alone, she rang for a nurse. We continued to chat. I thought, how small and impossible her world has become, but look at her, she's *smiling*.

No one came. "Shall I get someone?" I asked.

"Let's wait a bit," she said. "They're so overworked." It's unwise to be too demanding in a place like this. We continued to chat. I thought, under no circumstances would I ever allow myself to end up like this. But then, will I have any more choice in the matter than she did? Still no one came. I started for the door, but turned and asked, "What about me, can I help?" She hesitated, a long moment. "All right," she said, "yes."

Suddenly I was nervous. Last time we were together at a toilet, I was an infant. I wheeled her into the bathroom and helped her to stand. How could those spidery legs hold anyone up? I asked her to tell me exactly what she wanted done – surely she must have had enough of people doing things to her. Leaning on me, she turned her back to the toilet, in tiny, achingly slow steps. Would I pull down her skirt? I let it fall around her ankles. Would I pull down her panties? Baggy and soft, they settled on the skirt. Mollie covered her groin, but standing beside her, I could see her poor bum, shrunk to nothing. I helped her sit on the toilet, left her alone, and cried.

My nervous offer. Her hesitant consent. *This* is how people show their love.

Roles in the Hay

THERE OUGHT TO BE A WARNING: RELATIONSHIPS CAN BE DANGERous to your health. The rewards can be immense, but then so can the risks. And you can't get insurance.

Of course some relationships are more dangerous than others. The thing is, there are good queers and bad queers, and the risk tends to go up according to how bad a bad queer you are.

Good queers are model citizens and can hardly be distinguished from the straight version, except perhaps by what we do in bed – but then good queers tend not to talk too much about that. I'm a moderately good queer, so is Brian. We have a house, a garden, a car, and pets. Not having a highly evolved fashion sense, antiques, or a spousal dental plan, we can't claim to be top-notch queers. Still, we have decent manners, we can be quite presentable, and some of our best friends are heterosexual.

Bad queers are harder to define, the parameters tending to shift with time and power. In 1968 all queers were bad. Or so I was led to believe, and underwent a year of electric shocks to become heterosexual and thus good. It didn't work; nature triumphed over mad science.

A year later Parliament decriminalized certain sexual acts between two consenting adults in private, and many Canadian queers who had formerly been bad suddenly became good, or at least less bad. It was like those saints who get added to or deleted from the Pope's A list.

Bad queers would continue to have sex with too many people, or people of the wrong age, or in places the authorities considered insufficiently private. Or they would be too effeminate, or too butch, or they wouldn't have enough money, or they would be too old, or the wrong race, or they would dress badly, or. . . .

Good queers are encouraged to disapprove of bad queers, on the assumption that they give the rest of us a bad name. But I haven't been a good queer long enough to believe that our good name is all that secure. Perhaps if I had a dental plan.

For the meantime, in my book there are no bad queers, only ones at greater or lesser risk. Certainly queers can do appalling things, like abusing other people or supporting right-wing political parties that do it for them. But that's not because they're queer – it's because our hard-won equality includes the right to be as greedy, brutish, and narrow-minded as anyone else.

As the last sentence might suggest, I'm a little inclined to be judgmental. But when I go out from my workroom to meet people for a book like this one, an odd thing happens. Judgment seems to fall away, mysteriously, without will or conscious effort on my part. It's not that I like everyone I meet, or that I respect all their choices. But when I'm on the road, far from my comfortable den, I feel more vulnerable and thus perhaps more likely to notice the vulnerability in others, and some of the masks we wear.

We are, all of us, at best and worst, only works in progress.

20 **0977056: A Life**

On a cloudless day in June I'm winding through the plush green hills of Northumberland County in eastern Ontario. George said to watch for the spaceship. Suddenly it rises from behind a hill, an alien invader, bright orange and wavering in the afternoon heat. It's a water tower. Under it, down in a quiet hollow, that's where George lives.

From the field that serves as parking lot, it's a fair walk to the gate. Sun glints off twists of razor wire. When the wire-mesh walls were first electrified, George says, a sparrow, even a skittering leaf could set them off, but now it takes human contact. Inside the glass reception room a woman in blue-grey rummages through my equipment bag. Courteous, even pleasant, she slides my driver's licence into the dark mouth of a machine. "Why are you wearing gloves?" I inquire, in a carefully modulated voice I reserve for people who can do me harm.

"To avoid contamination," she says, with a smile. "This machine detects drugs. It's extremely sensitive. The most minute traces will show up on anything you've touched."

Nothing shows up. I pass through the metal detector, and another guard admits me to a tiny chamber. A loud buzz and I'm let into the visiting area, a spacious room with white concrete block walls and metal furniture. Every corner of it, including the 'private' glass-walled room I've booked, is clearly visible from a central booth. Here and there male inmates and female visitors talk quietly, in pairs. One woman leans forward, angry, wagging a finger at her companion. Another, pencil thin, speaks through a tiny window to one of the guards in the booth, and the two of them laugh. She must be a regular.

I set up my recorder and wait for George. I'm a little nervous, locked up like this. And though we connected nearly twenty years ago, we've never actually met. I don't know what he looks like. On the other hand I do know that when we're done I will return to the outside and the open road to other places. George Harvey Milne, #0977056, Dangerous Offender, will go to his cell for lock-up and count.

Thirty minutes later, I'm still waiting. When I arrived, a guard told me George would be along any minute. I ask her if she knows what happened. "I just called his unit," she replies. "They can't find him." I stifled a laugh. This is a *prison,* and George is supposed to be a *Dangerous Offender.*

A few minutes later he shows up. As usual in the afternoon he'd been working in the craft shop, and the official who booked our appointment had forgotten to inform him. His handshake is firm, but in faded denims and grey T-shirt, with Milne G 0977056 printed on the pocket, George looks old, pale, and rather haggard. He asks me if he can smoke. In such a small room I'm not keen, but surely he has enough restrictions as it is. His gravelly drawl reminds me of the older John Wayne. In January George turned sixty.

Some trouble with the law Born in 1939, he grew up in Scarborough, on the outer edge of Toronto. When his father died in 1949, his mother, Elizabeth, took on a variety of jobs to support her three sons. The older twin brothers quit school to work, but ten-year-old George, or Harvey as they called him, continued his education. He planned to enrol at teachers' college.

Through his teens, while friends dated girls, he found himself drawn to other males, but took it for a passing phase. "This was the '50s, the dark ages," says George. "No one talked about such things." Then one day in 1959 he picked up a hitchhiker, a teenager, and "made a pass," as he put it, reaching over to cradle the young man's crotch. Within hours George was arrested for indecent assault, a charge routinely applied in those days to homosexuals. The police warned him that if he contested it, his trial would be public; it would bring shame on himself and his family. He pleaded guilty. Since this was his first conviction, the judge gave him a year's probation, an order to attend psychiatric clinic, and the first entry on a criminal record that would haunt him for the rest of his life.

At the clinic they weren't interested in the age of his desired partners, he says, only that they were male. George's real crime was homosexuality. "One of them even phoned my mother," he recalls. "He told her I was gay, and it was her fault. Of course she was devastated. I only heard about it years later. It's just as well, because if I'd known he did that, I'd have been in here for a lot more than sex." Elizabeth kept the details to herself, telling George's brothers only that he had run into some trouble with the law.

Through his twenties, George ran into trouble several times. In the early '60s a simple unwelcome touch between males, or what would now be called sexual harassment, was sufficient grounds for many judges to convict on charges of indecent assault or gross indecency. Under common law, neither offence was clearly defined in the Criminal Code, giving judges a latitude of interpretation as wide as the continent. In George's case, since none of the incidents involved violence or coercion, indecent assault came down to touching without consent. One judge defined gross indecency as "a very marked departure from the decent conduct expected of the average Canadian." That rather loose definition remained in case law for more than two decades.

Police and the Crown prevailed on George to plead guilty to each charge. The judge would go easier on him if he did, they said, and the sentence would be shorter. Each time he pleaded guilty, his record grew. As far as he knew, no one had ever fought such charges, and what lawyer would take on a battle like this? Besides, he *felt* guilty. I know the feeling. In 1968, as George entered Joyceville Penitentiary on a three-year sentence for gross indecency, I consented to a year of electric shocks at the hands of a psychiatrist. It was meant to purge my own forbidden desire for men.

In 1974, two years after his release from Joyceville, George pleaded innocent for the first time to a charge of indecent assault. To his surprise, the judge acquitted him. While he was still in prison, studying for a diploma from the Radio College of Canada, the government of Canada had decriminalized some sexual acts between two consenting adults in private. Perhaps the dark ages were yielding.

For the next few years George operated an auto parts store and a do-it-yourself garage in Toronto, until the landlord called in his mortgage. "Without capital, it's hard to sustain a business like that," he says. In spring of 1978 he moved west to the Okanagan Valley in

British Columbia. There he bought himself a houseboat and set up a small business servicing air-conditioners. Soon he became friends, and lovers, with several young men. One of them, "Jeff," turned out to be a big mistake. "He swam out one day to the houseboat," George recalls. "And there he was in his Speedos, over six feet tall, quite well developed, and pretty wild. He fit in just fine with the others, who were sixteen or seventeen, and obviously he knew what he was doing." When autumn came, time to go back to school, George asked what grade Jeff would be in. Eight, he said. He was thirteen. George suggested that everyone might be better off if Jeff were to quit their little circle. The boy was not pleased.

Damage to the morals On February 1, 1979, two RCMP officers arrested George. He had just turned forty. They were acting on a complaint from a citizen, they said, and charged him with five counts of gross indecency. To George's misfortune, it turned out that Jeff's father was good buddies with Bill Bennett, the right-wing premier of the day. Even so, encouraged by the 1974 acquittal in Toronto, George thought his chances were fair to good. No one had been pressured, no one hurt. Three of the relationships had lasted more than six months, and Jeff himself had told George he was also carrying on an affair with a local teacher.

Legal age of consent at the time was sixteen to eighteen for heteros, depending on the circumstances, but for homos it was still twenty-one. After five months in the Kelowna jail, on twenty-four hour lock-up with no visitors allowed, George began to lose heart. As usual the police and the Crown urged him to plead guilty. With his record, they said, he didn't stand a chance of acquittal. Even his own lawyer advised a guilty plea: the sentence would be less severe. "Until you've actually felt that kind of pressure," says George, "it's hard to imagine it. After a while you're ready to do whatever it takes just to get the damn thing over with." Before another local dignitary, Judge G.S. Denroche of the Provincial Court, George pleaded guilty and was sent to the Occala Penitentiary. But the damn thing had hardly begun.

In mid-1980 George was informed that the Attorney General of B.C. would apply to the court to have him designated a Dangerous Offender under a section of the Criminal Code that allows for the indefinite incarceration of offenders who are likely in future to "cause injury, pain or other evil to other persons." But he had never done any harm to anyone, he protested. According to the police, said the crown attorney, he had "caused grave psychological harm to his victims." They weren't victims, said George, they were *friends*. Two of them had even kept in touch with him, through an intermediary. If they were called to testify, they had asked, should they disappear? No, George replied, that would only get them in trouble.

The mother of one "victim" offered to testify on George's behalf: he had often been to dinner with them, and he was probably the best thing that ever happened to her son. "He and I had been so careful," George recalls. "But one day I was sitting around with his mother, and suddenly she said to me, 'By the way, we've known for ages that Darrell is gay, and we're just happy he's with you instead of those other fellows he's been mixed up with.' You could've knocked me over with a feather!" However, George's lawyer informed the mother that her testimony would not be required.

Too late, George began to have doubts about his choice of attorney. A big name in a small town, Tony Peyton sponsored youth hockey teams, and he had political ambitions. "Imagine if he'd defended me successfully," says George. "What would that have done to his reputation around there? I should've fired him right off and got a lawyer from Vancouver. But what did I know?" As George recalls it, Peyton only got one psychiatric assessment, it was local, and it supported the police, saying that the boys had suffered "grave psychological harm."

Judge Denroche didn't take long to hear the Attorney-General's application. The defendant had been convicted on five counts of gross indecency and had a record of sex-related charges. According to the Criminal Code, gross indecency constituted a "serious personal injury offence," which satisfied one ground for Dangerous Offender status. Judge Denroche supplied the second ground: "He has, by his conduct, shown a failure to control his sexual impulses, a pattern that is likely to continue in the future and to cause injury, pain or other evil to other persons." "Evil" is not defined in the Criminal Code, but by precedent a judge can interpret it to include "causing damage to the morals of the victim." On these grounds Judge Denroche found George Milne to be a Dangerous Offender. George recalls that he was offered an out: chemical castration. He declined, and was sent to Matsqui Penitentiary. According to the law, he could be imprisoned for longer than if he'd committed murder, and possibly for the rest of his life.

Bad homosexuals When I heard of George Milne in 1981, I was writing for *The Body Politic,* a gay liberation journal based in Toronto. We were watching for such things; the sense of being an outlaw was still fresh with us. Until 1969 every one of us who had gay or lesbian sex, regardless of age, was still a criminal in the eyes of the law. Ironically, a pivotal event in bringing about the change to the Criminal Code was a case tried under an earlier version of the Dangerous Offender legislation. In 1966 Everett George Klippert was convicted of gross indecency for having had sex with several consenting males, aged fifteen to late thirties. Two psychiatrists testified that neither had he been nor was he ever likely to be a threat to anyone, but it was reasonable to assume that he would re-offend. Klippert was sentenced to indefinite preventive detention as a "criminal sexual psychopath."

The sentence was appealed, eventually to the Supreme Court of Canada. There the Chief Justice argued that, since Klippert posed no danger to anyone, the preventive detention sentence should be overturned and the law re-examined. But he was out-voted by two colleagues who said that the Crown had only to prove the offender was likely to re-offend. The decision sparked outrage in Parliament and the national press, and helped move the federal government to decriminalize certain homosexual acts in 1969. Still, the justice system does not correct itself easily. Everett George Klippert would not be released for another two full years, and then only on parole.

Under the revised law much had changed, and much had not. Justice Minister John Turner argued that his government had not legalized homosexuality, it had only exempted from criminal prosecution certain acts of private adult conduct. In other words, as sociologist Gary Kinsman argues in *The Regulation of Desire,* henceforth there would be "good homosexuals and bad homosexuals," a distinction that still endures. Good homosexuals are successful, law-abiding, model citizens, hardly distinguishable from good heterosexuals except in their choice of partner. Bad homosexuals, on the other hand, would include those like George Milne who had sex with people of the same sex but who were under twenty-one, even though the age of consent for heterosexuals had now been lowered to sixteen. Bad homosexuals would still be charged with gross indecency, as many were in the 1981 Toronto bath raids, for having sex in a private room at the steambaths, or with more than one partner at the same time. The law discriminated in other telling ways; while the maximum sentence for indecent assault on a female was five years, for the same act with a man, it was ten. Under a legal system like this, George and I were more alike than not.

We began to correspond in the summer of 1981. He wrote long, detailed letters by hand, with a fountain pen, in whatever colour ink he could find or mix. A few months before, some inmates at Matsqui Penitentiary had rioted, wrecking large sections of the prison, and now the whole population was forced to live in tents on the playing field. The guards would enter only during the day, with machine guns and in armoured vehicles, which the inmates would pelt with stones. Rock concerts, they called these encounters.

Life in Tense City, as George put it, was grim: "Two cold meals a day off cardboard plates, huddling over an electric heater, wearing parkas and boots trying to stay warm, being woken at all hours of the night by roving drunks, then having to get up to use a stinking portable outhouse that one of them had just been sick in." Much later he told me he'd seen gang rapes, terrible fights, heads smashed in with hammers. "After a while none of it fizzes on you anymore, you just block it out. In fact it bothers me more to think about it now than it did back then." One night someone set fire to the tent that George shared with three other men. The next morning he signed himself into The Hole – protective custody.

He missed Darrell, he wrote, his favourite of the Okanagan connections. "It's hard to explain, but until I met him I'd never had such a comfortable relationship. 'Comfortable' doesn't seem adequate, but I hope you get my drift." I did. By chance I had just met a man in whose company I experienced a degree of trust, or comfort, that was entirely new to me. It had, and two decades later still has the quality of a miracle.

A temporary inconvenience In the autumn George got good news. Two Vancouver lawyers, Richard Brail and Stan Guenther, had just appealed his DO status to the B.C. Court of Appeals. In a preliminary hearing the three judges had allowed the introduction of new psychiatric evidence, which made it clear that George was no danger to anyone. Though the actual hearing would be delayed until March, George wrote to me cheerily that our next encounter might well be in person, on the street. His letter concluded, "I will never, never accept this or any other jail as 'home.' It's only a temporary inconvenience that will eventually pass."

At the same time Corrections Canada had finally granted his request for transfer to medium-security Mission Institution. "The cells here are about 7x12," he wrote from Matsqui, "with a full-width sliding window with drapes and flat bars on the outside, a porcelain toilet WITH A SEAT, a conventional washbasin, a desk and a locker. It's taken me awhile to get used to sleeping again in a bed that isn't just a sheet of plywood." During the day he sorted boxes for the federal post office, earning $16 a week.

By now he had learned a basic prison survival tactic. "It's just too painful to get involved in here," he wrote. "I was with this one guy for almost three years at Joyceville. Of course I knew he'd be leaving before I did, and once a guy is out of there he's *gone*. You try to prepare yourself for that, but you can't. It's like having a relative die. No matter how prepared you are, it still hurts like hell. Eventually you don't want to be hurt anymore, so you just keep everything at the most superficial level."

Outside, the atmosphere couldn't have been worse. Since George's preliminary hearing, Clifford Robert Olsen had been tried in Vancouver for murdering two boys and nine girls, aged twelve to eighteen, and in January 1982 he was sentenced to eleven concurrent life terms. The public, the media, and politicians of all parties, even the Chief Justice of B.C., were demanding a crackdown on crime. Two months later George heard from his lawyers that the Appeal Court had turned down his appeal without discussion; they hadn't even bothered to hear the new psychiatric evidence. The lawyers reported that two of the judges on the original panel had been replaced by hard-liners.

Since the father of one of George's lovers in Kelowna was a close friend of the premier's, the lawyers suspected high-level meddling. But what could they prove?

Within a month George wrote a passionate letter of appeal to federal Solicitor-General Bob Kaplan, and Minister of Justice Jean Chrétien. Yes, he had broken the law, but in his case the Dangerous Offender legislation had been applied in an unjust way that Parliament could never have intended. At the same time he also applied for parole, for which he would soon be eligible, and for a transfer to Warkworth Institution in Ontario. He wanted to be closer to his mother, whose health was failing, and his brother Jim. He also believed that the atmosphere might be more liberal in Ontario, more amenable to a DO appeal.

I didn't want to discourage him, but replied that the grass over here wasn't quite as green as he might hope. In December 1977 police had raided *The Body Politic* and charged three of its principal creators with "possession of obscene material for purposes of distribution," and "use of the mails to transmit immoral, indecent and scurrilous material." One of the defendants, Gerald Hannon, had argued in a long, carefully reasoned article that it was time for a fresh look at the complexities of intergenerational sex. The defendants were acquitted, but over the next five years the provincial Tory government would appeal, again and again. So much for a liberal climate.

Meanwhile George's lawyers were preparing an appeal to the Supreme Court of Canada, provided they could get funding from the provincial Legal Aid plan. "They've always wanted to attack this legislation," George wrote, "and they feel that my case is a good example of the way it's been misused by the lower courts, especially here in B.C. I'm very fortunate that they both have a social conscience, and are interested in fighting inequalities in the law rather than just earn all the dollars they can, as so many in the legal trade do."

In August one of Chrétien's aides responded: There was nothing the minister could do. George's application for transfer to Warkworth was also rejected. There were too many young inmates, said the warden, and she couldn't accept the risk. George appealed her decision, as did his mother and brother. At the same time, the parole board turned down his application for parole. You're not ready, they told him, it's too early in your sentence. George appealed their decision. On August 10, B.C. Legal Aid turned down the lawyers' request for funding. In a nasty bit of irony, this happened to be Prison Justice Day. That night George's mother told me by phone that the lawyers were willing to waive their fees, but to take the case to Ottawa they would need their expenses covered, a minimum of $2,000. Elizabeth Milne didn't have anything like that kind of money. Neither did George, and neither did I.

Extraordinary measures Over the summer I had also written to the federal solicitor-general and the minister of justice, asking that George's DO sentence be re-examined. I included two recent articles by Cyril Greenland, a professor of psychiatry at McMaster University in Hamilton, Ontario, and a passionate critic of the DO legislation. He argued that it was the only sentence that could be applied not for what an offender *had* done, but for what he (or she, though it had not yet been used against a woman) *might* do at some point in the future. The legislation, he said, was "irrational, vindictive and a mockery of justice," used primarily and most harshly against nonviolent homosexual men. "Since no one seriously claims the penitentiary system operates on a rational basis," he observed, "it was not surprising to discover that the least dangerous sex offenders tended, on the whole, to be incarcerated for much longer periods than their truly dangerous counterparts." The only just and reasonable solution was to "replace the indeterminate sentence with fixed sentences commensurate with the seriousness of the crime." The federal Law Reform Commission has been saying the same thing, repeatedly, for years.

In his response to my letter, Solicitor-General Bob Kaplan informed me that the DO legislation had only been used nineteen times since its revision in 1977, and perhaps that wasn't enough. "I think that in some cases the indications of future violence are so strong," he wrote, "that the state's responsibility for protecting the public leaves no alternative but to employ extraordinary measures, such as indefinite incarceration."

I replied that violence was irrelevant to George Milne's case, and designating him a Dangerous Offender was an expression not of justice but of bigotry. The solicitor-general replied, "If Mr Milne is not in fact dangerous, I would not of course support his initial or continued incarceration as such. However, the determination as to whether or not Mr Milne is dangerous is made initially by the sentencing court, and latterly by the National Parole Board. It is not for a Minister of the Crown to try to substitute his judgment for those of the designated officials. I cannot interfere." Full circle, case closed.

In George's next letter, October 1982, he apologized for the delay, blaming "a dose of the blahs" that had made it difficult to get anything done. He was still sending out appeals, but aside from my correspondence, nothing had come back. To pay for the photocopies and postage, he'd sold a couple of wooden trays that he'd made as Christmas gifts for relatives. They would understand. "I'm fortunate," he wrote, "in having people like my family and you to raise a stink on my behalf out there. Some guys in here have no one, and are just about totally ignored by the system. I've spent considerable time helping some of them just to do simple things such as filling out the innumerable forms these places thrive on. Apparently the average educational level in federal institutions is grade 6, no doubt one of the factors involved in the repeated and continued incarceration of a great many of the guys here."

George had always loved the outdoors. "The scenery here, foothills and higher ranges beyond, is spectacular," he wrote, "if you ignore the double barbed wire fence and the gun towers at every corner. If I do go out for a walk in the yard, usually I don't stay long – too many thoughts of previous good times, like summer on the houseboat in Kelowna, and what should be. I'd really be happier if the weather was worse." Inside, "those of us who are sentenced to indeterminate time are constantly exposed to snide remarks or the silent treatment. It doesn't give a guy much to look forward to each day." He had made friends with a twenty-year-old inmate, but "as soon as he was seen with me in the dining room, several of the assholes here put pressure on him not to associate with me," he wrote. "Of late, I have difficulty getting up much enthusiasm for the future. I sometimes think I'm becoming devoid of all emotion except frustration and hate."

Finally in December, after nine months of "badgering and cajoling," George got his transfer to Warkworth Institution in eastern Ontario. "This is the first positive sign of anything happening in my favour," he wrote from his new cell. "It's been a long, long downhill slide for the past four years, so this is long overdue in my books." His brother Jim, who now lived in eastern Ontario, brought their ailing mother in for a visit. She was exhausted by the trip but glad to see him. George said he would also put me on his visitor list. After police clearance I could come down from Toronto for the interview I'd suggested, so that I could write his story.

Peace, happiness, and prosperity Time passed, as it does. When George didn't write, neither did I. In his next letter, dated 24 August 1983, he apologized for the lapse. "It hasn't been a very good year so far, and the first half has gone by in a kind of fog for me." His latest application for parole had been turned down by the board, and they informed him that they wouldn't hear another appeal from him for two years. He had also been sent to Kingston for an assessment at the Regional Psychiatric Centre. After interviewing and testing him for seven hours, the authorities there concluded that it was too early in his sentence to offer him any kind of treatment program, and in any case the only program they could offer was oriented primarily to rapists. They would review his case in another year.

Still, he had grounds for hope. Lawyers at Queen's University in Kingston had had some success in appealing other prison cases. "If a Supreme Court appeal is going to happen," George wrote, "it's important that it be well prepared. Should it fail, that would be the end of the road for me judicially, and I'd have no other recourse than to wait for parole, or the legislation to be changed." Professor Greenland and his wife offered to make a start-up donation to a legal fund for George, if one could be launched. George wondered if *The Body Politic* might help. But with the paper still under siege by the Ontario government, its supporters had other priorities.

In late June 1983 George's mother was put on life support in a Toronto hospital. For years Elizabeth Milne had suffered from rheumatoid arthritis and its painful complications. Finally on a Sunday morning in July she slipped away. "I declined to go to the funeral," George wrote, "preferring to remember her the way she was. The prospect of having two escorts in tow also had a bearing on my decision. I really miss her never-ending optimism and cheerfulness, but am relieved that her long, long suffering is over. No one will ever know the pain she suffered in total silence, with never a complaint."

The day after Christmas that year, George wrote to me that Ron Price, a professor of law at Queen's, had agreed to assess his case. And another federal study had recommended, yet again, that indefinite sentences be abolished. "At least *something* is going on," he wrote, "enough to make us all cautiously optimistic – once again. I've been picked up and slammed on my face too often now to get too wildly enthused about much of anything these days until after it's actually happened." He ended his letter, "My very best wishes to you for peace, happiness and prosperity in 1984. George M." He added a PS: "I'm aware that the demands on your time are considerable and appreciate hearing from you when I do. Don't be concerned if you can't reply right away."

I didn't. Life urged me to other tasks: radio plays, support work for Central America, a street theatre troupe, my first stage play and book, building a relationship, and our move from Toronto to a crumbling old house in the country. So much is possible on the outside.

Fifteen years later I began making contacts for this book. Since I could think of no one else who had paid more dearly for his chosen relationships than George Milne, I wrote to his old PO box at Warkworth. "I hope you're not there," I wrote, "but if you are, I'd like to see you." He replied within a week. The long interval had also been eventful for him.

Cruel and unusual punishment In 1984 Ron Price applied to the Supreme Court of Ontario to appeal George Milne's continued detention which, he argued, contravened the Canadian Charter of Rights and Freedoms. The application was dismissed. Price appealed the decision to the Ontario Court of Appeal, where it was also dismissed. But late in 1985, the Supreme Court of Canada agreed to hear the case.

Over two days in January 1987 a panel of seven justices heard *Regina v Milne*. Price argued that changes to the Criminal Code in 1983 had deleted gross indecency from the definition of "serious personal injury offence." Since this charge and definition had provided the primary ground for the appellant's Dangerous Offender status, his continued detention could no longer be considered lawful. In fact it constituted both "arbitrary detention" and "cruel and unusual punishment," in breach of the Charter.

The Court released its judgment in November. Justice J La Forest wrote the majority opinion. The appellant, he noted, had a record of sex-related charges over the last thirty years. On the 1979 charges he commented, "While there was no violence involved, and so no element of dangerousness in that sense, the evidence revealed that the boys involved had suffered varying degrees of psychological harm from these encounters."

La Forest argued, "Continuing detention is not premised on the status of 'dangerousness' under existing law respecting dangerous offenders." According to the Criminal Code, he said, it had only to be established to the satisfaction of the court that the offender "has shown a failure to control his sexual impulses" and that there was "a likelihood of his causing injury, pain or other evil to other persons through failure in the future to control his sexual impulses." The Crown had established both, La Forest concluded, and therefore the case had no merit.

Justice J Estey wrote one of two dissenting opinions. "There can hardly be a rational basis or a justifiable basis for the continued indefinite retention of the appellant," he argued. "The prospect of a person's serving an indefinite sentence in a penitentiary for an offence no longer attracting such a term of imprisonment under the Criminal Code is 'cruel and unusual' as this expression has been defined." Therefore, he concluded, "The continued incarceration of the appellant offends his right under section 12 of the Charter."

By a majority of five-to-two, the appeal was dismissed, and George would remain behind bars until the Parole Board saw fit to review his status. His appeals to the board continued to be rejected; since he had chosen to fight the DO status, it was clear that he had neither admitted his guilt nor learned his lesson. Still, the determined Ron Price won leave to represent him before the board, and finally in 1990, year eleven of his sentence, George was granted parole, first on a series of day passes, then to a halfway house in Kingston, and finally to "the street." Even though changes to the

Criminal Code in 1988 had lowered age of consent to fourteen for both sexes, a condition of George's parole was no contact with any male under eighteen.

Love doesn't work that way Within a year he had started a small business servicing travel trailers in the Portland area, northeast of Kingston. After being turned down for a government loan to expand the business, George asked his brother Jim and sister-in-law, Mary, to invest in it, along with several of their acquaintances. "That was a hardship for us," Mary recalls. "We're not well off, and our place had just burned, so already we'd had to take out a mortgage to rebuild, and now we had to take out another loan for Harvey."

Why did they do it? "We're Christians," says Jim. "It's the old-fashioned theory, I'm my brother's keeper. I did have my doubts. Every time Harvey would start up a business, he'd end up repeating the same problem, a weakness for beer and boys. But I felt that if I refused, and his business went down the drain, I'd feel guilty for letting him down."

Unfortunately, a disgruntled former employee set up a competing business down the road. Then in late August the same man informed the Ontario Provincial Police that George had someone living with him, a male, sixteen. At 10:30 a.m. on the Friday before Labour Day, OPP officers arrested George on his way to a service call, with Mike beside him in the truck. By 1:30 p.m. George was behind bars again, at maximum security Millhaven Penitentiary.

"That was such a huge disappointment," says Mary. "He'd waited so long to get out, we thought he'd never risk all that again." Regardless of the logic or justice of his parole conditions, I couldn't help wondering, as Mary did, *why*? I've done foolish things for the sake of lust, but never with the stakes so high.

"Mike was a good friend and a good lover," says George. "He was also very mature, he fit really well into the business. You only had to show him once how to do something and that would be it. Down the road I could see him running the business himself, and I could've stepped back, whether we'd continued our sexual relationship or not. It's easy enough to say in hindsight that I should have broken off relations with him, or never allowed it to happen in the first place. But love doesn't work that way."

Jim drove to Portland to retrieve George's belongings from the garage. He found clothes scattered on the floor, dirty dishes, beer bottles, a mess. "I was really surprised," says Jim. "I couldn't imagine my brother living like that. It looked like how you imagine a derelict might live. Or someone who's depressed, and just let things slide." Jim also encountered a very irate landlord; apparently George was behind on both his rent and the real-estate taxes, which he'd agreed to pay.

"He was always very handy," says Mary, "and he had great ideas, but very little of the administrative skills you need to run a business. We've wondered if it just got so hard to make a go of it financially, Harvey might have sabotaged his chances, unconsciously, somehow knowing he'd be better off back in jail."

One night at Millhaven George sat watching the TV news. The announcer reported that a dangerous offender on parole had been arrested after sexually assaulting a twelve-year-old boy. The offender's name was George Harvey Milne. "Within two days every paper from Toronto to Montreal carried the same story," says George, "and not one of them bothered to check the facts. Mike was sixteen, that's very clear in the court record. So where did the story come from? I'll give you one guess. Not long ago, that twelve-year-old thing came up again with a parole officer. It's still there, in that fucking police record." That night George checked into the Special Needs unit, a milder version of protective custody.

The police record he refers to is CPIC, the Canadian Police Information Centre. Maintained by the National Police Services at RCMP headquarters in Ottawa, this automated database gathers "tactical information on crimes and criminals." Apparently any encounter with police, whether or not it leads to a charge or a conviction, may be recorded here, with comments, essentially in perpetuity. "You might want to check on yours," says George.

"Mine?" I asked. "But I haven't had any encounters with the police. I've written about them now and then, but. . . ."

"That'll do it," he replies, with a wry smile.

For two weeks after the arrest Mike refused to admit that anything sexual had happened between him and George. "That was probably to protect us both," says George. "But finally his stepmother and the police coerced him into making a statement. They really must have done a number on him." The crown attorney told George that he had no defence against the parole violation, which was true, but also that things would go easier for him if he were to plead guilty to sexual assault, which had replaced indecent assault in the Criminal Code. Two days before the trial was due to begin, Ontario Legal Aid authorities informed George that they would not fund his court costs. In June 1997 he pleaded guilty, and three more years were added to his indeterminate sentence.

A stubborn old bastard Now finally I'm here with him in Warkworth. We have a lot of ground to cover and not much time. First I ask him about this place where he lives. I haven't forgotten what he said, that he would never, never accept any jail as home. A third of his life has passed since the arrest in Kelowna. Warkworth is high-medium security, he says, and badly overcrowded. Originally designed to house less than 400 inmates, currently it holds close to 700, and they continue to arrive.

George works in the arts and crafts section, cutting and staining glass for other inmates' projects and his own, mostly brooches and sun-catchers. After deductions for room and board, his available income is $34.50 a week. Since the re-arrest, he has retreated to a familiar cocoon mode. "I don't really have relationships any more that matter very much to me, so it's not hard to keep everyone at arms' length. I know that's not a nice way to be, and it's certainly not comfortable or satisfying. But you get your fingers burned often enough, you start to keep away from fire." Locked up in here with 700 men of all ages and types, surely he's drawn to it now and then? He shakes his head. "I haven't had sex, not once since the day I was separated from Mike. It's no big hardship really. My sex drive is virtually nonexistent."

He suspects that the number of inmates on indeterminate sentences is growing. "They're handing them out left and right. And though I don't have any statistics on this, I suspect that very few guys ever beat the DO thing. This one gay guy I know, four psychiatrists testified he was no danger to anyone, but one Crown psychiatrist said he was, and that was that. Since the re-arrest there's at least fifteen others in here that I know about. But most guys won't talk about it, it's too risky. Some of them will even tell you they're lifers, they're here for killing their old lady or something, when the whole joint knows it ain't so. Those are the kind of guys that run into problems."

Has he ever felt in danger? "Once, in Millhaven, I panicked a little after that story came out on TV and in the papers. But I've never had any problems, not from other inmates. I'm pretty up front about my charges, I don't try to hide or fudge anything, so no one can come back on me. Most guys will say to me, 'What are you doing in here? Your lover was sixteen, how can that be illegal?'"

George expects to see the Parole Board in August, as the law requires. But given his re-arrest, and current political trends, the prospects aren't good. His case management team hasn't made any moves to get him into a sexual behaviour program, and he hasn't pushed. In fact, I note, he seems to have stopped pushing altogether. He nods. "Everything I'd worked for got scooped out from under me when I got busted. $15, that's what I had in my pocket. Everything else was tied up in the business, and it's gone, all of it. I'm too old now to start up anything like that again, and how could I, with no financial resources? So what would I do out there – sit around in some boarding house, trying to survive on whatever pension they'd give me? I never thought I'd say it, but at this point in my life I'm starting to wonder if I might be better off staying in here. That's why I'm not pushing."

What about Jim, could he help? George hesitates, looks at his cigarette. Then he says, "Things have cooled off a bit there since the re-arrest. I guess Jim had enough on his plate. I've pretty much stopped asking him for anything. Too many trips to the well, you know what I mean?"

Later I asked Jim and Mary about the change. Jim replied, "The last time Harvey borrowed money from us he must've known the business was in trouble, but he didn't tell us. The other man who lent him money was very bitter about that too."

"That was the hardest part for me," Mary added, "Harvey's attitude. 'Tough, you knew it was a risky business,' that's all he said. He never seemed to take any responsibility for the pain he caused."

As if he'd never really grown up? I asked. "That's it," said Jim. Mary continued to write to George now and then, but they stopped visiting.

Now and then in our conversation George refers to his young lovers as his "victims." Is that how he sees them now, in retrospect? "No," says George. "That's what the system calls them, and I guess I've absorbed their language. I'd love to know how some of those guys are doing, twenty years later. Of course I wouldn't deny that my relationship with them affected their lives. You can't have a relationship with anyone without affecting their life somehow. But I think the worst effects came from the police and the publicity, letting the whole world know this young guy was hanging around with a cocksucker. Think what that would do to a teenager, especially in a little town where everybody knows everybody else. It would be devastating. But the police, the Crown, they don't care who they hurt. That was the only real assault that ever happened."

I wish that I could talk to them too, those guys, but by now they'd be almost impossible to trace. Instead I can only extrapolate from interviews I've done over the years with a number of gay men, now adult, who told me how deeply they craved sexual encounters with men when they were young themselves, as young as twelve. A boy in northern Ontario rode his bike to a truckstop on the highway, twelve miles there, twelve miles home, so he could have sex with men. Another boy in New Brunswick did the same at a nearby mall. "I needed those men,' he said, "and I probably used them a lot more than they used me."

The guard signals at us through the window: we have five minutes. Given the chance, is there anything George might change? "Yeah," he says, "the law. I know it's a terrible time for doing anything like that, with everything swinging to the right. But that's what I'd do. It doesn't make any sense that a guy can't have sex until he's eighteen. I guess I'm just a stubborn old bastard, eh?" He smiles.

There isn't time to catch him up on all the changes, including the drop in age of consent to fourteen, or recent pressures to raise it again to sixteen, or even eighteen, to recriminalize sexual acts that have no victims.

I've noticed other inmates and their visitors sitting and walking outside, in a sunny garden off the visitors area. Does George use it much? "Not really," he says, "not any more. I don't see the point."

I tell him that I'll visit again. I'll certainly have more questions. I pack up my equipment. He slips his cigarettes into his pocket. We shake hands. He goes through one door, and I through another to open air, a shining June afternoon and the road home to my lover.

Near suppertime on Saturday, September 11, a Reverend Franklyn Andrews calls. He's a chaplain at Warkworth, and he regrets to inform me that at 2:04 p.m. George Milne, aged sixty, was pronounced dead. His heart failed.

Mine was the only name on his visitor list. Mary and Jim had recently applied to renew their lapsed security clearance. Jim asked the chaplain, as I did, to let them know when the funeral would be held. A prison official called him three hours before it began, and neither Jim nor Mary could leave work on such short notice. No one called me.

Not that any of this would have greatly bothered George, or so he led me to believe. At one point he said, "After my dad died, I asked my mother why we didn't go to the cemetery. 'Whatever for?' she answered. 'Life is for the living.' She was so practical, so down-to-earth, my mother. It's the same with me. Shit, when I go, they can throw me in a dumpster. It makes no difference to me."

His body was cremated. Jim and Mary plan to bury the ashes beside their church, when the ground thaws.

21 Exodus

Arriving from east Vancouver, the bus dips into the downtown east side before ascending again to its destination, the throb and glassy towers of the city centre. That short dip is another country. Its inhabitants, the homeless and the addicted, prostitutes and psychiatric survivors, are exiles from the New World Order, with nowhere to go but here.

On a cold, grey spring morning in 1999, a few dozen people circle quietly with placards in front of First United Church, a building as worn as the locals. Police watch from several cars. Over the past year more than twenty prostitutes have disappeared from these dangerous streets. A serial killer is suspected, but police and city officials have remained indifferent. What do you expect, they say, they're whores. One official even suggested they would not be missed. At the same time, police launched a major offensive in a more comfortable part of the city, where valuable property – car stereos, gas barbecues – had been stolen from a number of private garages. One of the roughly lettered placards here today reads, "Prostitutes aren't disposable women."

Inside the church the complement to this public outcry is a memorial service for the women who've disappeared. It's a chance for relatives, friends, and the community to mark their absence, to acknowledge the value inherent in each of their lives, and to remind the authorities that out of sight is not out of mind. For Chris Morrisey, hearing the names of the disappeared ring one by one through the sanctuary, it feels an awful lot like Santiago.

Under the yoke Through the 1980s Chris and Bridget Coll lived and worked in a *poblacion*, a crowded shantytown near the centre of the Chilean capital. They were Franciscan nuns, Missionaries of St Joseph. Their work was to help build authentic Christian community in the shadow of tyranny. "The central idea for us," says Chris, "was that you can't separate religion from politics, you can't go through the motions of Christian piety on Sunday, then ignore poverty, injustice, and oppression the rest of the week. The scripture story that guided our work was the exodus, the long journey by which the enslaved got out from under the yoke of the oppressor."

The yoke was imposed in September 1973, when the CIA-backed Chilean military overthrew the democratically elected socialist government and murdered its president, Salvador Allende. Since then the dictator Pinochet and his thugs had ruled the country by terror. Thousands of Chileans were imprisoned, tortured, and disappeared. By the early '80s the "economic miracle," as it was called in Washington, had taken hold in Chile. As usual with such miracles, the rich got richer and the poor more numerous and hungrier.

By then the oppressor's yoke, though no less pervasive, had become more subtle. "To an outsider things might have seemed almost normal by then," says Chris. "The military presence was much less overt. You rarely saw soldiers with machine guns in the streets anymore. The secret police had done their work so well that people had come to police themselves. No one trusted anyone, you could never tell which of your neighbours was a spy. You never asked the last name of anyone you worked with, so that even if you were tortured you couldn't reveal their identity." Everyone knew the particular houses in which the torturers plied their trade.

A few blocks away the Franciscan nuns and their allies helped organize food co-ops, community kitchens, and health teams to provide first aid and basic care, also to promote nutrition, better hygienic practices, and birth control. "None of this was charity," says Chris. "The last thing we wanted was to take more power from people. Our goal was to support them any way we could in defining their own needs and creating their own solutions."

On days and nights of escalating protest in the later '80s, the meeting hall at the back of their house turned into a first-aid station where they would patch up the injured. For more serious cases, they knew where to find discreet doctors and nurses willing to help, and to do what they could for victims of torture. Chris and Bridget also joined the growing national movement against torture. Once a month a small group of people would protest outside one of the known torture houses in Santiago. "We'd plan very carefully," says Chris, "so that we could be there for three minutes, just long enough for it to register that there were people prepared to speak out. Then we'd clear out before the police had time to arrive."

As the women of the *poblacion* learned to organize co-ops and run meetings, they began to find their own voices and to talk more openly about their private concerns, which often involved men. "They'd hear the men give speeches about the dictator," says Chris. "Then these same men would demand to be fed, and sometimes they'd even beat the women. By talking these things out with each other, women started to make connections between the reality of their own lives and the larger picture." A team of women, natural leaders in the community, led a series of monthly workshops on women's sexuality, reproductive rights, and violence against women and children. "That was an amazing process to see, how something would suddenly click for women at those workshops. Eventually they came up with a new slogan for the protests: 'Democracy in the Nation and the Home!'"

With the two nuns living and working together so closely, their relationship had ripened over the years, almost unnoticed in the day-to-day struggle. As they "accompanied cohorts and friends on their journey to liberation," as Chris puts it, she and Bridget began to question their own situations. "I had recognized and struggled with my sexual orientation since my early twenties," says Chris, "but I had no experience, I didn't even have any language to understand or express it." At retreats with feminist theologians from the United States, she began to acquire the necessary language and to understand more clearly the life implications of being a woman, and a lesbian, in an institution that reviles both.

The only birth-control clinic in the neighbourhood was controlled by the Catholic church. The authorities there refused to distribute condoms and forcibly removed intrauterine birth-control devices from any woman who had managed to get one. Abortions, of course, were anathema. As a result, women stayed away from the clinic, and left their IUDs in place much longer than was safe. Self-abortions were common, often with disastrous outcomes. "Looking at all of this and at our own relationship," says Chris, "it was hard for us to see how this could be a whole – or holy – way to live, as we had vowed to do. We knew that if we stayed in the church we would have to remain closeted, which could only become more dishonest and stifling as time went on. We were too much at odds within ourselves, we needed more congruence." In due course both reached the same conclusion as many of their sisters before and since: the only way they could hope to find that congruence, and wholeness, was to leave the church.

Bridget was fifty-five, Chris forty-six. "I loved Chile," says Chris, "and I could imagine living there the rest of my life." Bridget was less certain. From here on, Rome would no longer provide them with a survival allowance. How would they make their livings? Community organizers either worked for the church, or they volunteered. Chris had been a teacher, but the only jobs available were in teaching business-people to speak English, which seemed a little close to the oppressor's yoke for comfort. At the same time, after several years of escalating protests, in 1989 General Pinochet and his backers held a national referendum on their continuing rule. They assumed that a compliant population would confirm their dictatorship, but to their astonishment, a substantial majority of Chileans voted a resounding NO. With the oppressors due to retire, at least back to the barracks, Bridget and Chris felt it was time for them to move on too. But where?

Compañera Bridget Coll was Irish-born and an American citizen. Chris had worked in the U.S. but lost her right to residency there when she moved to Chile. That left Canada, of which Chris was a citizen but Bridget was not. With her experience working with adults who have mental and physical disabilities, and help from a sympathetic immigration officer who happened to know the agency she'd be working for, Bridget got a work permit to enter Canada, good for one year and subject to annual review. Each year it got harder to renew and at year three the Immigration Department told her that was the end of it. Already it had been made clear to her that she had neither the financial nor professional qualifications to qualify as an independent immigrant. That left one option, used by thousands of heterosexual couples each year: Chris would sponsor Bridget, as her spouse.

They checked with a lawyer, who said go ahead and try, the law won't allow it, but we'll challenge the law. If nothing else, they could buy some time to be together. Chris announced her intention to the Immigration Department. Don't bother, said the department – spouse means a person of the opposite sex. How about life companion, they asked. It was the closest they could come in English to *compañera*, the richly nuanced term of affection and respect they would have used in Chile. No such category, said the department. In January 1991 Chris and Bridget filed suit against the Immigration Department, challenging its restrictive definition of spouse as contravening equality provisions in the Canadian Charter of Rights and Freedoms.

Quite suddenly a government lawyer asked why Bridget hadn't applied as an independent immigrant. Because, their lawyer replied, they had already told her she didn't qualify. Apply, said the government lawyer. They did. The application was accepted immediately. Apparently there was a compelling need for Bridget's skills after all, and no Canadian citizen could provide them.

Bridget and Chris never had their day in court, nor did they need it. Each bureaucratic obstacle that arose disappeared as soon as they challenged it, and by September Bridget had her papers. "It's clear that the Immigration Department doesn't like legal challenges," says Chris. "They prefer to deal with these things case by case, so they don't have to change the system or the law." If they had fought their way through the courts, they learned afterwards, it could have taken up to seven years and more money than they could imagine, with Bridget working at a group home and Chris part time in a transition house for battered women.

Having won their own private battle, they could be expected to relax and enjoy the fruits of victory, but that's not how these women do things. They had, after all, defied one of the world's more brutal tyrants. In 1992 Chris and Bridget held a press conference, announcing their intention to confront an unjust law that discriminated against same-sex couples. The resulting media stories attracted the notice of other gay and lesbian couples in similar situations. Some had been in Canada for years, hanging on by student visas and work permits or by disappearing underground. All felt trapped, and didn't know how to proceed. And so was born LEGIT, the Lesbian & Gay Immigration Task Force.

Now in its ninth year, LEGIT provides information on immigration options to gay, lesbian, and, more recently, transgendered people, both inside and outside Canada. Most apply from the U.S., but the group has also heard from people in Asia, Africa, Europe, the Middle East, Central and South America, and the Caribbean. It may direct them to appropriate lawyers or advocate on their behalf to Ottawa or the consulate where they're applying. In one of its early campaigns LEGIT lobbied successfully for changes to federal guidelines on how immigration officers in Canada's embassies, the first point of contact for most would-be refugees and immigrants, should use their considerable discretionary powers in processing applications from same-sex partners on "humanitarian and compassionate grounds." These changes would bring their practices more into line with equality provisions in the Charter of Rights and Freedoms.

The ultimate goal of LEGIT is to eliminate from the law and the Immigration Department any policy or practice that discriminates against lesbian, gay, or transgendered applicants. This would render obsolete the case-by-case approach, which still leaves queer applicants at the mercy of individual officials and politicians. To this end the group submits reports and proposals to the department and pursues ministers responsible for justice and immigration as well as local officials in a position to help or hinder applicants. It also participates in national consultations to update the Immigration Act. Proposed changes currently working their way through the legislative machinery would finally put same-sex and common-law partners on an equal legal footing with opposite-sex married applicants.

Maricon At a LEGIT meeting in March 1997 Chris and Bridget met a young couple in their mid-twenties, Jose Manuel Enriquez Ramirez and Jorge Arturo Villanueva Villalpando, who had just arrived in Canada. They could see no safe future for themselves as gay men in Mexico and had heard they might find safe refuge in Canada. Chris suggested they consult with barbara findlay, a lesbian lawyer who specialized in queer cases and has a reputation for challenging unjust laws. She recommended that Jorge and Jose apply as refugees. They would have to make a very good case, findlay warned; the refugee board turned down many more people than it accepted. It would not be enough to argue that their lives in Mexico were unpleasant; they would have to prove actual danger. In the meantime, the two had very little money – Jorge had sold his car to pay for their airline tickets – and their tourist visas wouldn't permit them to work. Jorge had learned English in school and on the job, but Jose had none.

Jorge's journey began in 1971, in Guadalajara. The youngest of five boys, he grew up knowing he was attracted to boys. But with no one to talk to about it at home, in church or at school, his only source of information was his friends. These are the facts of life, they said: Boys go after girls, and anyone who doesn't is a *maricon,* a faggot, a fate worse than death. Jorge assumed that his own inclinations would pass and kept to himself. "As I got older and the phase didn't end, I got more lonely and more depressed," he says. "In the last year of high school I tried to be friendlier, just so I could be with boys that I was attracted to. But then I would fall in love with them and want more from them, which only made me feel even more dishonest and guilty."

At eighteen he followed his parents to a small town in northern Mexico where his father had found work building a railroad to serve a new mine. Jorge trained in computers and got a job in the office. "I concentrated on my job," he says, "often working double shifts so I could keep busy and get over these feelings. But it was hard. There were thousands of men there, working on the railroad and in the mine, and the men in that part of Mexico are gorgeous. On the weekends I would watch them in their tight pants, playing softball." He talked to a company psychologist, but when Jorge asked an indirect question about sexuality, the psychologist immediately changed the subject.

By the time he turned twenty-one, Jorge had returned to Guadalajara, moved in with one of his brothers, and got computer work at a Motorola factory that manufactures cellular phones and pagers. After a year or so he became friends with the human-resources manager at the plant. One day Jorge stopped by his house. The man was surprised but invited him in. Other friends were due, he said, but Jorge was welcome to stay. When the friends arrived, all male, they kissed their host on the cheek. "I thought that was strange," says Jorge. "It was very intimate, even for Mexico." They settled to a game of cards. "After a while one of them started to talk to me as a female, he called me Jorgina, bitch, and so on. My friend said he would make him stop if I wanted. 'It's okay,' I said, 'it's funny.' Then he said, 'You must realize by now what me and my friends are.' I said, 'No problem, as long as no one touches me.' Then we played a game where the others get to ask you questions. Someone asked me if I was gay. So many things went through my mind – should I trust them, who else will find out? – but finally I said yes. That was the first time in my life that I acknowledged it to anyone." He was twenty-three.

Shortly after, Motorola transferred him to Mexico City. He had his own place and a car, he was financially independent, and, on the suggestion of his friend, he picked up some good books on homosexuality on work trips to the company head office in the United States. Then he undertook to follow his friend's advice: Get out there, meet people, and find yourself a lover. Terrified, he found his way to a gay disco in the northern reaches of the vast city. "I arrived much too early," he says with a smile, "and there was no one there but waiters. But later I saw guys dancing and kissing and grabbing each other. I was amazed, I was excited, and I was very scared. What if I was seen by a co-worker? What if the police came and arrested people, which they often do – how would I explain it to my boss?"

On his fifth visit he found the courage to send a drink over to another man, but as soon as the man approached, Jorge fled. The next time, he allowed a man to kiss him. "I didn't like him much," he says, "and I wish it could have been someone different for my first kiss. We danced for a while, then I invented a story to get rid of him." A couple of months later Jorge had sex for the first time. "The next day he couldn't even remember my name. But just after that I met my true love, Jose."

A romantic movie Jorge and I are talking over soup and a sandwich at Harry's Cafe, a queer hangout just off Commercial Drive in east Vancouver. It's quiet on a Monday night, just us, the young man behind the counter, and on stools in the window two women, one with purple hair, the other draped with chains heavy enough to pull a tractor. Jorge has a fine-boned Aztec look about him, or perhaps I just imagine it.

When he and Jose Manuel Enriquez Ramirez were introduced in a bar in 1995, Jose took him for a snob. "I was so nervous," says Jorge, "I didn't know what to say to him." He did manage to get Jose's phone number and called the next day and every day after. When Jorge returned to Mexico City from a business trip, Jose met him at the airport. "All I could hear was the music," says Jorge, smiling. "We ran to each other through the airport. It was like a romantic movie."

They decided to be boyfriends, the old-fashioned way, and held off kissing until they had dated for two weeks. Then Jose said he wanted Jorge to come away with him for the weekend, to his sister's place in a small town. He neglected to mention that he would bring along a carload of relatives, including his mother. Since the sister's house was too small for everyone, the two men had to stay in a hotel. They didn't dare ask for a room together, so Jose's mother booked it for them. "She's very spiritual," says Jorge, "what you might call a paranormal. Every time she read Jose's cards when he was younger, a guy would appear. It made him quite nervous. He would say, 'Oh, it's nothing.' Finally when he was eighteen she said to him, 'I know you're gay,

I love you, and I will help in any way I can.'" Later Jose asked her what she thought of Jorge. "He's a good person," she replied, "and I love him already."

In October Jorge moved into Jose's flat. To the neighbours he was "a cousin from Guadalajara." By then, thanks to another economic miracle, the North American Free Trade Agreement, Mexico's economy was in meltdown, the peso collapsing. Motorola "reorganized," and invited Jorge to resign. No one was hiring. Jorge fell into depression, got an infection in his mouth that made it painful to eat, and within a few weeks lost nearly half his weight. Jose took him to the hospital, where a doctor told him that until he ate, he would not release him. Jorge ate. Jose and his mother nursed him back to health and out of his depression. Eventually he found a job in Guadalajara, at half his original salary, and Jose joined him there. Now they would have to face Jorge's family.

One brother said he didn't understand, but he loved Jorge anyway. Another quoted metaphysical theory, saying that by their nature, homosexuals are closer to God, and therefore it was okay with him. The other two brothers, born-again Christians, told Jorge and Jose they were bound for hell. One threw them out of his house, and the other told Jorge privately that they would be glad to help him get rid of Jose, then Jorge could take hormones to become more of a man. If he didn't, he couldn't enter his house because he would be a bad influence on the kids. Jorge's father was surprisingly relaxed about it. "You're financially independent," he said, "so you have the right to live how you like." "So that's why you were so depressed," said his mother. She was disappointed – now he wouldn't be giving her any grandchildren.

As the Mexican economy continued to implode, life became more perilous for homos in Guadalajara. Local politicians declared there are no *maricons* here, but just in case, they passed a law forbidding any open display of affection between men, such as holding hands or kissing. Jorge and Jose knew well enough to be discreet, but their house and car were both marked *Maricon,* and vandalized. It was time to get out. "We were still young," says Jorge, "so if we couldn't stay in Canada, we could still come back or try again somewhere else." On March 8, 1997, International Women's Day, they flew to Vancouver.

They stayed first with a friend in a small town to the south, then rented a room in an inner-city apartment. The Inland Refugee Society provided food, clothes, and advice. While Jose went to school to learn English and job skills, Jorge looked for work, but as soon as employers learned he was a refugee claimant, that was the last he'd hear from them. He took any job he could find, gardening, painting, all at less than minimum wage. Once he and Jose had applied for status as refugees, they were able to get social assistance, though ironically, they were caught in a Catch-22 of gay progress – the social assistance officials recognized them as a couple, and thus provided even less support than they would have got as two individuals. They dipped into their food money to pay the rent, and waited in line two to three hours at the food bank. "It's not good to feel dependent like that," says Jorge. "You start to think you have no abilities, and no options." At Christmas their friends Bridget Coll and Chris Morrissey gave them a new bed.

Into the labyrinth In the meantime Jorge and Jose had been preparing their case for the refugee board, documenting the vandalism in Guadalajara and other incidents familiar to Mexican homos. A week after Jorge picked Jose up from his office job, where he had an impeccable record, Jose was fired without notice. No *maricons* wanted here, they said. Jorge was arrested outside a gay bar, and as usual the policeman demanded money. The alternative was arrest and very likely assault. Now that the policeman knew where Jorge lived, he might drop by any time for further payment. The same happened in Cuernavaca, when police arrested everyone in a gay disco, including Jorge and Jose, then released the ones who could pay. Two policemen followed a friend of theirs home, stripped his apartment, and warned him that if he reported them he would be killed. They beat another friend almost to death; his crime was dressing too flamboyantly. This is what Jose and Jorge would face, routinely, if they were forced to go back.

By now their lawyer, with too heavy a caseload, had referred them to another, who reviewed the refugee board's decisions on Mexican claimants. The chances were 60/40 that they'd be rejected. Chris Morrissey explains, "Unfortunately, refugee policy tends to be shaped by government attitudes to the current regimes in other countries. Mexico is now a major trading partner of Canada. So how could it be a place that people, homosexual or otherwise, have to escape from in fear of their lives?" The lawyer suggested that, given Jorge's computer skills, he might have better luck if he applied for a work permit under NAFTA rules, which facilitate the cross-border movement of workers with particular skills, especially in computers and other high-tech fields.

With uncanny timing a Vancouver software company had picked up Jorge's business card at a computer exposition, and after an interview, they offered him a three-month contract. He dropped his refugee claim and reapplied for a NAFTA work permit. Since immigration rules require that he apply from outside the country, he and his lawyer crossed into Washington State and presented his application to a Canadian immigration officer at the border. "I was so nervous," says Jorge. "He dragged it out every way he could, looking very carefully at every page of every document. We even had to phone my employer to fax some other papers. All the time I kept wondering, will he turn me down, will I have to go back to Mexico? It's a very strange feeling, your life being so much in someone's hands like that." After five hours the officer issued Jorge a one-year work permit, subject to annual review.

Jose remained in jeopardy. Their lawyer doubted that he would be accepted as a refugee. If the board rejected him, he would automatically be deported and might then be ineligible to return to Canada, even as a tourist. Nor did he stand a chance of being accepted as an independent immigrant. Jose had taught jazz dance in Mexico and represented his country as a folkloric dancer at festivals in Europe and Israel, but none of this shows up on the Canadian government's list of marketable skills. So Jose dropped his claim, got a cheap charter ticket back to Mexico, and after three months away, returned to Vancouver on a two-month tourist visa. "It was painful to be separated for so long," says Jorge. "We spent so much on phone calls, it would have been cheaper for me to just go there for a visit."

By this time Jorge's employer had offered him a permanent position as a systems analyst, and under NAFTA regulations he could apply for permanent residence as a professional worker. With his status secure, Jose could then apply for permanent residence as Jorge's partner. Humanitarian and compassionate grounds is the usual route for married applicants and blood relatives, and now thanks to LEGIT, increasingly open to same-sex applicants. Until then Jose would have to commute between Canada and Mexico, returning each time on a short-term tourist visa. In Mexico he would get what part-time jobs he could, and Jorge would support him in Canada.

In December 1998 the two exchanged rings and vows in a commitment ceremony. "We called on a powerful being to guide us and be with us," says Jorge. "We promised to stay together through good and bad, as friends and companions, to love and take care of each other until we died." Their friends Chris and Bridget officiated. Aside from affirming their relationship through the enforced separations, this would help prove to the Immigration Department that they were a bona fide couple, a requirement for same-sex applicants but never an easy task for homos from other countries. It's another issue that LEGIT has taken on with immigration officials. "If the rules require proof of cohabition in the country of origin, that's often out of the question for us," says Chris. "Partners aren't always from the same country – Bridget and I weren't – and in some countries for two women or two men to live together as a couple in an open enough way to produce proof, that could be very difficult, sometimes even fatal."

Jose and Jorge have agreed to be monogamous. "That's how we think our relationship should be," says Jorge. "My love is for him, and his is for me. We don't need to sleep with anyone else. It's harder when we're apart, and there are so many handsome men here in Vancouver. But for me it's easier to be faithful to Jose than to have to hide it if I slept with someone else. It's the same, I think, for him."

And life goes on Aside from his job, Jorge does volunteer work with LEGIT, and with the Vancouver Regional Health Board on the gay/lesbian/bisexual/transgendered advisory committee. "We are trying to make it easier for minorities to access the health-care system," says Jorge. "It also helps me to become more aware of the diversity within my own community." He would like to get a university degree. Jose has started a Mexican dance group that performs in and around Vancouver. He's studying English, and hairstyling. "Our dream," says Jorge, "is to adopt a child. Jose wants to live on a ranch, or in a small cabin in the forest. He would love to grow our own food and have a cow or two. I have to be here for my work," he says, then adds with a laugh, "I'll visit on the weekends."

Last I heard, Jose Manuel Enriquez Ramirez and Jorge Arturo Villanueva Villalpando are in, both of them permanent residents of Canada.

LEGIT's work goes on. The federal government has started an experimental partnering program, in which agencies and groups can sponsor refugees from other countries. The minimum grouping is five people, with a minimum collective income of $100,000. "That's not so much when you have five or more people involved," says Chris Morrissey. "So we're starting to look for people who'd be interested in doing something like that, as well as people in other countries who might need to claim refugee status."

Bridget continues to work with people with mental and physical disabilities who used to live in institutions but can now live in the community with the right kinds of support. Chris works in an emergency shelter for women and children on the downtown east side. "We try to provide an environment where people can be safe, feel respected, and get treated with dignity. That doesn't often happen in their lives," she says. "I'm an administrator, so mostly I push papers. But given the prevailing attitude to poverty and welfare, it's a challenge just to keep the place alive and maintain a decent quality of service. It turns out the issues aren't that different, really, from the *poblacion* in Chile."

From where Chris stands, north and south are looking more and more alike. One night on the TV news she saw the Vancouver riot squad at work. "They had the same helmets, same shields, same clubs as the police in Santiago. One guy was felled by a rubber bullet – we used to deal with injuries like that all the time in Chile. And now here we are doing the same things in Canada. It's hard to believe."

The increasingly homogenous voice of Canadian mainstream media also has a familiar, haunting ring. "In Chile it was so clear to us there was no free press. We knew it was all controlled by business and the state, except for a few underground papers that managed to elude the police, and the one radio station we listened to that kept pushing the edge. What I find so frightening here in Canada is to see exactly the same control thing happening, with nearly all the media owned by a handful of people. But here it's so subtle that hardly anyone seems to notice we're getting the same narrow perspective almost everywhere we look. It's so easy to ignore these things until it's too late."

Bridget's and Chris's own financial situation doesn't give them much more cause for comfort. Neither has been a high earner at the best of times, and Bridget faces retirement with little pension or savings. "We're living with the consequences of the choices we've made along the way," says Chris. "It's a bit scary, but then lots of people are facing the same pressures, particularly now when the social net is being dismantled so quickly and with so little compassion. I wouldn't change any of the experiences I've had, not one of them. I'm very grateful for that."

Given such tenuous circumstances both at home and in the larger world, what on earth sustains her? Chris hesitates, a long moment. Finally she says, "Conversations like this one that give me the chance to reflect on what I'm doing and why, which isn't easy in the heat of the day-to-day struggle. Healing meditation with a circle of women that helps me to find some quiet and to touch deeper levels of my own spirituality. The immigration work. A lot of it deals with systemic injustice – of course, that's the long haul – but now and then we can do specific things that get direct results for people like Jorge and Jose. At work I love to see a woman's face after a drop-in session, to see her relief at feeling safe and valued by somebody for a change. And the openness of those women, their willingness just to be there in all their vulnerability, that's very precious to me."

"Yes," she says, as if to confirm her own thinking-out-loud. "These things I find sacred. They give me a sense of purpose, and the feeling of making a difference, sometimes in such small ways you'd hardly even notice."

22 Out There

Michelle, Brenda, and a couple of friends are heading back to their hotel in Edmonton. Ginger is the designated driver. At 3 a.m. the long straight roads are almost empty. Then an oncoming car squeals into a U-turn and slides in on their right side. Teenagers, boys, liquored up. Ginger wants to floor it, get the hell out of there. From a small northern community, he doesn't get out much, at least not as Ginger, and he's never even been close to a jam like this. Besides, he's not used to driving a standard, what if he stalls? "You won't," says Michelle, "And if we get into a high-speed chase, somebody's going to end up dead. Just maintain a steady pace."

He watches the other car. In the back seat three adolescent males fall over each other to get at the window. "Fucken faggots! We're gonna fucken kill ya!" The driver looks at Michelle. He can pass, but it's been a long night and half a day since he shaved. The driver says, "Are you a real girl?" "No," says Michelle. "Do I look like one?" "Not really," says the driver. "Why do you do that?" "Do what?" says Michelle.

Stay calm, buy time. The driver seems cool. At this speed, with no stops, they're still a couple of minutes from the hotel. "Why do you dress like a girl?" The driver has to yell to be heard over the chorus behind him: "You're fucken *dead*, cocksucker!"

"See those big trees coming up?" says the driver. Something has shifted in him. "Which one of them do you wanna to be part of?" He swerves closer.

"Hey, come on," says Michelle, "lighten up." One more block, a traffic light, green, and then a quick right turn to the hotel. But the other car is on the curb side, blocking the way. The light turns orange, red. Michelle says quietly to Ginger, "Speed up, but be ready to turn." Ginger accelerates, 60, 70. The other car speeds up to keep pace. Almost at the light. Michelle says, "Step on the brakes – NOW." Their car screeches. The other driver slams on the brakes, but now he's ahead of them, nearly through the intersection. Michelle says, "Turn right – NOW." Ginger veers hard to the right. "Keep going," says Michelle. "But here's the hotel," says Brenda.

The other car backs into the intersection. Michelle replies, "We don't want them to know where we are. Keep going." The other car stops. Then it squeals off, the same way it came.

Harbouring secrets On my western travels for this book, I met Michelle and Brenda Hart one spring evening in the parlour at the Black Orchid bed and breakfast where I stayed in Calgary. It's owned and operated by three men who are lovers, a threesome. One of them raises orchids, including a rare purple-black variety. The house is quiet tonight, I'm the only guest. Barry is out of town for the weekend; Ron, who starts his day job early, has gone to bed, and Don is out at the movies with a friend, a member of the family they call 3SM. More about them later. Don, a carpenter, is a client of the business that Michelle/Mike and Brenda run, making wood components for cabinet and furniture manufacturers. It's a small world, queer Calgary.

Four years ago the Harts moved to a small town south of the city, where they live on a five-acre property, with their workshop next door to the house. Brenda is forty, Mike fifty-one. Wanting to meet me tonight as Michelle, he began to prepare in mid-afternoon: shave, bath, breasts, clothes, makeup, nails, hair. He's wearing an auburn wig, a long, patterned skirt, denim jacket, white pantyhose, and sensible shoes he left at the door, wet from the rain. Brenda, in white hose and a tangerine sheath, crosses her legs neatly at the ankle.

Born in Nova Scotia, Mike Hart moved with his family to Alberta when he was twelve. At his new Catholic school he was treated as an outsider, an instant target. "The teacher would make me say the rosary. He'd stand beside me and tap me on the head until I started to stutter. Then he'd call me a dummy. Of course the other kids lapped it up. They assassinated my personality. By the time I got to college I had no idea who I was. I'd gone missing."

One Christmas his sister got a go-go wig, the latest girl craze. A headband with a fall of fake hair down the back, it had a nice perky bounce to it when you danced. "When she unwrapped it, it was like a thunderbolt, " Michelle recalls. "I wanted it." As soon as he was alone in the house, he tried it on and liked what he saw in the mirror. He was fifteen. After school, before anyone else got home, he began to try out his sister's make-up. Eventually he became a "partial dresser," putting on girl clothes whenever he could. "I was very secretive about it. I'd get the urge, I'd dress up, then I'd masturbate. I felt disgusted with myself every time. I'd undress as fast as I could, and put it all away. I tried to stop, to purge myself of it, and then of course I'd do it all again, the whole cycle."

His father, a member of Alcoholics Anonymous, warned Mike and his siblings that if they harboured secrets, it would do them harm. "That always wore at me," says Michelle. "I kept wondering what damage I was doing by keeping all of this to myself. But who could I tell?"

Mike married at twenty-three, fathered a daughter and a son, then told his wife he was a cross-dresser. "I hoped that being honest about it might save the relationship, but it was already too late for that. To her credit, she never used the cross-dressing thing against me." When they divorced, Mike was twenty-six. He'd been through college by then and had a degree in graphic design that would come in handy down the road.

In 1979 he told his next-door neighbour he'd like to go to a dance in the village where they lived, but not alone. She suggested he invite her sister, Brenda. They've been together since, and married now for two decades. In the first decade Mike built a successful woodworking business, eventually employing thirty-five people. Then he sold it. It was doing the job for his clients, but not for him.

By the late 1980s Mike had heard about the Illusions Club, a hybrid of showcase and support system for cross-dressers and transsexuals in Calgary. He was also fed up with the dress-up, jerk-off, and disgust cycle. "One day I said to myself, My God, you are one sick puppy. Either you quit this whole thing right now, once and for all, or you finally do it right." He began to build a wardrobe, bits and pieces from here and there, shoes and make-up, and stashed them away in a dark corner of the basement. He found his first wig in a Salvation Army dumpster. Brenda had no idea; neither did Lisa, Mike's daughter who was living with them at the time. He started to experiment with falsies – water bags, balloons, oil-filled sacs, whatever it took. "I really wanted to go to the Club, but I was afraid if I didn't look good, they'd throw me out," he says. "It was a ridiculous thought, but that's how insecure I was."

One day, tidying in the basement, Brenda found a pair of skin-tight stretchy jeans. Too tight for her, too tight for Lisa. Mike admitted that they were his. He liked wearing tight clothes, so what? Shortly after, he came out to Brenda as a transvestite, and asked her to see him, at least once, fully transformed. If it was intolerable to her, he wouldn't stop, but he wouldn't do it in her presence. She agreed to see the other Mike, but kept stalling. After several weeks he finally announced: he would dress for her that evening. While he did, Brenda watched TV, and fell asleep. Michelle recalls, "I couldn't wake her. I still think she didn't want to wake up. So I just took everything off."

"When I woke up," says Brenda, "Mike was sitting there."

Says Michelle, "I told her I was really offended that she'd done that. It's the first time in our relationship that I had ever said that."

The next time, Brenda stayed awake. "I didn't understand," she says. "I had no idea how to deal with this, so I guess I just hoped it would go away."

For the next few months Mike continued to cross-dress, and Brenda continued to ask, "Is it ever going to stop?" No, said Mike, it is not. But it was Brenda who came up with his girl name: Michelle. When he made his debut at the Illusions Club, she was there. Neither of them got thrown out.

The coolest thing Over the next few years Michelle came out to selected people, one by one. "My criteria for coming out is simple," he says. "If not telling someone changes the normal pattern of my relationship with them – if I have to lie and make up stories all the time to cover up – then it's time to come out." Most of his relatives know Michelle, including his son and daughter. "His daughter thought it was the coolest thing," says Brenda. "She told all her friends. She knows a lot of people in Calgary, so the biggest problem was setting some reasonable limits on who she should and shouldn't tell." Brenda was hesitant to tell her father.

"He's a retired farmer, and what you might call a bit of a redneck. But he's been wonderful."

Michelle adds, "He comes to stay with us for a few days now and then to help out on the acreage. If it wasn't for him, it would have taken us a lot longer to get settled."

In their Calgary social circle, some people have never met Mike, only Michelle. Cross-dressing friends call him Michelle, gay friends either Mike or Michelle, and lesbian friends Michael. Among his business contacts, most have only encountered Mike. "I'm almost at the stage where I don't care who knows about Michelle," he says, "but neither do I want to cause us any financial harm. At this point we want to keep the waters relatively calm until we retire." Still, Michelle continues to evolve, with pierced ears, longer nails, the moves a little softer, the voice a shade lighter. "Sometimes people will notice that something is different. But they can't quite figure out what it is, and I don't see any need to explain."

No one in their town has met Michelle, not yet. "The trouble with being a tranny in a small town is you never know when a neighbour's going to drop by for coffee," he says. "You can't just throw on some old sweater and suddenly you're Michelle. It takes time." Michelle has her own dressing room and a closet next to the bathroom; both are kept locked. "I hope we get to the point where they know Michelle and it's not a problem. But for now they're still getting to know us as Mike and Brenda. By the time we've proved ourselves, whether they accept Michelle or not, still they'll know us as a viable part of the community."

Brenda adds, "I don't see that happening for a few years yet."

Michelle adds, "We don't have a timetable. It will happen when it happens."

Their caution is justified. Incidents like the encounter with the teenagers in Edmonton are rare but remind them sharply how vulnerable they are. One night they were touring Calgary pubs in a small group, women and cross-dressers, to promote latex dresses made by a friend of theirs. A man called Brenda "a goddamn fucking queer." She laughs. "Me! I was wearing this low-cut latex dress that showed lots of real cleavage. And I was sitting right next to a cross-dresser! That really pissed me off. Couldn't they tell I was the real girl?"

"That's what you get for hanging out with trannies," says Michelle. "It's guilt by association."

I wonder about Brenda. She married Mike; Michelle wasn't part of the deal. How does this "other woman" fit into her life? "I actually told him a while ago that I liked Michelle better than Mike," she says.

Michelle smiles. "It's what every cross-dresser wants to hear from his wife. You're so afraid they won't like the girl expression as much as the boy expression."

I've only met the girl expression. What's the difference? "Mike is quieter," says Brenda. "Michelle is more expressive, she uses the hands more. And Mike can be a little hard. He used to have quite a temper. But when the make-up goes on, that person is softer, and easier to get along with."

"It made me start to wonder, so what's wrong with Mike?" says Michelle. "When I realized that they're not two people but two expressions of the same person, I started a project to bring the two closer together. For instance, I tend to go at problems a little differently now, a little less head-on. Of course if things go badly, Mike can still throw a wrench across the shop."

"Michelle would never do that," Brenda adds. "She wouldn't be caught dead anywhere *near* a wrench!"

"Mike can also be more expressive now," says Michelle. "I find that I can talk with women in a more personal way than men usually do."

"Sometimes when we're out, even when Mike isn't dressed," says Brenda, "I'll see something, maybe a gesture, and I'll whisper to him, 'Michelle's here.'"

I notice that Brenda is picking at her pantyhose. "Got a run?" Michelle asks. Brenda nods. "Well," says Michelle, "better you than me! That's the advantage of wearing a long skirt, you can get all the runs you want and who's to notice?" They both laugh.

Are there aspects of Mike that either of them wouldn't want to lose along the way? "Oh yeah," says Brenda, "there's one big one."

Michelle smiles. "That's part of it. If I took female hormones it would wreck my libido, and I like my libido the way it is, thank you. But it's more than that. So many trannies when they first come out will immediately declare, 'I'm a woman, this is so cool, bring on the hormones and the knife!' I keep telling them, slow down, sister, relax. This isn't like getting your hair done, it's for the rest of your *life*. If you're totally dissatisfied with your previous life, and you can't think of a single aspect of your old self that you'd like to carry forward into the new one, that doesn't give you much of a foundation to build on, does it? There are lots of things about Mike that I'd carry on, habits, interests, all kind of things."

According to Brenda, hormones and the knife are touchy subjects among the wives. "What you fear is that the person you married will disappear, either gradually with the hormones, or snip, just like that."

The two of them have talked about it. "I'm quite aware of the process and the technology," says Michelle, "and I've seen a few people go through it. It's not for me, hips popping out, voice changing and all that."

Says Brenda, "I've made it clear that if Mike ever went through with that, I'd try to be supportive, but it would certainly end the relationship. Michelle isn't the person I married, and I don't consider myself to be a lesbian. Most wives I've talked to feel that way."

"Fortunately, I'm happy just being a plain, garden variety transvestite," says Michelle.

"Garden variety perhaps," I reply gallantly, "but hardly plain."

"Thank you very much," says Michelle, with a smile and a slight tilt of the head.

Has Brenda ever wondered if her husband might be gay? "In the beginning, yes, most wives do."

"Though I hang out a lot with gay people, I've never thought of myself as gay, " says Michelle. "I suspect that a lot of cross-dressers may be bi, and I guess I could be open to that under the right circumstances, but it's really a moot point because it could only happen if I stepped outside this relationship, and I'm not prepared to do that." Early in Michelle's public career, an attractive man asked if he could buy him a beer. He consented, but before the suitor returned he fled. "Not too subtle," says Michelle. "I made the decision right there that I would never do that again. Now I'll talk to guys, and if they want to go where I don't, I just say no. Usually I can't imagine being kissed by this person, but every now and then – " He makes an airy gesture with his hand, brushing aside the rest of the thought.

Blushes, brushes, and boobies With Michelle and Brenda being so out in the tranny scene, they tend to attract people in search of mentors. Next month Michelle will give a workshop at the Illusions Club on shaving, foundation techniques, and haircare. When men come out as cross-dressers, their wives often seek out Brenda for information and support. One man in his sixties, Audrey, keeps asking her what he should do about his wife; she knows he cross-dresses, but doesn't like it. "He seems to think I can offer some kind of magic solution," says Brenda. "But everybody's situation is so different. All I can do is tell them about our own experience and how we manage."

Other couples see their enduring relationship as a model, and a sign of hope. "They want to know our secret," says Michelle. "Well, I'm sorry, but we don't have one. We're just two people, we work out our own problems as we go."

Still, Mike hasn't forgotten his own long struggle to release the Michelle within. "It's so important for people to have good information, and they also need to stay in contact with each other. There's nothing more destructive than isolation." When the Illusions Club newsletter folded a few years ago, it left a void, and Michelle watched the group that had helped him come out disintegrate. Three years ago he decided to fill the void. Volume 1, Issue 1 of *Crossroads,* a magazine for transgendered people and their friends, appeared in autumn of 1998. The publisher/editor announced his intention to publish quarterly, and to finance the magazine with subscriptions, ads and, if necessary, his own money. "I am capable of doing it financially," he wrote. "Also, my life is compartmentalized in a way that will allow the time for it. *Crossroads* is my way of giving back to a community that gave me so much."

The ads in the magazine promote local groups and bars, the Black Orchid ("a gay bed & breakfast, transgendered-friendly"), an Edmonton distributor of "high-heeled shoes, specializing in large sizes," wig care and cosmetic make-over salons, and a Calgary emporium offering "beard covers, blushes, brushes and boobies." Mike designs and produces *Crossroads* on his computer and prints it on his photocopier. He gets material from trannies – cross-dressers and male-to-female transsexuals, pre- and post-surgery – that he's met in Saskatchewan, Alberta, and British Columbia. With each issue the reach expands. No one is paid. Someone asked Michelle how he planned to spend all the money he makes with the magazine. He laughed, then told them if he made any at all, it would finance a new printer. At this point *Crossroads* just covers its costs.

The magazine is a lively mix of letters, news, chatty personal commentaries, a column for wives, and abundant advice on make-up, fashion, and hormones. Issue 2 includes an account of Britany Renard's first appearance as a girl on her job in the men's wear department at the Bay. "It was a busy sales day, but I was urged by my supervisor to tour the store first. Reactions ranged from mild shock to wild disbelief. The girls in cosmetics said I had better legs than they did, and wanted me to work with them for the day. I received compliments on my wig, make-up, short-skirted business outfit, shoes and ankle chain. Amazingly, most of the guys were as supportive as the girls."

In the same issue, Cassandra, a.k.a. Michelle Hart, offers tips on hair. "There is absolutely nothing that will turn people off faster to your *en femme* presentation than male body hair showing in the wrong places." He suggests shaving the face, neck and upper chest, also plucking hair from knuckles and wrists, nose and ears, and possibly the eyebrows. "You might want to reshape them a bit, or if they are big and bushy you may desire to thin them down. You can do this progressively over a six to eight month period and avoid comment; people will not notice if you do it a little bit at a time."

Issue 3 includes a column on washroom etiquette, written by Jodee. She asked a Calgary police officer: If you were on patrol in a mall, and a woman reported to you that a man dressed as a woman had just entered the women's washroom but there was no allegation of any bad behaviour, what would you do? Regardless of the trans-person's behaviour, the officer replied, he could be up for charges of invasion of privacy, or even assault. "The woman who complained only has to feel afraid for her own personal well being. But she would have to press charges and be prepared to go to court." Jodee recommends, "If you do have to use a washroom, then use a unisex. If there isn't one then go in as quickly as you can, do your business and get out. Don't primp your hair, don't play with your lipstick." She also sought comments on an

Internet chat line. Katrina, a cross-dresser in Minnesota, writes, "I use the restroom I'm dressed for. If I use a ladies room, I DO primp, fix lipstick, smile and make eye contact. Anything else and you WILL get read." Bottom line, says Jodee with crisp finality, "I think most of this is using your head and not being just outright stupid."

Last time I checked, *Crossroads* had more than 100 subscribers, and newsstand sales had just begun. "We need to reach out to new readers," says Michelle. "Especially people in the closet, they're especially hard to reach. It's so good for people to know they're not alone."

Don Bastian has arrived home from the movie, and Michelle switches to shop talk. He had to fire a wood supplier, he says, because the idiot sold a load of basswood to another client after promising it to Mike. His voice doesn't change, doesn't deepen or harden. I can hear both of them now, Mike and Michelle. Then he and Brenda head off home; they have an early day tomorrow.

3SM Don and Barry met in the mid-1980s, in a Calgary bar. "He walked in, and I said, 'That's the man,'" says Don. "I don't know why, I just knew." For six years they were monogamous, then they began to experiment, to see what they could add to their mix. "It didn't happen that often, because usually it didn't work. You'd have breakfast and that was it, goodbye."

One night at the bar Barry met Ron and invited him home. Ron refused. "I didn't see how it could work, with the two of them," he says. On Barry's third invitation he changed his mind. "Then we couldn't get rid of him," says Don.

"They wouldn't let me leave," says Ron. They both laugh. Two years later, the three of them bought this three-storey Edwardian house on a huge corner lot in Crescent Heights, a quiet neighbourhood overlooking the city centre. "The bed & breakfast was Barry's idea," says Don. "None of us had a clue how much work it would turn out to be."

They all have full-time jobs outside the house, Don as a carpenter, Ron as operations supervisor at the Hudson's Bay Company, and Barry as a teacher. At home, they share the work. Don does most of the renovations, and Barry most of the cooking, but Ron will do both. Barry and Ron take care of the gardens, which are large and elaborate, though it's still too early in a prairie spring for anything to show in the raised beds. Don and Barry enjoy having guests come and go, but Ron tends to be more private. "That's why we built the little house out back," says Don. "That's his getaway." It's out there beyond the sheltered deck and the hidden garden for nude sunbathing. In the big house they've just finished renovating the third floor, their collective retreat from the guests.

"The Black Orchid fills an important niche in our community," says Don. "For men from small towns or in closeted jobs it's a refuge, a place where they can feel free for a change. Mostly it's men, though we do welcome lesbian, bi and transgendered folks too. The only straight folks we get are friends of our gay clients, so they know what they're getting into. We won't join the B&B association because we don't want Ma and Pa Kettle complaining about the artwork and wanting to know what all those naked boys are doing in the hot tub." Photos and drawings of hyper-men adorn the guest rooms and the bathroom. Tom of Finland's book *The Art of Pleasure* sits heavy on a side table in the parlour. But the male principle is in check here: the curtains are lace, the beds have skirts, the dining room and parlour dance with floral appliqués and decorative plates.

I had a chat with Ron before he went off to bed. Their threesome, or triad as they call it, how does it work? In the early days Ron didn't believe it would, it was just too complicated. "I lost a couple of friends over it," he says. "Most of them thought it was just a sexual thing. I was also making a commitment to a leather lifestyle, and that was too much for them. But I was in love by then, so damn the torpedoes." Unlike Don, Ron believes in monogamy. Under the circumstances, how does he define it? "I'd say it's a quality of commitment, or intimateness with my partners." All he did was add an "s."

Ron is not unaccustomed to facing torpedoes. When he came out on his previous job as an electrician, things got a little rough with his brothers in the union. "I got a lot of flack. They asked me not to eat with them in the lunchroom, and one time I got punched out. But I stuck it out, and I got respect for that. If I'd turned tail and run, it would have confirmed what they thought about gay men. By the time I left, they'd say things like, You're a pretty good guy, for a fag."

People ask Ron if he loves one of his partners more than the other. "Sometimes I need one more than the other, or I might be closer to one for a while, but then it's the other. I know I'll never have the same kind of bond that Donny has with Barry. They had eight years together before I even met them. But I'm not jealous of either one."

Depending on purpose and destination, they will travel solo, in any combination of two, or all three together. At a leather gathering in 1995 they were asked to identify their group. One of them improvised, turning their threesome into the tidy but suggestive acronym 3SM. Since then it has widened to embrace a chosen family of seven. "One way or another all of us have been outcasts," says Don. "It's a wonderful thing to choose your own family, and to have a group like that for emotional support, especially when you've been abandoned by your birth family as I was." He grew up on a ranch in southern Alberta, strict Lutheran family, traditional German background. When he told them he was gay, they disowned him. "I knew I was gay from age four, but like so many others I went and got married anyway." He has two children from that marriage, now twenty-two and eighteen, both of them at university.

Late in the evening Don and I sit at the kitchen table to talk. A tattooed chain winds around his left bicep. His T-shirt features the same insignia as a stained glass window in the front hall, a leather pride flag, black and blue with one white stripe and a heart. When we made contact, Don described himself as a leather activist. "I stand up and say it's okay," he says. "I'm out there in support of the leather lifestyle, and BDSM [bondage, domination, sadomasochism]."

Out there he is. Don wears his chaps in the Calgary Pride Parade. "You don't have to say a word or carry a sign," he says. "People will just come up to you and say, I'm interested, I can't come out, but I'd like to talk." He's written for international leather magazines, several pamphlets, and a book, not yet published. A website is in the works. As an executive member of the International Leather Association, he helps organize events like the upcoming Ms Calgary Leather. Next weekend he flies to Chicago to judge the International Mr Leather contest. He's the only Canadian to have won two International Male of the Year awards. In Calgary he and other 3SM members lead workshops on topics like Sensory Appreciation ("covers everything from sandpaper to feathers to pattern cutters as tools for making an impression on your date"), Bottoming ("tips on training for Tops, as well as exploring how to get what you want as a Bottom, through negotiation and signals of consent"), and Mentoring ("grooming the next generation of leatherwork through the lessons of respect and honour within the BDSM culture").

Being out there has its price. "When you say SM, everybody goes nuts," says Don. "I get a lot of criticism, some of it from our own community. I've had trouble crossing the border into the U.S. – my name comes up on their computer, for buying the wrong magazines. And my picture keeps showing up in the *Alberta Report* [a right-wing magazine], usually around Pride week. The guys in the lumber yard will say, Hey, your picture's in here. It's not a problem, it doesn't bother me. In fact the longer I keep on saying the things I do, the more respect and credibility I seem to get." It sounds like Ron with the electricians: If you can take it, you're okay.

What is it that Don keeps on saying? "Do you really want to know?" he asks. That's why I'm here.

"I had to ask," he says. "I can talk all night on this. But only if you're serious." I'm serious. "All right then." He settles in for some mentoring. "What people react to is the visual, the guy in chains, the dominatrix in her boots and tight corset waving a flogger. When you don't know what lies behind that visual, and what it really means, of course you're going to be alarmed by it." Behind the potent image, Don argues, there's the code of conduct that governs leatherfolk. The short form of it is "safe, sane, and consensual, know and respect your own and others' limits."

"People think BDSM is all about sex and pain," says Don. " Sometimes it's about sex, but it's always about power, an exchange of power between equals. Everyone does it. Every human relationship is a power exchange. I respect that you have power to exchange, and together, as equals, we'll determine where that exchange starts, and where it stops. If I don't respect those limits, then it's abuse."

Communion Don is a Top. He worked his way up, so to speak, from being a Bottom. "The fellow that brought me into the community was a very powerful personality," he says. "He scared me good, but I knew that I would never be in serious trouble with him. With him as my mentor, I grew through my own fears, and in the process I found something to believe in, something to belong to." Back to the code, and the community that defines it. "The culture we live in is built on young and pretty. But age and beauty don't count for much in the leather community. We work on what's inside, your potential, your sense of honour. When we do workshops, it's a huge investment of time and we never make any money, but it's amazing to watch the lights go on. Maybe they came for the image, but suddenly something clicks, and they start to discover the deeper components. We rescue people, that's the only way I can describe it. A fair number of the people who come to us are loners, they can't find a place for themselves anywhere in the gay community. When you find a space for them where they can belong, they blossom, they become whole people."

It sounds rather religious. He nods. "Lots of BDSM players talk about the spirituality of it. It's rooted in your belief in other people, the trust you build, the common ground you find – some people describe it as communion. One of the closest images I know is the aboriginal elder. It's a cultural attitude based on honour, and the idea that we learn through longevity, and what we learn we pass on to others." In *Mentoring,* his booklet, Don compares the mentor or Top role to that of the shaman, "the keeper of an exceptional body of ancient wisdom and techniques for healing and empowerment." The Top also functions as "psychologist, props master, choreographer, set designer, playwright, and caregiver."

I notice that "respect" and "honour" come up frequently with Don. In *The 3SM Runbook*, a collection of thoughts and advice, he writes, "Honour. Such depth in that simple word. Complicated. Intangible. Honour carries no price. It cannot be bought, or sold. It cannot be given, but it may be bestowed. It cannot be pursued, but must be earned. Nor may it be solicited, but well rewarded. Honour acknowledges the integrity of the bearer, and stands above indifference. A badge, and a shield. Armour. Honour mirrors our culture, certainly recognizable, but singular in definition. Proud but not arrogant. Respect amid conflicting views. Secure. Self-reliant. Special. Honour among Leathermen."

It's easy enough for a Top to talk about honour, equality, and consent. I wonder where the Bottoms stand. My first inclination would be to organize a union. The *Runbook* includes "A Bottom's View," written by a man who describes himself as "a longtime wordsmith and political activist." He writes, "i wish to please my Top, i am aroused by having Daddy enjoy me, i get a rush when i sink to my knees and am permitted to fondle Sir's boots. But this is during a scene and in specific social settings. At the risk of sounding arrogant, more than one Top/Dominant has been taken aback by my highly vocal reaction to being dismissed, talked down to, or treated rudely in a social setting simply because i happen to flag right [a Bottom signal]. i speak with friendly respect and approach others as social equals. i expect no less in return."

Every couple of months 3SM will put on their leathers and make an appearance at the bar. Their image, particularly en masse, both attracts and keeps people at bay. "We create lots of elbow room for ourselves, even in a crowded bar," says Don. "Usually there are two kinds of people – some will rush over for a hug, they seem to want others to know they know us, and then there'll be others who want to approach, they'll cruise heavily, but they hang back unless you speak first."

"My God," I interject, "it sounds like the queen!"

"And I am," says Don. "Don't you dare print that," he adds with a laugh. "I'm far too butch for that, or at least my image is."

For a week or so after their appearance at the bar, they get calls saying: I want to get involved, what do I do? "The gay phone lines and a couple of psychotherapists also refer people to us," says Don. "We educate a little, clear up misconceptions, point them in the right direction. First we'll ask, is this a sex thing, do you just want to beat off, or do you want to go deeper and really get into the honour, the integrity, the code of ethics of the community? Then we'll take it from there. If you want good, solid information, not your hot videos and one-handed literature but boring old clinical information on how a scene works, the safe words, the out words and so on, we're there. Among the seven of us we have over 150 years of experience. But we're still learning. Your own mistakes are your best teachers."

Recently 3SM accepted their first pledge. As in the post-World War II biker clubs, the template for many leather groups, a member sponsored him as an apprentice. For a period of time he will be absorbing the values of the family and the code of the community. At some point the family will meet to decide either that he's ready to belong as a full member, or he still needs more work. "Everyone's learning curve is different," says Don. "With this fellow I'd guess it'll take at least a year." I'm surprised to hear that the man is straight. And one member of 3SM is a male-to-female transsexual. "We preach a pan-sexual ethic," says Don. "The only thing that matters is the commitment to shared values. We don't have group sex, let's get that out of the way. But we do love each other. I don't know anyone who grew up in a so-called normal family, but each of us holds some ideal image of that. All we did was create our own ideal, one that works for us."

When Don goes out into the world as a leatherman, he takes nearly as long to dress as Michelle Hart does. "Leather is drag," he says. "I change when I get dressed, it's a ritual." Ritual is a crucial element in BDSM. It serves many purposes, Don writes in *Mentoring*: "It signifies intent; it focuses the conscious mind; it serves to communicate by way of symbol or gesture." He begins to dress at least an hour before he goes out. "I put on my armour, my shield, and I also put on the value system that I want to project. As I get dressed, I slip into my role. I'm a leatherman. That's how I identify myself, first, before anything else. That's my heart and soul."

Michelle Hart also takes the role of mentor quite seriously, but as Mike and Michelle gradually merge, his approach has changed. "When I was on the town council where I used to live, I'd try to pressure others to come around to my point of view," he says. "Now I'm more inclined to think that just because I say it's a good idea, that doesn't necessarily mean it is, so now I'll try more for consensus. Sometimes it's hard to know where we're going, as a community. Because I've been consistently involved with our group at Illusions longer than anybody else, people will say to me, 'Oh, you decide.' But I keep saying, 'No, it's the group that needs to decide.'"

Before Michelle and Brenda headed off home from the Black Orchid, Michelle mentioned that she'd always loved the circus arts, and Mike once owned a travelling carnival. A remnant of this passion is the practice of eating fire. She doesn't do it professionally, just for fun, to mark special public events. She sent me a photo to prove it: tall and stunning in a latex sheath, Michelle, a tranny dragon, spews a mighty tongue of flame.

Seems a dangerous hobby, I said. "Not if you know what you're doing," said Michelle. "And how else are you going to have some excitement in your life? You can only go so far with the clubs, but then what? Okay, so I'm Michelle, I'm out and about, is that all there is? What's next?"

Without missing a beat, Brenda jumped in. "Hollywood."

23 You Gotta Have a Gimmick

BILL'S WORKPLACE NESTLES IN A ROW OF TIDY BUNGALOWS, ON A busy street in east end Toronto. The entrance is hardly visible, up a walk that snakes through a jungle of shrubs. Bill greets me at the door, an elegant wisp of Renaissance dog curled in his arms. Michelangelo, an Italian greyhound, sniffs my hand with a certain *hauteur.*

The jungle motif continues inside, with a twenty-three foot anaconda skin draped over the rafters, a stalking lion, zebra-striped bedspread. The open interior, very compact, is a stage-set in white, black, and silver. Huge framed photos ascend to the vaulted roof: studio portraits of Bill, the two dogs, James Dean, a brooding Garbo, and image after iconic image of Marilyn Monroe. Fountains burble and plish by the bed and in the bathroom.

The priest/altar-boy fantasy begins in the bathroom, Bill tells me, there behind the black and silver curtain. The altar boy takes a shower, then asks, please, Father, will you towel me dry? "Having been an altar boy myself," says Bill with an impish smile, "I happen to know all the lines."

He has cleared the morning for me, no clients till noon. At sixty-four he's still blond or, as he puts it, fair. If it's a dye job, it's very well done. In shorts and a white polo shirt, his arms and legs are lightly tanned and very smooth. Two small gold rings twinkle on his left ear.

We sit on the deck, tree-shaded and relatively cool for a steamy day in mid-June. As soon as Bill settles, Michelangelo bounds, weightless, into his lap. The uproar of a thousand wired kids rolls in from the schoolyard across the lane, then a siren wails, the kids go in to class, and the din fades to urban grey noise. Bill tunes the radio to classical CBC, uttering Vivaldi at the moment. "A sound screen," he explains. "I have nothing to hide, it's just more private for talking."

The American dream At twenty he got his first teaching job, he tells me, in Ottawa so that he could continue his relationship with a married fireman there. A few years later he suddenly set off to California with some men he met in Letro's, a Toronto gay bar, and $500 he'd borrowed from his mother. This was the late 1950s: Diefenbaker was prime minister, Eisenhower the U.S. president, Elvis king, and Marilyn Monroe had just married Arthur Miller. *I Love Lucy, Father Knows Best* and Ed Sullivan ruled the airwaves. "This was my big chance at the American dream," says Bill. "I had a burning desire to wipe out my past. As a child I was fat and unattractive. I became convinced that I really should have been somebody else, I'd been born in the wrong place, to the wrong parents. Just as Norma-Jeane turned herself into Marilyn Monroe, in California I would transform myself into someone entirely new and I would make it, I would be a success. I chose the name Scott. That represented exactly who I thought I was meant to be." Scott was young, attractive, and didn't carry an ounce of fat.

He lived various places in the Golden State, fell in love, it went sour, and Bill imploded. "I had no friends, no identity – the only friends I had in California were Scott's, and no one even had a clue who Bill was." He fled back to Toronto, dangerously underweight, then recovered and tried New York. But as the war escalated in Vietnam, the American dream faded further for Scott. Or rather it blurred into alcohol, though he would continue to deny that for more than a decade. Back in Toronto again, he settled into teaching English. Scott receded with the American dream. "But I still keep an S on my licence plate," says Bill. "Just a reminder."

At fifty-five he retired with full pension. "After thirty-three years there wasn't much more I could learn about teaching," he says. "On the other hand, I had always wanted to model and do theatre. Now I was free to do both." With help from storyteller Helen Porter, he developed *Me & Marilyn,* a solo theatre piece. "I've always been fascinated by Monroe. But only in recovery did I begin to understand the Norma Jeane-Marilyn connection to Bill-Scott. How do you meld the created persona with your own, and what happens if you don't? Norma Jeane always spoke of Marilyn in the third person, she never got beyond that, and it's pretty clear to me that if I hadn't got into recovery, I would have come to the same end as her." He toured *Me & Marilyn,* got some decent reviews, and will still give the occasional private performance for a small group at his house.

Bill came to his current career by a process of elimination. He had split with his last lover at the end of the '80s. "It was a mess, and I was devastated. I'd been sober two years by then, and I needed to figure out how could I have got myself into such a disaster, what was wrong with this picture?" Kicking the booze brought him some clarity, so why not try the same with sex? After a year, he was surprised how easy celibacy could be. "It was so liberating to be free of all that pressure, it was like stepping out of the game." He would remain on the bench for another seven years. "Then I started to think, well, this can't go on forever, so now what? I wasn't interested in going to the bars. I tried ads and the phone lines, but as soon as you tell them your age, forget it, not a chance. It's so sad the way that age thing permeates our culture."

He decided that what he needed was something to sell. As the three strippers sing in *Gypsy,* You gotta have a gimmick. Bill's would be massage. "And why not charge a little," he says, "maybe $20, since I had no experience. Money is a powerful aphrodisiac for me, it always has been." In Bill's early twenties, a man in a Detroit bar offered him cash for sex. "I wasn't interested, but he kept upping the offer. And this was U.S. dollars! Finally it clicked with me, what control, what *power*! Friends were horrified at what I'd done, but for me it was a huge rush. I've always been kind of vain. I want to be desired, to be accepted – that was the goal for Scott, and it still is for me. I believe that if someone pays you for sex, it's the highest compliment, the ultimate proof of your desirability."

Condoms by the gross His first classified ad specified that Bill's clients would have to be smooth, fit, and under forty. "I know that was odious, but I did it anyway. Well, in no time a young, very handsome black man called me on it, he said it was blatant discrimination, and how could I deny it? Anyway, people kept showing up who didn't fit what I'd said in the ad, but I couldn't turn them away. To my surprise I found that I could minister to anyone, by locating the good in each one of them."

Minister? Bill nods. "We are talking about men's most vulnerable area here. They have so many anxieties and so much shame around it, and they're starved for affirmation. I'm in a position to do great harm or good." An attractive Asian man asked Bill if he knew how to make his penis bigger. Bill suggested a few tips to make it *appear* bigger, and referred the man to his favourite Toronto sex store, Come As You Are, where Bill buys his condoms by the gross, and the man could find a selection of vacuum pumps and other devices. "I also told him I must have seen about a million penises by then, and his certainly wasn't the smallest. I told him what's between his ears is his most important sex organ, and whatever he did, he should not submit to surgery." The teacher lives. "Absolutely," Bill nods. "It's amazing how much I use of what I learned in teaching – sensing what's behind a question, dealing with someone's nervousness, performing, counselling. In this case the right man certainly found the right job!"

He advertises in the *Toronto Star* (expensive, but gives the best returns), *Eye* and *Now* magazines, and *Toronto Life* – it reaches an upscale market, has a long shelf life at doctors' offices and such, and only one rival advertiser in his particular field. He also runs a regular classified ad in the Oshawa *Buy & Sell,* "to reach the suburban blue collar market." Callers tell him they were scouting for used golf clubs and happened to see his ad.

I'm surprised he doesn't run ads in any of the gay publications. "I used to," he says, "but the first thing most of them want to know is how big is your dick. Or they want a catalogue, chest size, cock size and so on. You can ask me anything else on the phone, but for some reason that crosses a line of vulgarity with me, it cheapens the thing. Here you get a whole package, the house, the music, the atmosphere.

Can it really matter *that* much whether a person is 155 or 157 pounds?"

More than 90 per cent of Bill's clients are married. "Sex is such a fluid continuum," he says, "it's really inadequate to state categorically that they're gay or they're not. Most of them speak very positively of their wives, they love that world, and they feel it's where they belong. It's just that this is one area they need to explore outside. They need my world for forty-five minutes every two weeks." Forty-five minutes in Bill's world costs $50. "It's strange," he says, "but in this culture you tend to be judged by your price, and $20 was just too low. Some people think I should charge more, but $50 seems fair to me, at least for now."

The clients range in age from eighteen to eighty-two. It startles me that such young men would pay for sex. "Oh, they come with shopping lists of things they want to try! I suppose that to some of them I must represent a kind of father figure, or an older man with experience. I also get men in their forties who've been turned off by encounters with young men. They may have the body, but no compassion, no empathy, no patience – they want to get in, get out, and gimme the money. What I offer is a bigger frame, a well-rounded, more nurturing experience."

With all this talk of ministering and nurturing, I begin to wonder what Bill's work has to do with sex. In fact he never actually calls it that, at least not to me. "The best way to describe what I do is to say I facilitate fantasies." One client is a cross-dresser. His wife disapproves; the deal is that he will only indulge when she's out of town. "It's obvious that he spends a great deal of mental energy and money on his clothes, make-up and jewelry – he wears *exquisite* lingerie," says Bill. "His dates with me consist of him showing me what he's wearing and having a glass of wine. He gives me money when he comes in the door, and every time he says the same thing: 'When my time is up, throw me out.' But he never stays that long. All he really wants is for someone to acknowledge the effort, to admire him, to say 'Those are *beautiful* stockings, what a *gorgeous* necklace.' And that's it, he's gone." Even in retelling it, Bill's flattery sounds quite sincere.

Facilitating fantasies Is there anything he won't do with a client? "Less and less," he says. "Things I would have thought pretty disgusting ten years ago, now I can find quite exciting – with the right person, and under the right circumstances." For example? "Water sports. Minor bondage and domination." What constitutes minor? "Well, I don't have a dungeon, I don't do wax, or cutting, or electric. I'm really not interested in doing damage to people." One client worries, what if his own SM fantasies progress? "I can't see into your head,'" Bill tells him. "But you can be sure I would not allow anything to become dangerous, physically or psychologically, to either of us.'"

Immediately after orgasm, another cross-dressing client is overwhelmed by shame and guilt. "In five years it's hardly changed at all," says Bill. "I'd love to help, but if he's going to work on it, first he has to acknowledge that he has a problem – not the cross-dressing, but the shame." Another client could only have an orgasm if Bill scorned his penis as tiny and pathetic. "I must admit, the sadistic part of me did enjoy that," says Bill, "especially since it wasn't true, his penis was average or above. But what I miss sometimes in this work is the chance for a debriefing. I'd really like to know how this fantasy came about, why is it such a turn-on?" Why not ask? "The thing is, they don't hire me as a therapist. If someone asks me, I'm only too happy to articulate how I feel, or even to make suggestions. But basically my job is to facilitate their fantasies."

Some of his clients want to play out their fantasies in a more public arena. The cross-dresser with the gorgeous clothes wants to hire Bill as his escort for an evening, to take him out to a restaurant and a play, in fact to show him off. "I would definitely have to choose the venue, for his safety and mine," says Bill, "but for the right fee I'd do it. Same with someone who wants me to take him to a fetish night, in a slave/master situation – if the fee and the conditions are right, why not?"

What about his own boundaries: how much will he allow clients to do to him? "Not much. I have to be in control. This is my home, so there are safety issues. For instance, I'd never allow anyone to tie me up – they could just leave me here, and who knows what might happen. Also, I used to be so often out of control in my own emotional life, I'm not likely to let that happen again. Actually there's very little submissiveness in me. I really enjoy control and power, no matter how velvet-gloved it may be."

Has he ever been afraid of a client? "Only once that I can recall," he says. "This man's fantasy was so unhealthy, I felt frightened and sick. He was violently, viciously angry with his wife, and his fantasy was all about abusing her and getting back at her. He brought what I took to be a man's G-string, but it turned out to be a pair of her panties, and his fantasy also involved a plastic gun. I was so alarmed I had to insist on checking what else might be in his gym bag. He wanted me to say all these horrible things about his wife while he was masturbating, but I drew the line at that. And of course I wouldn't see him again."

Does he ever let clients evolve into lovers or friends? "There are a few," he says, choosing his words carefully, "that I might like to have as friends. But the financial transaction is a real barrier. Early on, if I liked someone I would give him extra time. But then if the relationship changed, that was hard to reverse. They'd say, you made an exception for me before, why can't you now? It's so much easier if you don't allow any exceptions in the first place."

Would he like to have a partner or lovers outside his work life? "It's a rare man who can deal with what I do, and still establish an intimate relationship. They don't seem to understand, this is just what I *do*. It doesn't matter how much I assure them that I have special feelings for them. But then I've never been particularly successful in one-on-one situations anyway, so what are the odds it will happen now?"

Me and Heidi Fleiss On a deck two houses along, a chatty cleaning woman gabs with her friend, a little louder than the CBC. After a few minutes Bill mutters under his breath, "Will you get inside and dust the damn furniture!" Then he relents, with a smile, "Well, at least she sounds happy."

If I were in his place, I'd worry about how the neighbours might react to the parade of gentlemen callers at all hours. He has no such qualms. "If you run a legitimate, quiet business," he says, "if you don't irritate people and you don't step on their toes, most of them don't care too much what you do in your own place." What are the ground rules? "I never allow a client to take anyone's parking space. Nothing upsets people more than coming home tired from work and finding someone in their spot. That and having their sleep disturbed. So I never have a new client arrive after eleven p.m. Repeat clients know enough to be quiet."

It's mid-morning. Glen leans out from the dark interior to offer tea and croissants. I met him briefly when I arrived, a slender young man in shorts who slipped away after being introduced. Since then I've noticed his discreet presence from time to time, up a ladder cleaning the eavestroughs, in the shadowed garden below.

Bill has few legal concerns about his clients. "Of course I'm careful on the phone. If someone asks me what I do, I just turn it around, I ask them what they like. And if I have any doubt about their age, I ask for proof. I do get calls now and then that I think may be set-ups. For example, I tend to be suspicious if someone says he's only sixteen, can he come over? Absolutely not. I'm familiar enough with young people to know that if you're really sixteen you don't say so, you want to pass for older." But what if he did run afoul of the law, as others have done? "If they ever charged me, they'd have a real fight on their hands. I wouldn't go quietly. I'd go public, do lots of talk shows, make a big noise – I'd go out Heidi Fleiss-style." Fair warning.

Some of his clients are more fearful. What if they were to meet Bill by chance in some public situation, what would he do? "Nothing," he tells them. "Unless you speak first, I don't know you." One client was petrified that he might carry some telltale fragrance home with him on his clothes. "This was in the dead of winter, it was bitterly cold, but he insisted on stripping outside on the deck. He took off every stitch he was wearing and left it out there in a bundle until he was ready to go home! I find it hard to understand how anyone could live in a relationship like that, with so much fear. Why would they *want* to?"

But accidents do happen. A client with a van volunteered to pick up a large photo that Bill had got framed, for which he needed Bill's credit card number. "I gave it to him – I trusted him, and still do today." In a rush, the man tossed the number into his glovebox. A few days later the man's wife grabbed it by mistake to pay her cell-phone bill. The embarrassed client reported the mishap to Bill, who was more amused than distressed. But the wife discovered her error, and then her husband's. She left the marriage and her children for another man, citing her husband's relationship with Bill as the cause. She has since charged a second phone bill to Bill's account, which the client dutifully reimbursed.

Maintaining Bill Glen brings Earl Grey tea, croissants, and jam. Then he's gone, back to his chores. His call was the first that Bill got in response to an ad he ran in *Xtra,* the Toronto gay paper, seeking a jack of all trades. "From his voice on the phone, I thought he might be a dyke – the name could be either gender – which would be fine with me. So Glen came over, and I liked him instantly. He took the job on one condition: that he could bring his own Filter Queen vacuum. I couldn't imagine a better recommendation!"

Jack of all trades is an apt job description. Though it makes Bill squirm, Glen prefers the title personal assistant. "Basically he does everything I don't want to do, or can't," says Bill. "He gardens, cooks, buys the groceries, brushes Michelangelo's teeth and coat, cleans the car, sets up for the business – he remakes the bed, tidies the bathroom, puts on the fire, turns on the fountains, that sort of thing. He never meets the clients, doesn't want to, and that makes it easier for him to be discreet. Also he looks after my clothes, he makes phone calls – he's catching up on some this morning while I'm not taking calls for the business – and I'm sure I'm forgetting all kinds of things he does, he always seems to have a million items on his list. And then there's me. He says I'm high maintenance, what with my pedicures, and my waxing – I have this fetish, I don't like body hair, so he waxes me from top to bottom, front and back. It can take all day. There have been times I've actually had to do clients with one leg waxed and the other hairy! Glen says, 'Couldn't I at least do the two fronts so they match?'"

Glen is thirty. It's clear from Bill's tone that he's more than the usual houseboy. When Bill had to get an uncomfortable medical procedure done, Glen offered to drive him to the hospital, then took him home after he surfaced from the sedative. Since it was Glen's day off, Bill offered to pay for his time. Glen refused. "I thought that was amazing," says Bill. "Especially since he doesn't have a lot of money. What he does have is a really sweet disposition."

Beyond that, how would Bill describe their relationship? "Tumultuous. Tumultuous but rewarding. And really hard to define. I have no physical desire for him. And though I can see that he's influenced by me, for example in the way he decorates his apartment, you wouldn't call this a father-son relationship. And even though we do social things together, we're not the usual sort of friends – after all, he is my employee – though we do describe ourselves as friends. We've been through some pretty tough stuff together. Glen is an alcoholic – he and I have discussed this, I have his permission to talk about it – and occasionally he'll go on a binge. Twice he's asked me to take him to the Donwood [rehab clinic], but each time he's backed out at the last minute. It used to bother me a lot, with my own AA background, but for some reason I'm less disturbed by it now. However you define it, our bond is quite close, and very strong."

Contessa and Michelangelo Beyond the trees and across the lane the children have been let out for mid-morning break. It sounds like a riot. A moment after I start eating my croissant, Michelangelo alights on my lap. I can feel his fine bones and sinews under my hand. He's clearly more interested in the croissant than in me. "Mike!" Bill admonishes, "Stop that!" But he rips off a corner of croissant and offers it to Mike. A dog's life indeed. The photo gallery inside features Michelangelo and another Italian greyhound alongside the Marilyn icons.

As a child Bill never owned a dog, but he decided that when he bought a house he would have one. "Friends of mine doubted that I'd be willing to take responsibility for a dog. But how would I know that if I never had one?" It couldn't be just any dog. "I spent a whole year researching breeds. My first requirement was that it had to be beautiful. Well, Italian greyhounds aren't just beautiful, they're exquisite. You see them in the Renaissance art books, and sculptors love them as models."

First he acquired Contessa, or vice versa. A previous owner had returned her to the breeder, and there was evidence she'd been mistreated. Full of doubts, Bill went to see her with a friend. "She was gorgeous, very quiet, and quite regal. But as soon as her crate was opened she leapt into my lap, and that was it." Contessa was nine months old. Over the next eleven years they became constant companions. Contessa lived with him, slept with him, and almost everywhere he went – out for the evening, off to AA meetings – so did she, by his side, in his arms, or in an open travel bag. "She became absolutely fundamental to my happiness and well-being, to a degree that I could never have imagined possible."

In September 1998 Contessa was recovering nicely from minor surgery to her nose. "Running to greet me at the door, she went to jump on the footstool by the fireplace, and instead she just sank underneath it. I raced her up the street – the vet is only 500 yards away. She went on life support, but he said there was no hope, and he didn't want her to die hooked up on the table. So he unhooked her, and I laid her across my lap. He went to get the hypodermic, but by the time he came back she was dead."

Bill struggles to control his voice. "I had no idea that anything could shake me so badly. I've been through other deaths – when my brother committed suicide, and my parents died – but I was drinking at the time. Once in a while people who still don't know will ask, how's Contessa? Sometimes I can be quite balanced about it, but then other times the grief will just grab me, I never know when."

A year before Contessa died, her nephew Michelangelo joined the household. "I had no intention of buying a second dog, but the breeder insisted on showing me this eight-week-old puppy, already so cocky and full of himself. And he was stunning, with gorgeous markings. He was much more forward than Contessa, and very hard to train, a real alpha. But a joy and a treasure." The treasure is nearly two years old now and barking at a squirrel we can't see, up in the tree. "Mike!" Bill scolds. After a few more barks Michelangelo settles down, and soon falls asleep by Bill's chair. "When Contessa died, he was still training and he would always sleep in his own crate. But when I came home from the vet that day with her empty collar and lead, I said to him, 'Well, Michael, this is it. Regardless of what happens to the house, you have to take her place.' For the first time ever, I took him to bed with me. Of course I was sleeping fitfully, and every time I'd wake up he'd be sitting there looking at me as if to say, 'What is going *on* here?' It was truly amazing, he seemed to grow up virtually overnight."

Michelangelo travels almost everywhere with Bill. The mutual friend who led me to Bill has witnessed the magnetic pull that the dogs exert. "Complete strangers will stop Bill in the street to ask about them," she told me. "I've seen grown men fall on their knees to pet them." "It's true," says Bill, "they really are a great entrée to all sorts of places, and everybody notices them. I feel like Jack Kennedy tagging along after Jacqueline!"

It's almost noon. Bill checks his messages. There are nine of them, all from the same man, a first-time would-be client calling anxiously from his car phone on the rim of Toronto. How soon can he come? Earlier, Bill told me he has to think twice before taking any time off during work hours, whether to talk with me or to go cruising for antiques with our mutual friend. But surely he could live quite nicely on a full teacher's pension? "Not the way I want to," he replies. "To begin with I couldn't afford Glen. I couldn't afford Michelangelo. Nor could I buy the art and antiques that I want, or donate to causes that matter to me, like Fashion Cares." Coming up soon, the glamourous event raises buckets of money for AIDS research.

"I also think it's a pretty remarkable testament that a man of sixty-four can still be considered desirable enough to pull in this kind of money," he says. "It proves you don't have to be young and buffed to make it in our world. Many wouldn't believe that possible. They think old men can't even give it away, let alone market it." On a good day, it's not unusual for this one, a year shy of the old age pension, to pull in $300.

He dials the hungry driver. Bill will be ready for him in fifteen minutes.

24 Roaming with Roxy

WHEN ROXANNE HASTINGS AND HER DRAG KING DOMINATRIX FRIEND made their entrance at the Edmonton Symphony concert, the elegant crowd parted like the Red Sea. The dom wore a tuxedo and all the gear that goes with it, Roxy a shimmering glamour gown, stratospheric heels, an array of glittering jewelry, and huge, astonishing hair. "We were decked out rich," says Roxy. "You absolutely could *not* miss us."

As they mounted the broad steps to the hall, an older gentleman in formal attire locked eyes with Roxy. "I knew that look," says Roxy. "He was thinking, oh my God, what a gorgeous girl, and he was cranking up the charm." But as they got closer the smile froze, the eyes widened, and the formally attired gent turned into a rabbit caught in headlights. "He was so shocked he fell over, he actually hit the ground!" Roxy laughs now in telling it, wickedly, like a boy who's just farted in church. "My friend said to the guy, 'You took him for a girl, didn't you?' He turned beet red, I'd never seen anything like it. My friend and I nearly wet ourselves laughing. That sonofabitch had to go home thinking about how he'd been attracted to a male, and what did that say about his own sexuality? I like that. I want to challenge people to think. That's the adventure."

And that's Roxanne-Ross Hastings, something of a missionary when it comes to gender. Roxy is also curator of botany at the Provincial Museum of Alberta, specializing in the evolution and ecology of mosses. I asked about pronouns, she or he. "Doesn't matter that much to me," says Roxy, "though more and more I prefer to be treated in the female role, even when I'm looking like a guy." Today she's a mix, in moderate make-up, a full but restrained wig, and a long, loose dress that moves easily and doesn't inhibit her stride. At forty-five, she has chunky shoulders, a strong grip, and a light male voice, more jock than siren.

The power of glamour Roxanne remembers being drawn to a farm equipment calendar at her grandparents' house in rural Alberta. A beautiful cowgirl poses by a John Deere tractor. "The other boys expected that when they grew up they would drive that tractor," she says. "I knew just as surely that I would be the calendar girl. And knowing that, I hated myself." Ross Hastings was four.

For the next two decades, dressing in his bedroom, then in his own apartment, he kept his hateful habit secret. Around 1970 a racy *Penthouse* article on transgender offered cold comfort: he was not the only one, he learned, but he was a sexual freak. Not considering himself to be gay, he didn't seek contact through any gay channels. For three years he lived with a woman; they were lovers, until she discovered that he was cross-dressing. "I don't put any blame on her," says Roxy. "If you're miserable about your own life, how is anyone else supposed to love you for it?" Now he was free to dress as he liked, at least at home, but he was also increasingly isolated. "I spent thousands of dollars on clothes and wigs, then I'd throw them away. I thought that would solve the problem. Then I'd go out and buy new ones."

Finally in June 1995, at age thirty-nine, Ross picked up a copy of *Illusions* magazine, for transvestites and transsexuals. Soon he ventured out to the association's social club in Calgary. "It was amazing. For the first time in my life I was with people like myself! There were boyfriends, girlfriends, wives, straight people, gay people, and they weren't freaks, they were just ordinary people living their lives." Over the ensuing summer he erupted from the closet, coming out in a giddy rush to friends and family.

One bright, hot day in August, Ty Morgan, Roxanne's drag mother, asked if she was ready to make her public debut. She was. "It's hard for me to express how important Ty was to me," says Roxy. "She didn't just teach me about hair and make-up, as many drag mothers do, she told me about the life, and how to survive out there." For Roxy's debut, Ty would do her up so big, tarty, and dangerous that no one in their right mind would dare mess with her. She emerged in full daylight on a busy downtown street, a stunning spectacle in towering heels, spandex micro-miniskirt, tight gold top, show biz make-up, and hair to match. She had to walk four long blocks to reach her car. "People literally stopped in their tracks," says Roxy. "Guys whistled from cars, construction workers hooted and hollered. But no one hassled me, not once, they just parted to make way. I had never experienced that kind of power before. It's the power of glamour and drama."

That same evening Roxy performed at a dyke bar. "Most of the lesbians had been pretty tough on transgendered people," she says, "but I'd made some friends by then, selling drinks to help them raise funds at their dances and that kind of thing." For most of the evening a young woman stayed close by Roxy, but said nothing until they sat down after the show. She didn't know whether she was a boy or a girl, she said, but either way she hated herself. If only she could look as gorgeous as Roxy, even for one night, she'd be happy. "I just started to cry," says Roxy. "She was so broken. Within a few hours I was hit by both sides of the beauty thing – in the afternoon by its power, and then by the pain it can cause when you don't meet the standard. It took me a while to figure it out, but I knew there was something there that I wanted to challenge " Shortly after, she signed on as the first transgendered peer counsellor at the Lesbian and Gay Centre in Edmonton.

As Roxy evolved, she pierced her ears, plucked her eyebrows, and started growing her nails, occasionally even wearing a discreet polish. Now and then she'd turn up at the museum with residual traces of make-up from the night before. One day, Ross's fortieth birthday by chance, his supervisor asked a couple of vague questions about how his research was going, and then, was there anything else he'd like to talk about? Ross introduced him to Roxy, showed him before and after photos, and mentioned current research papers s/he was writing, in both gender roles. "I see the world quite differently, depending on which one is dominant at the moment," said Ross. Did he want to come to work as Roxy? the supervisor asked. Definitely. Then start telling people, said the supervisor, and we'll make sure it happens. The two had become allies, and then friends, in a recent battle to prevent senior bureaucrats from reading museum employees' private e-mails. Both knew that current human rights legislation in Alberta offered no protection whatsoever to the likes of Roxy.

For the staff Christmas party that year Ross's section decided to stage a Marilyn Monroe number, with Roxy as Marilyn, two women as backup singers in glitter gowns that Roxy managed to extract from drag-queen friends, and enough competent musicians to make up a small band. They rehearsed for weeks. A few days before the party the museum director got wind of the act. Furious, he ordered them to stop. How dare they put drag queens on display, he ranted. This was a family institution! What if the minister showed up? They could all lose their jobs!

Letting Roxy be Ross informed personnel that he wanted to come to work as Roxy. Aware that his research work was unique and widely respected, both within the museum and beyond, the official consented. The case worked its way up through the bureaucracy. In due course the deputy minister called. Roxy could come to work, but if she did, Ross would no longer be welcome. It had to be one or the other: both would be "too confusing, and too disruptive."

For almost a year only Ross went to work, or so it appeared. Roxy continued to evolve outside, building an increasingly high profile as a drag performer and community activist. She served on the boards of PFLAG, the Gay & Lesbian Community Centre, and Equal Alberta, and got elected as Princess to the Imperial Sovereign Court, a local gay social and fund-raising organization. "As Roxy grew and became more powerful in the community, it became impossible to keep her down," Ross says. "I was miserable at work, I'd bite people's heads off for the littlest things. It got far more disruptive than just letting Roxy be." In December he told his supervisor that from then on he would be coming to work as Ross and/or Roxy, his choice, and at whatever level they tried to stop him, he would sue.

Without protection from the Human Rights Code, Ross had no option but to seek support from a psychiatrist. "I hated going that way," says Roxy. "Now that I'd sorted out and accepted who I am, a psychiatrist was the last thing I needed." His lawyer agreed. You're not sick, she said, so let's fight this on the equality provisions in the federal Charter. But such a case would take years, and bags of money. Roxy had neither. On the other hand, the one thing the Alberta government would find very hard to oppose was medical treatment deemed necessary by a doctor. Roxy would have to find a psychiatrist willing to state categorically that for Ross Hastings, necessary medical treatment must include the right to live and work as a transgendered person, Ross and Roxy.

After waiting four months to see the psychiatrist, Roxy's first appointment started badly. The psychiatrist arrived an hour late, and Roxy lit into him for being rude and disrespectful. The doctor retorted, "I can see we won't need to check *your* testosterone level." Says Roxy, "That's the ultimate insult to a tranny, saying your testosterone is high." She giggles. "I've even used it myself on occasion, it really gets them flying." She told the psychiatrist she didn't need him, only his signature. After a quick assessment the doctor concluded that Roxy was "a transsexual in denial" and suggested hormones. Roxy agreed.

He referred her to an endocrinologist and promised he would write the letter she needed for work.

It took another four months to see the endocrinologist, but when she did, he wrote her a hormone prescription on the spot. By this time Roxy had begun to have second thoughts. "It was too fast, too easy. I know people who've had to fight for *years* to get hormones. And neither of those guys did a proper evaluation as to why they considered me a transsexual in the first place. That really bothered me, both as a scientist and as the person with the most at stake." Roxy's trans friend Stephanie recommended another psychiatrist. After a more thorough assessment, Dr Brooks concluded that Roxy had a "gender identity disorder," a psychiatric grab-bag that's less restrictive than 'transsexual.' "As far as I'm concerned, I don't have any kind of disorder at all," says Roxy. "But if that's what it took to get what I needed for work, I was prepared to go along with it."

Dr Brooks wrote the letter. This time the minister called in person to say that from now on both Ross and Roxy would be welcome at work. Once again, nothing was put in writing. Co-workers thanked Roxy for coming out, and for courage under fire. "They also started to talk more freely about issues of their own," says Roxy. "It's as if my being open had given them the freedom to get some of their own stuff out. I actually wound up counselling a few people." But the battles took their toll.

When I meet Roxy, she's in the middle of a stress leave. Her tasks, according to Dr Brooks, are to get out of the fray for a while, rest, write, and settle into Roxy, deep enough to sort of who she really is, and what.

A perfectly good body To the psychiatrist it's simple: If she would only stop denying that she's a male-to-female transsexual, Roxy could take the hormones, get on with surgery, and in time would feel whole again, with a body more in harmony with her mind.

Not so fast, says Roxy. First, she's ambivalent about the hormones. On the one hand, she admits they have a certain appeal. "If I take estrogen and testosterone-blockers, I get boobs and hips, less facial and body hair, and a higher voice – in other words, I get to look and sound more like a girl. I would also *feel* more feminine, like some of my MTF friends say they do. And the hormones seem to cut tension, they calm people down, almost like a tranquillizer. Aside from all that, if you choose to undergo sex reassignment, they won't do the surgery unless you've had the hormones."

On the other hand? For Roxy, the pros are inseparable from the cons. The downside of the calming effect, for example, is a loss of drive. "I can't think of any transsexual friends where I liked the effects after transition. One of them went from being a $100,000-a-year executive to being a shopgirl on minimum wage, and she says she's perfectly content just to be accepted as a woman. That's not female, it's passive, and it seems more drug-created than any kind of natural state. I work with women who have lots of drive and ambition. I don't want to lose that, I like pushing myself, and being out there, on the edge." The psychiatrist says not to worry, drive has nothing to do with taking hormones. "I asked him if I could still be a bitch," says Roxy, with a wry grin. "'In your case,' he told me, 'no problem.' But I don't really believe him. Since he diagnosed that I'm a transsexual in denial, of course he has a vested interest in pushing the medical solution."

Roxy has good grounds for being suspicious of chemical solutions. "In the '70s I did all kinds of drugs, and it really messes with your brain. I was in the top 1 per cent of Canadian students. I've been clean since, and of course I can still think, analyse, write, but I know that I lost some intellectual power. I would never trust drugs again, legal or illegal – and anyway, look who decides which is which. If I went on the hormones, how would I know what was real and what was estrogen induced? And even if I went off them, would I ever be the same? Now that I'm winding down from all the tension of fighting, I'm just starting to get my clarity back. I can't afford to toss that away. I need to be clean, and I need to be clear."

As an evolutionary and ecological scientist, Roxy has to grapple with an even deeper dilemma. "I've lived and studied a lot in the field, and I see how plants and animals evolve characteristics that allow them to survive over time. It's the same with us. Gay and transgendered people have been around since the beginning of time. If we were fundamentally unnatural, if there was no reason for us to be here on this earth, selective pressures would have knocked us off a long time ago. But we're still here, we've survived every attempt to wipe us out. Now western corporate society tells us it's too confusing and disruptive to be both genders, we have to choose, one or the other, male or female. That's all this culture has to offer, the absolute dualism of either/or. With hormones I can buy my right to be a woman. Without them, I can't. That's so crazy, so narrow. If you've got heart disease, fine, maybe you should go for a medical solution, but if you're not sick, why the hell would you want to muck around with a perfectly good body?"

We're sitting at the kitchen table in her small house, on a quiet street in Edmonton. Her long dark dress drapes over legs spread wide. It's a solid stance, like a wrestler not easily thrown. The sound system in the next room plays smooth New Age native flute songs. "Indigenous cultures go at it so differently," says Roxy. "In their eyes the world isn't ruled by dualism. There's all kinds of room for ambiguity, and transgendered people have a natural place in the whole ecological and social pattern. In fact it's a place of honour. Shamans have often been transgendered people, with a particular sensitivity that gives them access to kinds of wisdom that other people don't have. If I submit to the western technological solution, I betray thousands of years of evolutionary history, and I betray all transgendered people, my spiritual ancestors. It isn't us that need to be fixed, it's a society that can't see beyond its own walls. But can you see me telling all this to the psychiatrist? He'd have me locked up!"

As Roxy evolved, she was shocked to discover it wasn't only the straight world that maintained and defended the prison walls. "Some lesbians have a hard time differentiating between transgendered people like myself and drag queens, who they see as parodies of women. They also think, as many straight women do, that you can only be born a woman. If you haven't been raised female and gone through all the stages, you can never emulate that. Even if you're on hormones, you don't get the cycles, so how can you be a woman? I wouldn't argue with that. But if I'm not a woman, and I'm not a guy, what am I? I'm something in between. So don't worry about trying to fit me into one package or the other, just ask yourself, do you like the *person* I am? When you can accept me like that, as a *person*, we'll both feel better."

It's not only gender that the walls imprison, but orientation too. Roxy encounters gay people who regard trans people as basically straight, and therefore "on the other side." "So how do you define gay or straight? If I'm with a guy as Roxy, and we both think of me as a girl, is that straight? If I'm with a woman, it would only be as Roxy – Ross hasn't had sex in years – so isn't that gay? When I look at a woman I'm not thinking, boy, would I love to go to bed with her, I'm thinking, what a gorgeous body, I envy her beauty. But I also like having the strength of a man. I love the endorphin rush when I'm working with weights, which is related to testosterone, and if I went on blockers it would really inhibit that. In fact my natural testosterone level is actually quite low, and my FSH [follicle stimulating hormone] is well into the normal female range, so already I'm set as authentically transgendered, or intersex. That's where I am, and that's where I want to be."

MAMA! What does Roxy look for in a potential lover? "If the right guy came along, I'd have no hesitation about forming a partnership with him. The men I'm attracted to tend to be academics, or writer-artist types, guys who are out there on the edge and likely to get kicked around a little for having risky views. But my sexual preference has been mostly for women. As Ross I met some fascinating women, but I didn't have the courage to pursue them. As Roxy, on the other hand, I don't have to pursue them, they seem to be drawn to me. Especially bi women. A lot of straight women get uptight about being seen in public with a tranny, but bi women really seem to get off on us. This way, I suppose, they can get it all in one package!" One straight girlfriend, a seamstress for strippers, did enjoy roaming with Roxy or Ross, either way. "She and I wound up in some really dangerous biker bars. With me in a micro-miniskirt and done up big time, and her being a mouthy, bitchy sort of person, I was always grateful in those situations to have a male muscularity and a brown belt in karate. Never had to use them, but I was always glad to have them, just in case."

On one front where many trans people have to do battle, Ross Hastings has been blessed. Not only have his parents accepted Roxy, they've told the whole family, even their neighbours. They pass around photos of Roxy as Princess to the Imperial Sovereign Court as proudly as any snapshots of their other kids. "Now they'll get people wanting to talk to them about all kinds of things," says Roxy. "And these are Alberta farmers, rural people who don't reveal much of themselves to anyone, but now they feel safe enough to follow my parents' lead and open up. It really comes down to the fundamental belief that family comes first, and you have to look after your kids, you have to stand by them." Roxy smiles. "I guess you could call it family values."

Roxy has a whole other family, and she stands by her young as steadfastly as her own birth parents do by her. Technically, she says, your drag mother is the first person who gets you into drag, but the role adjusts to fit the occupant. "Some drag mothers have hundreds of daughters. They just make you up in the bar, and you may never see them again. But the best kind of drag mother will really take you under her wing, she'll tutor you in how to perform, what to do when a guy hits on you, or how to go after a guy that you want – pretty much how to survive and get by as a queen. Many young people who get into drag don't have accepting parents, so for some of them this may be the only family they know."

Roxy has three drag daughters. Two are twenty-one, the other twenty-eight; one is a drag queen, two are transgendered. One is manic-depressive. One had already been on the streets for four years before she connected with Roxy at seventeen. "That was pretty dangerous stuff," says Roxy. "She was underage, I wasn't out at work, and the Klein government was making a big noise about gays being child molesters and all that crap. But she really needed a lot of support to get on her feet. She had terrible taste in men, and it got her into a lot of trouble. One time I had to go after her in a hotel and face down her pimp, this scary guy with a gun, to get her out of there. It's almost like adoption, where you really look after the kid as your real daughter, on and off stage, in her relationships with men, school, jobs, whatever. But I don't let them run away from their problems. That's like trying to run away from yourself." Sounds like a mother.

What's in it for her? "It's like having kids later in life," says Roxy. "You get to watch them grow as people, and you go through the suffering and the joy that goes with that. It's a way to extend my love and help a few younger people get through life a little easier. In return, they're extremely loyal. They keep me informed of what's going on in the community, and they've worked hard on my campaigns. I love walking into a club and hearing 'MAMA!' from way across the room. They're my closest relationships in the community, as strong as most blood relationships. I know that if I ever got attacked in a bar, my drag daughter would be the first one in there, swinging for me."

25 And the Walls Came Tumbling Down

At his parents' home for Hanukkah, Mira Goldberg happened to catch a TV documentary on Jesus, whose name in Hebrew translates as "he who helps." Given Mira's work and approach to life, the phrase had an immediate appeal. "But can you imagine introducing yourself?" says Joshua: "Hi, I'm Jesus." And how would people ever manage the Hebrew version, Yeshua? He settled for the anglicized Joshua. Joshua as in the Bible, and the gospel song, the fellow who brought the walls of Jericho tumbling down? "That's the one," he says. "I guess you could call it my moment of grandiosity."

But why shed a perfectly good birth name, Mira (pronounced "Meera"), and the life history it embodied? "It struck me that the pressure to take a male name was entirely socially constructed," says Joshua, "and on that basis alone I had to resist it." But by then his voice had dropped; when he talked on the phone, there would often be confusion at the other end: who was this Mira person, man, woman, boy or girl? "I'd also been through twenty-five years of having my name mispronounced and misspelled. Did I really want it to be misgendered too?"

Joshua Mira Goldberg grew up in Vancouver. His mother, Dianne Goldberg, recalls, "Mira taught herself to read by the time she was three, and she always asked far more questions than other children. In school she was so much more mature than the others that teachers tended to give her extra responsibilities, like making sure a child in a wheelchair got out for the fire drills. Like most children, Mira really didn't want to stick out so much. She wasn't very physical, and she wasn't that comfortable with other kids her own age. Mostly she preferred to do things on her own, or with older children or adults. The way we saw it, there's only so much energy in one body, and in Mira's case most of it went to the intellect."

Mira was a very feminine girl, says Joshua, but from age ten or so, schoolmates started to label her a lesbian. "I was never happy at school. Being Jewish and being queer are inseparable in my mind; both of them isolated me. I had a really hard time being social."

In her teens Mira discovered that alcohol and drugs increasingly smoothed her way in social situations. At fourteen she told a few friends that she was a lesbian. "In fact I really didn't know what I was," says Joshua. "I was having sex with boys, so how could I be a lesbian? But on the other hand what I thought I really wanted was sex with girls." The mother of a girl she knew at school turned out to be a vital connection. "This girl was ashamed of her mother because she was a lesbian, but to me the woman was a good friend, I could talk to her about anything. She provided one of the few anchors I had in those years."

Mira moved to England with her parents for three years. After they returned to Canada, drink and drugs remained her social lubricants. By the time she was nineteen she realized that the only way she could live was to get clean and sober, quick. She dropped out of university and came out to her family, first as a lesbian, then as bisexual, since she was still having sex with men. With her parents' support she moved to Victoria, and threw herself into an herbal medicine course. "It was very intensive, five days a week, and it kept me out of trouble," says Joshua. "It probably saved my life."

How did her parents react when their elder daughter came out to them? "I guess I was a little confused," says Michael Goldberg, "since she'd have boyfriends sleep over, but – well, whatever. I'm not that reactive a person in general."

"We didn't have much choice in the matter," says Dianne. "Most of Mira's moves tended to be pretty absolute, and it would be up to us to adjust. Even as a child, whether she was playing with Lego or painting on the easel, her approach was always, this is what I'm doing, and that's that. We always tried to negotiate things and give the children options, that's the kind of parents we were. But in Mira we were dealing with a child that we might refer to now as severely empowered." She laughs, but it sounds half serious.

In any case, Dianne wasn't entirely surprised by the news. Some time before Mira made her announcement, she had read up on homosexuality, just in case. "I couldn't put my finger on it, but there was something, maybe in the kind of relationships she had with men, that just made me wonder." In her own growing up, acceptance of diversity was the norm with her progressive parents. "When I was in high school," she says, "a couple that my parents knew split up, and it turned out she was a lesbian. I remember hearing some surprise at that, but there was no stigma attached, and my parents stayed friends with both of them, the man and the woman." As a social worker in the '70s, Michael worked with several out gay men; the Goldbergs would be invited to their New Year's brunches. "Those were the best parties," says Michael. Dianne adds, "The girls loved it, the food, the music and dancing, the people. They never seemed to notice it was all men."

By now in her early twenties, Mira still hadn't made peace with herself. In and out of depression, she attempted suicide and had to be hospitalized. A few months later she was back in hospital, this time for gynecological surgery. When she surfaced from the anaesthetic, something had shifted in her, deeply. "I don't understand what happened," says Joshua, "or why or how, but from then on I was profoundly uncomfortable being female." She cut her hair short and began to wear more conventionally masculine clothes. People took her for a butch lesbian. "That was okay, but after a while it wasn't enough. I started to realize that rather than being seen as a masculine woman, I wanted to read as male but still also to be feminine somehow. It was hard to put all that together, to make sense of it. I didn't have the language."

The only transgendered person she knew had moved the other way, male-to-female. Then Mira read *Stone Butch Blues,* a passionate, detailed account of Leslie Feinberg's transition from female to male. "That book was an explosion for me," says Joshua. "Finally I had the language to understand what it was that I really wanted." Early in 1996 Mira Goldberg embarked on the long, arduous journey of sex reassignment.

Joshua Through the Internet she connected with FTM trans people in Vancouver, who advised her to start by finding a doctor familiar with the issues and process. To get funding from the B.C. medical plan for any surgery she might need, Mira would have to get a referral to the gender clinic in Vancouver. Her new doctor sent her to a psychiatrist and an endocrinologist for assessment. In Victoria there was only one psychiatrist willing to see transsexuals. "I had a rather dim view of the profession in general, but he turned out to be quite compassionate," says Joshua. "He accepted that I was clear and confident about what I wanted and acknowledged that what I really needed wasn't therapy but the means to get on with my life."

A year later, Mira began to take a daily dose of testosterone, the male hormone. In sufficient quantities it also suppresses production of the female hormones, estrogen and progesterone. "It's ironic," says Joshua. "I've been through some quite profound physical and psychological changes, and yet I really haven't changed at all." After a year and a half of hormone therapy, he looks and sounds like a boy in his mid-teens: the facial hair is patchy but should fill in over time, the voice has dropped as much as it will, the hips are a little slimmer, the muscles a little heavier. Visible side-effects of the hormones are minimal: some acne, and a thinning of head hair. "I knew that would happen," says Joshua, "and it's not a big concern for me. My mother's father is bald as a billiard ball."

The shift in hormone balance also forced Joshua's body simultaneously into a version of menopause, due to the drop in female hormones, and the equivalent of genetic male puberty, due to the infusion of testosterone. "It's very weird. At the same time that you're getting hot flashes, your voice is also cracking, you're sprouting body hair, and you get these wild fluctuations in libido that teenage boys experience. I'm really glad I'm going through this as an adult. It also gives me a certain empathy for adolescent males – there's so little support when you're going through all the confusion that these changes can cause." In an odd paradox, the hormone shift also appears to level out mood swings, which Joshua describes as "a pleasant change."

When we talked, he was due to take the next step in his transformation, chest reconstruction. "It's a two-and-a-half hour procedure, a cross between a mastectomy and breast reduction," he says. "I should come out of it with a more masculine-looking chest, squarish pectorals, smaller nipples, and as little scarring as possible. I'll be able to take my shirt off without getting ogled." He chuckles. "Except when I want it, of course."

It sounds so easy, but the journey from F to M is a long one and littered with obstacles. Prevailing psychiatric standards require that candidates for transition surgery live openly for two years in the chosen gender. During that period hormone-induced changes are dramatic, but others don't occur until surgery. "It's a Catch-22," says Joshua. "How, for example, can you live as a man with triple-C breasts?" For FTM candidates, the provincial medical plan will fund chest reconstruction, a hysterectomy, and removal of the ovaries. Currently, it will not fund the construction of a penis and external genitals, nor will it cover the cost of hormones, without which no candidate can proceed to surgery. Fortunately, Joshua's insurance plan at work pays for the hormones, which he will have to continue taking for the rest of his life.

The other side For Joshua, such visible body changes clearly required a second coming out. Reactions were mixed. "Some people were confused because it seemed so sudden. I didn't fit the stereotype of the tortured transsexual who's known from an early age that they're trapped in a body of the other gender. Lesbian friends were alarmed because I'd been such a strong feminist, and here I was going over to the other side – what if I turned into this asshole man who suddenly denied everything I'd stood for, and who they couldn't possibly hang out with anymore? I think most of them started to relax when they saw that I hadn't really changed, I was still fighting sexism, only now it was from a different perspective. In fact, I suspect that finally coming to terms with who I am has made me more effective as an activist."

At work and at acupuncture school, Joshua made it clear that he wanted no bullshit, and no tiptoeing around – any honest question was valid. People were a little stunned, he says, but supportive. The school invited a local professor who does research on FTM transsexuals to give a talk to the students. "At work, clients were very supportive," says Joshua, "although it took some of them a while to sort out my new identity. At first some of them thought I was male-to-female, because that's the only kind of trans people they knew."

After a front page story on him and another transsexual in a local magazine, he expected some backlash, or at least a chill in his day-to-day encounters. Instead he got compliments. "I was shocked," he says. "People said that's great, it must have taken courage. I'm quite fortunate to have chosen fields where gay and lesbian people have paved the way, and acceptance is more the norm than discrimination. I know this isn't the typical story for transsexuals – far from it. It's quite unusual not to have any problems in your employment situation, to lose so few friends, and not to lose any family members."

However, the family reaction wasn't quite as smooth as he had hoped. "I expected the same sort of response I got when I came out as a lesbian – yeah, so? Well, I was wrong, it was a complete shock to them. They'd always had gay and lesbian friends, but they didn't know any FTMs. And they were alarmed that I was taking testosterone, they thought I'd end up looking like Arnold Schwarzenegger. My father didn't say much, but he did try to be supportive. My mother said, 'Why are you betraying the women's movement by becoming a man? Why can't you just be a butch lesbian?' I think what she really meant was that I was letting her down somehow, and the bond we'd shared."

Michael Goldberg recalls that he had two reactions. "The idea of a radical mastectomy really freaked me out. This family doesn't relate well to the medical system in general and especially not to hospitals and surgery. When I was a teen, a neighbour had a breast removed due to cancer, and I remember how long it took for her to recover and how phenomenal the scarring was. So my first thought was, why would anyone want to do that to themselves, voluntarily?" His second reaction: "Given the politics of gender, why would anyone want to become a man? I said that to her – him. I still find it hard to get the pronouns correct. But I think we're forgiven when we mistakenly call him Mira, we've been doing it for so long."

Was Michael disappointed with Mira/Joshua? "Not at all. For me the real disappointment would be if either of my kids became a raging capitalist!" He laughs. "Really, that's the important stuff to me, being politically aware, opposing greed and injustice." A little context: at fifty-eight, Michael is the research director for a nonprofit social planning organization, and Dianne Goldberg, fifty-five, works with a nonprofit social service agency. Both have been committed for most of their adult lives to building a more just and equitable society. Mira and her sister remember being taken in their strollers on peace marches, picket lines, and rallies. "I'd like to think that we exposed them to opportunities," says Michael, "but also that we never forced them to adopt our way of seeing things. That would have gone against everything we believe."

Dianne's reaction was more turbulent. "It was extremely difficult for me. Just before she told us about the transgendered situation, Mira was the kind of feminist that I'm not and nor would I ever want to be. Certainly I think of myself as a feminist, but my world includes men. For her everything was women only, men were the oppressors and blah blah blah, on and on. Now suddenly she was telling us this is what she wanted to be, a man. For me it was a huge disconnect, I couldn't put the pieces together. I also had tremendous fear of what might lie ahead for her. I only knew one transgendered person, and I had the clear sense that her life was pretty difficult. Of course both kids would say, oh, that's just Mum, she always worries. Well, why not? As a mother it's only natural to want your kid's life to be simple, and nice."

Dianne urged Mira not to tell her grandfather, Dianne's dad, who was eighty-three at the time. "She was afraid it would kill him," says Joshua. "But there was no way I could hide the changes from him. As always, he was incredibly supportive, and an advocate for me. He was one of the first people to call me Jo. It's not Joshua, but close enough."

Says Dianne, "My father has four granddaughters, and his comment was, finally, the grandson he'd always wanted! He told other people long before we did. So I found myself thinking, well, if he can handle it, what's wrong with me? As both kids know, it takes time for me to adapt to change. My father also says all the struggles with Mira were just payback because *I* was such a pain in the ass!" She laughs. "My mother, on the other hand, says I was just lovely."

At her own pace and in her own way, Dianne is working through her maze of reactions. "I'm incredibly proud of the way both our kids live their lives as young adults," she says. "Maybe it would have been easier in some way if Joshua hadn't made this decision, but she was in so much turmoil for such a long time that probably it's much healthier this way. Now I see someone who's happier, someone who's made a commitment to schooling, and someone who follows through on her – his – decisions. I still worry about the physical side, the long-term effects of taking steroids. I can understand it from his point of view: even if there's a risk that your life might be shorter, still it could be a better life. On the other hand, as a parent you want your children's lives to be both long and healthy."

A big sissy In terms of relationships, this is a good time in Joshua's life. "I'm really fortunate to have a great biological family that gives me a sense of continuity and strong support even when we're struggling with each other. As I get less dependent on them, it allows our friendship to develop, and I actually find myself choosing to spend more time with them. I'm also finding that the sense of responsibility I have towards my biological family is growing in relation to my chosen family too."

In Victoria his chosen family centres around the two women who share his house – a close friend who also happens to be his landlady, and his partner. The friend is the mother of a woman he dated for a short time. "It's strange how these things happen," says Joshua. "That relationship was quite short, but Valerie [the mother] became deeply important to me. One of the reasons both of us stay in Victoria is that moving away would mean the end of our living together."

Joshua's partner entered his life about three years ago, in the midst of the hormonal transition. "Our relationship is unusual," says Joshua. "We share finances, the house, and our lives in the most profound ways I could imagine. She's incredibly supportive of whatever changes I'm going through. But we're not sexual with each other. My primary sexual identity is still with men, and as the gender changes proceed, I still want the chance to explore having sex with men, as a man."

What is he waiting for? "The right man," he says, with a laugh. "That's only half true. I'm still going through huge physical changes – I still have breasts, though not for long, and I still have a vagina. I find that straight men still see me as a woman, which is not how I want to be perceived, especially not in sex. And not surprisingly, most gay men are a bit leery about my genitals. I mean, where would a gay man's identity be if he had sex with someone with a twat?" He laughs. "Of course I'd love it if my vagina miraculously inverted itself into a great big penis, but that's not how it works. The surgery is very expensive, and it's not really all that good yet. And I've still got a huge student loan to pay off. Anyway, if I had $40,000 I'm not so sure I'd buy a penis with it. There could be all kinds of other things I'd rather do. Who knows, that could change with time. We'll see."

The first time I heard Joshua's voice on the phone, he sounded like a gay man, maybe a seven on the macho-to-swishy scale. Exactly right, says Joshua. "My desire is to be a male, but I also want very much to be *read* as feminine. So I walk and talk in ways that typically read as fag. As my gay friends put it, I'm a big sissy!" He laughs. "I don't wear skirts at the moment, but I intend to again, as soon as I look masculine enough not to be perceived as a woman. I've always enjoyed wearing what are generally defined as feminine clothes, and I'm certainly not going to stop now just because that's not allowed for FTM transsexuals. Why would I go through this incredible struggle and change only to end up as someone who can't be myself, *again*?"

Where does the removal of his breasts fit in this complex evolution from radical lesbian to swishy fag? "It makes me sad that society judges people so narrowly by body type, so it's not possible to have breasts and still be regarded as a man. In time, I expect we'll be able to define and choose our gender much more fluidly, but for the moment, it's not a free choice. State funding helps to maintain the boundaries, for example, by not allowing for a simple breast reduction. The rule is that any real transsexual will want those breasts *gone*. Some of us would like to change that kind of external pressure, so people could make their own decisions more freely."

Yet he's still choosing to shed the breasts: Why? "Even though I want those contradictions in the way I'm read, I also need the congruity of having a body that approximates my sense of self as a man," he says. "That just means I'll have to find other ways to express the contradictions, by wearing skirts and so on. It's a really crucial part of my identity to be on the margin. I don't know if that's altogether healthy, since I know in identity politics you can get extra points for the degree to which you're marginalized. Maybe I'm afraid I'd have to let go of some bonus points if I become too fully a guy." He laughs. "I guess I'll have to sort that out."

It makes me dizzy. "I'm not surprised," says Joshua. "Going through all these changes, I've become very attentive to the signifiers, the ways that people perceive you as male or female. Some things about me won't change. I will always have teeny, girly hands, and my big hips aren't going to suddenly disappear. But now I have facial hair, and if I let it grow, people will think, ah, must be a guy. That's a default setting in our society. I know women who don't shave their facial hair, and even in the absence of any other signs, they're often assumed to be men. If you have breasts, you gotta be a woman. No matter what I do with my hair, or how I dress, I see people looking at my chin, my chest, my chin, my chest – you can see the wheels turning: Now what the hell is *this*?"

In the community of struggle that's so important to him, Joshua has been looking for a home. At the last women-only event he attended, invited to speak by old feminist buddies, he felt profoundly out of place. When he tried to get involved in a pro-feminist men's group, they still knew Mira, the radical dyke, and suspected that s/he was spying for the women. "Also, though I appreciate what they're trying to do," says Joshua, "in working to undo the conditioning you get being raised male, those guys are coming from an experience that's very different from mine."

Now he works for the inclusion of trans women in the wider community of women. "It's another way to support the feminist project of being whole and fully diverse. I also want to counter sexism in the FTM community, where I've seen some folks embrace aspects of masculinity that just plain suck. It's the same old struggle, really, to fight our way out of the stereotypes of who and what we're allowed to be as women and men."

Having been born and raised a genetic male, I have some experience of the territory. Thought I don't feel much at home in a culture that seems to idolize the most brutish expressions of manhood, still, it's where I live. In the same way I'd wonder what a newcomer to my country thinks of it, I'm inclined to ask Joshua: what is a man?

For him, manhood is a work in progress. "I see how much damage it does when men compete with each other to decide who's more of a man, who's got the biggest cock. There's no end to the violence that comes from that contest. I've seen how it cuts men off from each other and how hard it is for them to form good relationships with each other – with me, for example, not because I'm a tranny but because I'm another man. I think gay men and trans men can have a powerful impact in opening up the definition to embrace many more kinds of men who are excluded now. Look, if someone who was a woman can be a man, who can't?"

The journey is a gift Last time we talked, in autumn 2000, Joshua was thirty and working as a research assistant/secretary for a community health unit. "Now I'm able to live as a man, without all the questions and stares I got prior to the surgery," he says. "Now I'm perceived as an effeminate man." This was his goal. On the other hand, because nerves were severed in the surgical process, he's lost tactile sensation through most of his chest.

Any regrets, second thoughts? "It's been an incredible learning experience. I've gone from feeling quite disconnected emotionally from my breasts to feeling physically disconnected from my chest. I do wonder if I could have learned to manage the gender dysphoria – the gap between the gendered aspects of my body and my internal gender identity – without surgery. I wonder if I could have learned, with the right kind of support, to cope better with that original disconnection."

One of his grounds for wondering is a new relationship, now over a year old. His lover, another FTM, still has his breasts. Says Joshua, "He and I have had to navigate what kinds of touching, looking, or other acts involving his chest are okay for us to do. Being sexual with him like this, I wonder what it would have been like with my body as it was, before all the modifications occurred."

As he has always done, Joshua still uses his personal experience to challenge the larger picture, the status quo. "I do question the pressure on us to have surgery. The medical system classifies us as either/or: either you're a transsexual who wants to change all gendered aspects of the body, or you don't, in which case you're not a real transsexual, and you're denied access to funding for any surgery at all. But my gender identity is quite in the middle, between masculine and feminine, and I think now it would have been more accurate to have my body also somewhere in the middle of that spectrum."

To move towards that middle ground, he's stopped taking testosterone. "I still look like a man, but now I look more effeminate. My facial and body hair are starting to lighten, my head hair has stopped thinning, and I'm menstruating again. I had thought that would feel quite uncomfortable, but other than having to think about what to wear – no white undies in the middle of the month! – it's actually quite reassuring to have the mixture of physical gender." Undies aren't the only challenge. "It's a bit embarrassing to navigate things like buying menstrual products, or changing tampons in a men's room. I've very conscious now that I have to consider a 'bathroom schedule,' and locate single-use washrooms to avoid that kind of awkwardness."

Complexities like these are now being addressed by Transcend, a community agency that Joshua helped start and currently chairs. It provides education and resources on transgender issues, as well as support and advocacy for transgendered people and their families. It also aims to build working alliances among women's, men's, and transgender groups, hoping to head off inclusion/exclusion conflicts that have arisen in other places.

And another wall comes tumbling down. All this by age thirty.

Dianne Goldberg says of her elder daughter, now her son, "It always seemed to me that if there were two paths to choose from, one of them smooth and the other one hard, Mira would never choose the easy one. Sometimes it's hard to sit by and hope for the best. But I've learned, and there are times when I just keep my mouth shut."

Says Michael, "You do?"

"More often than you think," says Dianne, and they laugh.

"It's a strange society we live in," says Joshua. "It does everything in its power to avoid the discomfort of internal struggle. We're supposed to be happy and free of tension, in a way that can ultimately make everything feel quite flat. A life without struggle and questioning certainly isn't the kind of life I want. People say, 'Oh, how horrible that you have to go through all this,' but I don't see it as a problem. The obstacles and bumps are problems for sure, but not the journey. The journey is a gift."

26 Walks with Smudge

ONE BRIGHT, HOT DAY IN JULY 1998 SMUDGE AND I WENT OUT FOR our morning walk. For me, who sits so much, these daily walks are beneficial, but to our Smudge they are compulsory. Only a couple of times in her life has she declined a walk, and then she was so ill we feared she must die.

As usual, she began to agitate shortly after we arose in the morning. Indoors, she paced, wagged, whined, then escalated to a sharp bark that could not be ignored. Exiled to the outside, she barked louder and bounced, literally, off the porch door. She weighed only eighteen pounds, but the impact of this determined projectile on the glass door made her point. Some days, when I face a hard deadline, or I want to hide, or just sit quietly with my tea and Brian, it occurs to me that I've created a monster. But really it's simple genetics; one of Smudge's parents was a terrier. I can see how the word has come to signify persistence.

We walked up the lane – I walked, she ran, as she does, madly off in all directions – and crossed the neighbours' field to circle around the back of their vacant land. As we came close to the pond, Smudge took off after some tantalizing scent, yapping, *I'm onto it!* Probably a rabbit, but could be a deer; she doesn't discriminate.

Our Smudge was never a great hunter. She certainly had the nose and speed for it, but not a clue about stealth; as soon as she picked up a scent, she made it known for miles. She inherited the noisiest, most exuberant attributes of both parents, a terrier and a cockapoo, a cross between cocker spaniel and poodle. Even in her fourteenth year, she still functioned almost entirely at two settings, high and off.

Suddenly her yaps changed to ferocious growling. I knew the sound – she had caught the prey but it was fighting back. Raccoon, fox? Both would be more than a match for her, but she would never yield. One day I ran to growls like this and found her lock-jawed with an adult raccoon, bigger than herself. Neither would give. Without thinking, I lifted the whole snarling mass into the air. Startled, both released. The raccoon dropped to the ground and shambled off. Left to their own devices, they would have kept at it until one or both had bled to exhaustion, or death.

Now I shouted her name and ran toward the growls. My shouting could either help or hinder. If the other animal turned to flee, Smudge might renew her attack. But occasionally it had happened that if Brian or I yelled loud enough to command her attention, she would come, and the other animal could escape.

The growls changed to screams – her voice, in panic or pain. She was deep in cedars too dense for me to penetrate. I started to shriek, a wild sound I hardly recognized. Then through the trees I saw a tawny blur, big shapes, more than one, and fast. Wolves? At least they were going the other way. I found Smudge in the pond, half submerged and shaking so hard her teeth rattled. I could see a small bite on her face, and a gash on her shoulder, but neck and belly seemed intact. I carried her home, soaked and shuddering. The vet said they must have been coyotes, hunting in a pack. I don't hold it against them; they were just doing their job.

After a few days on antibiotics, and aloe on the open wound to soothe the itch, Smudge's raw flesh began to skin over and heal. But not, I think, her spirit. As we resumed our walks, over time it became clear that her worldview had shifted radically. Nothing like this had ever happened to her before. One more second, and she would have been lunch.

Enter Smudge In September 1984 Brian's sister Linda told us that friends of hers, expecting a second child, thought it best that their puppy go to another home. We found her hiding under a coffee table, her refuge from the first child, who mistook her for a toy. Not surprisingly, she hasn't been fond of children since. Less than a month old, she was a small mass of high energy and black woollyness, with one ear straight, the other bent, and deep shining brown eyes. They had named her for the white smudge under her chin.

Brian and I had talked about adopting a dog. As a child I had to care for one that was supposed to be my brother's. It should have been a joy, but instead got tangled in a messy knot of resentments. Brian and I agreed that, though we would both care for Smudge, he would be primarily responsible for her. As with everything else, we would work out the details as we went. Obviously she was very bright, and *very* determined. Within a week she had become indispensable.

Before long Brian and I revealed quite different parenting styles. I'm inclined to be permissive. If Smudge wants something, and I can think of no good reason why she shouldn't have it, she gets it. Brian is no authoritarian, but he does draw lines. If the dog indicates she'd like to go out, I let her out, regardless of what else I'm doing. Brian, on the other hand, tends to wait until he's ready. While I can see advantages to his approach, it has never occurred to me to try it. Since he's calmer and more competent in such things, he clips nails, administers pills, and tries to set reasonable limits on my indulgence.

When we moved to the country, Smudge was young still, and loved to prowl the woods. Sometimes she'd be gone for hours, even into the night. Of course we'd worry, but we couldn't imagine tying or confining her. When we'd call her in for the night, if she was engaged out there she would simply ignore the call. Eventually we'd go to bed, but like anxious parents we'd lie half-awake until we heard her at the door. Our irritation vanished in a second under the wash of relief.

Someone suggested we give her a dog biscuit each time she responded to our call. Being a quick learner, she soon realized that all she had to do for the reward was go out and come back in. As her turnaround time shrank to less than a slow count to ten, Brian drew a line. "You just came in," he would tell her, "you're not going out again." I continue to provide the reward on cue, a conditioned response as finely tuned as hers. Brian accuses me of pandering to them, Smudge and Willy the cat, to win their affection. I'd like to claim some higher motive, but he could be right. At the same time, as the drawer of lines, cutter of nails, and giver of pills, he frets sometimes at playing the mean parent to my indulgent one.

Willy has been with us almost as long as Smudge, and we suspect he's older. He's a tall, dignified cat, elegant in orange and white. All the other cats at the Humane Society clamoured, *pick me, pick me,* but Willy sat calm and aloof, above this maudlin display. How could I resist? At home, after a few sharp swats to the nose, young Smudge learned to leave him in peace. Over the years Willy has become increasingly affectionate, at least with us, but always and only on his terms. He prefers to hunt solo. Some visiting friends have seen so little of him, they doubt that he exists. He's upstairs sleeping, or under a lilac bush, minding his own business.

By contrast, Smudge is descended from wolves, and wouldn't survive a week without her pack, Brian and me. Or so I like to think.

Getting on Until the coyote attack, she seemed immune from the normal signs of aging. We kept wondering what she might be like when she grew up.

It's likely she had already lost some hearing before she encountered the coyotes; otherwise she would have known to keep her distance. But over that summer she lost more of it, until she could only hear loud, sharp sounds like a high whistle, a bang or a clap. The loss of this crucial sense has tended to isolate her from the world, and us, and that in turn has made her more anxious. If we touch her from behind without warning, no matter how gently, or make any sudden move on her periphery, she cringes for a second like a dog who's been abused.

In her eyes the woods have changed from a place of adventure where she'd play at hunting to a place of menace where she could as easily be the prey. One winter day she stopped and gazed into the deeper woods, sniffing the air. In the snow I could see rabbit tracks. Before the coyotes, she would have given instant chase, but now she had second thoughts. She stays very close on our walks, often just a foot or two ahead. Because she can't monitor my presence by sound, she stops often and suddenly, to look back and confirm that she's not alone. Sometimes to avoid tripping over her I have to make leaps or pirouettes I would have thought long gone from my repertoire.

We've had to work out new forms of communication. If I'm going to change direction, I wait until she looks, then wave to indicate the new route, and usually she runs to get ahead. If she seems bent on going her own way, I follow. In this pack there is no alpha; we muddle toward consensus.

One rainy grey afternoon I stopped to signal a change of route. By going my way, we would miss a tangle of juniper roots that could trip her up. By the time she turned to check, I was partly hidden by a cedar. She sniffed the air, this way and that, then headed back along the trail. I moved into the clear, yelling and waving my arms. Still she didn't see or hear me. She stopped, increasingly alarmed, started back the other way, stopped again. Finally she saw me, and she ran, full throttle, to rejoin the pack. Such are our negotiations.

On another walk I stopped to pee. Smudge rambled on, and this time she didn't look back. I yelled and whistled but got no response. With a gusty autumn wind and dry leaves rattling, I couldn't hear well either. My pulse quickened. So did my pace. Here was the pond, and the stand of red cedars where she'd been attacked. I had wondered sometimes, when she'd be out of sight for long stretches of a walk, what if she was injured, or attacked out here? I might not get to her in time to help. We might never find her. We come across the skulls and bones of other animals, even cows, that have died in these woods. But I could just as easily slip and break a leg, and how would Brian know where to search? Would Smudge race home like Lassie to report, *Johnnie's in the well!* I retraced my route, almost running now. Smudge knows this land better than I do, I reminded myself, and if she was attacked, surely she'd let me know. If she could. Probably she was home by now. Over the years, whenever she lost contact with us, this had become her default setting, head for home. But what if she wasn't there?

She was. As usual, relief and delight came in a giddy wave, like being mildly drunk.

Smudge's century The next summer we got another sharp reminder of her mortality. After our walk one day she got quite sick, probably from eating something dead and rotten in the woods. By next morning she could hardly lift her head, and a walk was out of the question. One of the vets at our animal clinic suspected acute pancreatitis, common in dogs who have ingested rotten food. He prescribed an antibiotic and gave her an injection of prednisone, a cortisol steroid, to reduce inflammation. Within a couple of days her energy had picked up, but now suddenly she was drinking and eating frantically, peeing and shitting in the house, which she had never done before, also panting and trembling almost constantly. A younger vet at the clinic thought this odd cluster of symptoms suggested "pituitary dependent Cushings syndrome." A urine test supported his conclusion.

Alarmed, I did a search for Cushings on the Internet. Apparently one or more microscopic tumours form inside the pituitary gland in the brain and stimulate the adrenal glands to produce an excess of the natural anti-inflammatory cortisol. Aside from the symptoms we had already seen, the syndrome can cause a potbelly, decreased muscle mass, lethargy, hair loss, bruising, and infections to the skin and urinary tract. If a tumour gets large enough, it may lead to behaviour changes, loss of appetite, and blindness. The vet told us it could also cause seizures of an increasingly destructive nature.

To treat it, apparently we had four options. If we took a holistic approach, my first choice, we would be on our own, and we had no idea how much time we might have. Conventional veterinary medicine offers three drugs. One is experimental, expensive, and unpredictable. Another, which kills the adrenal cells that produce cortisol, requires close monitoring and frequent, invasive testing for the rest of the animal's life. Already we minimize visits to the animal clinic: Smudge starts shaking the moment we turn off the highway into their parking lot. The third drug, l-Deprenyl, was originally prescribed and then rejected for Parkinson's disease in humans. By blocking a particular enzyme and enhancing the production of dopamine, apparently it helps to regulate the cortisol. Since it also carries the least known side effects of the three, this became our drug of choice for Smudge. According to the literature, if it's going to work, improvement should be seen within six weeks.

Brian and I had a talk: What if it didn't work? We agreed there would be no aggressive medical intervention. Our Smudge had already lived fifteen of our years, or by the standard formula, more than a century of hers. Whatever time was left to her, we would make it as full and comfortable as we could. I cried a little, in practice for mourning.

Within a week she stopped panting, she no longer peed or shit in the house, and her eating and drinking had returned to normal. Astonished, we began to wonder if she might actually have the iatrogenic version of Cushing's, caused by drugs like prednisone that suppress the body's cortisol production. Normally it takes chronic use, but still, Smudge's symptoms seemed to come on so abruptly – could the culprit have been that injection for pancreatitis? If that were the case, once the drug had cleared her system, she would recover from the Cushings symptoms, as she did. But with her dramatic recovery only having occurred since we started the l-Deprenyl, we were afraid to stop it long enough to experiment. What if we did her some irreparable harm? The two of us became drug dependent on her behalf.

I also found a Cushings discussion list on the Net. Primarily used by dog owners in the U.S., it's a good source of information, support, and debate on how to make sense of this bizarre condition. Often the discussion is sad – so much suffering and death, in dogs too young for such things – but as often it's encouraging. Two things impress me in particular: the depth of grief that people can feel when a companion dog dies, and the financial resources that some are prepared to invest in their animals' health. Some even talk of mortgaging their homes to pay vet bills, which can include procedures like MRIs that cost thousands of dollars. Grief or guilt notwithstanding, neither of us was prepared to mortgage the house.

In time Smudge saw through each of our crude strategies for concealing the bitter little dose of drug in her food. Then it came down to Brian wrestling it into her mouth every day. But we started to wonder: all the anxiety that this fight induces in her, won't it generate more cortisol, which is what we're trying to *reduce*? One morning we skipped the pill. Next day we gave it, next day we didn't. A few days later Smudge had her last pill.

Autumn In the woods, most of the leaves have fallen. This morning the gardens are glazed with frost, and the last of the roses nipped in the bud. Later this week we'll plant next year's garlic, and then we'll cut our firewood. Winter is close. In the seasons of Smudge's life, it's the same. From month to month, and day to day, we watch the bright spark in her flicker and fade.

Her sight is failing, which heightens her anxiety. At a familiar place on one of our routes a wire fence blocks the way, but a break close to the ground is just big enough for her. A year ago I would climb over the fence, and she would dart through the opening, hardly breaking stride. A few months later she approached the fence and stopped, stymied. For a while I would indicate the opening, and she would pass through. Later on, even when I showed her, she couldn't make sense of it but stood and fretted. So I climbed the fence to the other side, beckoned to her through the opening, and she came through. Now we don't go that way anymore.

She can still take my breath away with a beautifully choreographed running leap over a small stream or a fallen tree. But she can also miscalculate, smack into the water or tumble over the log and plough into the ground, face first. I gasp and cry out as if I'd taken the fall myself. I lean left or right, as bowlers do, trying to will her past the obstacle. This summer, heavy rains made the wild grasses taller than usual, rendering some of our normal routes inaccessible to her. Creeping wild raspberry canes grab at her coat, making her twist and roll in panic to evade the attack. As the autumn deepens, mauve asters, goldenrod and Queen Anne's lace lay down to die, thwarting her further. Either she charges into them until they tangle in her legs and send her tumbling, or she simply stops before them and waits. In her eyes I read: Do something, make it go away. I bend the obstacle out of her path and encourage her to proceed.

On good days she can still climb the two steps into our house. But now, nearly always, she waits to be lifted. There's no clear evidence she can't do it, or that it hurts; she seems to lack confidence, or motivation. Most of her waking life has been defined by action. Now she stands and waits. Waits for her walk, waits to be fed, waits to be let out, waits to be let in. After she peed this morning, she stood facing the garden, shivering in the early chill, until I went to her side and urged her to come in.

Smudge used to alert us when cars or people approached. With her high-pitched bark she made her wishes well known, as soon as she knew them herself. A friend dubbed her "the autocrat." Now the autocrat has gone silent. She just waits. Sometimes when I watch her standing like this, especially as day fades into night, I imagine she looks sad. I wonder if she regrets the passage of each day, as one more used up from her mortal allotment. Projection? But who knows what or how other animals know, think, or feel?

Now and then I get flashes of irritation with her increasing dependency. Once or twice, tired or particularly fretful myself, I've even wished for a moment to be freed of the burden of her. Then I'm overcome by shame. In fact I'm far more patient with the animals than I am with most people. This anger-shame sequence is familiar to caregivers, I gather, especially ones involved with the terminally ill. The other day we turned down a request to take in a younger dog; it would be much too taxing for our Smudge and Willy. We hesitate to leave home overnight. When we do, a good friend takes care of house and animals, but as they get increasingly geriatric, less and less do we like to presume. At the same time, I know these burdens – inconveniences, really – are small price for the delight our Smudge and Willy give so freely. In sickness and in health, 'til death us do part.

I can also see in them my own future, and Brian's. Each of us has fewer days left than he's already spent. As our capacities diminish, we will also become more dependent on the kindness of others, strangers even, in an ever more frightening world. Even now, some mornings when my body hurts or my spirit is unwilling, the only thing that compels me to move is Smudge's demand for a walk. And each day, irritated or not, it still pleases me to watch her out there, on better days still prancing like a show pony, still eager to be in this world, as alert to its signals as her fading senses will allow.

One day she stopped at a familiar tree, and looked up, wagging. Raccoons live here, or they have. I've seen her wag like this at a nest of voles, tiny bite-sized rodents in the grass. I read in her gesture: *Come out and play – you run, I'll catch you and eat you, won't that be fun?* But why here, now? I can't detect any sign of animals in this tree. Perhaps she's caught a scent. Or is she having a flashback?

After our walk one morning she paced, circling through the kitchen, living room and my office, all of which connect. Round and round she went, for hours, driven by dog demons or her own brainstorms. By noon I wanted to scream at her. She and I function at close quarters; she sleeps under my desk. With deadlines looming, mine on this book and Brian's on a kitchen he's building, both of us are up before dawn, and the household is not relaxed. Dogs, I understand, are empaths, sponges for our emotional states. Are *we* the demons driving her?

Brian suggested building a den for her in the passage between my desk and the kitchen. I balk at leashes, fences, and such, all of them fetters on the free spirit. But I do have to work, and as wolf descendants, they say, dogs do love a den.

Next morning after our walk, I beckoned her into the new den. She stood in there, watching me. I closed the low gate behind her, and sat to my work. For twenty minutes she gazed at me over the gate. A year ago she would have jumped it, but now she just watched. I saw, or imagined, reproach in her eyes, or sadness that it had come to this. Finally she settled to sleep.

Sometimes, watching Smudge or Willy eat what we've provided, I feel a sort of maternal glow. I suppose it's rooted in a very basic connection: if we don't eat, we die. A couple of months ago Smudge, always an easy feed, went off the dry dog food she's eaten all her life. One day she sniffed at it and walked away. Her teeth are failing, but at this point it's unthinkable to subject her to the dangers of a general anaesthetic for dental work that would be temporary at best. When she balked at canned food too, I started to cook for her: chicken livers, turkey backs, rice, carrots. For a while Brian put her food through an old hand-cranked meatgrinder he'd salvaged from his youth. She gobbled the resulting goop, geriatric baby-food. On days when she refused all of these, I've made scrambled eggs, anything. Some days I practically count the mouthfuls. There is a balance, says Brian quite reasonably, between neglect and obsession. I haven't found it, and if truth be told, neither has he.

Yesterday she didn't eat in the morning, she didn't eat after her walk, and she didn't eat at midday, as she often does when we do. At tea Brian and I had another talk about her life and death. Of course we wish for her, as we do for ourselves, a quick, painless end. Out on a walk, her heart will stop. Or one night she'll slip away during a gentle sleep, and that will be that. If, on the other hand, we have to end her life deliberately, will she give us a sign when she's had enough? And if she does, will we know how to read it? She's been taking her leave of us, I think, for some time. She sleeps most of the day and may not even notice when visitors come and go. In sleep her little body contracts as she inhales, some kind of spasm. But she doesn't seem to be in pain, or suffering in any overt way that we can discern. How will we know?

Then she and I went out for an afternoon walk. In a forest radiant with golden light, we rambled through paper-dry, pepper-scented leaves. She trotted ahead, a perky bounce in her gait. By my current measure this indicates a good day, a very good day. Her plume of a tail has thinned, and it droops now when she stands, but out here in the woods, it curls over her busy body, dancing as she goes. Who knows how many days we have left, or walks, but I'm overwhelmed by how much evident *life* still remains in this life of Smudge.

I cry, watching her. This too, I know, is what it means to love.

And there I meant this chapter, and book, to end.

But lately I've been bargaining. This cold, snowy brute of a winter has made it hard for Smudge to walk anywhere but on the ploughed road or when snowmobiles have packed our lower trail. I've been bargaining for one more spring, so we could walk on the thawing earth again, and she could smell the tracks of deer and fox and rabbits one more time.

As her capacities continue to decline, our afternoon excursions gradually fall away, but she continues to insist on the morning walk. I don't know what it means to her – pleasure, habit, duty to me? – but each day I note how far we get. To me it's a measure of her life force, and where we stand in terms of the bargain. She never complains but eventually lags behind to indicate when she wants to turn back. One morning we get to the second oak past the neighbour's lane, another day to the top of the hill, some days only to the end of our driveway.

As our walks change, so do other routines and the house. Somewhere along the way Smudge has forgotten how to go into reverse. Each time we find her marooned between washer and toilet, or a chair and a lamp, we block the gap, draw lines, make her world simpler and smaller. To prevent her stumbling into her food and water, Brian builds a little three-sided corral she can approach only from the front. He pads the porch glass, so that when she flies heedless off the top step, instead of crashing she just bounces.

In the last week of February Brian awakens several nights to hear her scrambling on the kitchen floor. Her hind legs have started to fail, and she can't get enough traction with her front feet on the smooth floor. Once we get her up and moving again, she can carry on by herself.

Tuesday morning I continue to bargain, another walk. Smudge takes a playful bite at my coat sleeve, a muted version of the excited vertical leaps she used to make. We reach the first shrub past the neighbour's lane.

That night I awaken to Smudge crying. The only time she speaks these days, she's in high distress. On this night we had confined her to her den, with a rug on the floor for traction. When I reach her she's fighting to stand, her hind legs crossing helplessly. She cries, not in pain, I think, but from the effort. We put her in the living room, which has textured carpet wall-to-wall, and we lay a mattress on the floor to be with her through the struggle.

She doesn't sleep but battles the whole long night to stay on her feet. She manages to stand, takes a few tottery steps, then her rear end collapses. She fights to her feet, again and again. We imagine it a deeply primal urge: once you're down, you're prey. In any case our Smudge, a terrier, never let go easily of anything. Brian tries to hold her, for comfort, but she has to keep moving. At one point she slumps exhausted into the crook of his arm. But she won't let her head down, not once. Near dawn she comes close to my face and licks my nose. By now we're used to her smelly old-dog breath.

Wednesday morning I prepare to call the vet but can't manage it coherently, so Brian makes the call. Visits to hospital cause Smudge such distress that Steve James has already agreed he'll come to the house. We trust his gentle, quiet presence. He'll be up around midday.

Smudge goes out for a pee. It's a bright, cold day. In the absence of her regular patrols, the squirrels and rabbits have become scandalously bold; she rarely sees them anymore. Since she came down the stairs without help, I invite her to go for a morning walk, even a short one – still bargaining. She stands her ground, just looks at me. Enough. We go back inside, and while she sleeps, worn out by the night's labours, we wait.

Steve and his assistant Amanda arrive shortly after twelve. Sometime during the night, I thought of Brian's mean-parent concern, and suggested that he be the one to cradle her today. She's nervous – who *are* these strange people in my house? Steve gives her a sedative. We sit on the sofa where she used to sleep until she could no longer jump. In a few minutes the drug takes hold and she settles into Brian's arms, letting go her own weight. But then she starts to squirm, and struggles to stand. She pees from the effort. I tuck a blanket under her rear end. Suddenly she throws her head back and lets out seven or eight quick, sharp yelps. A reflex, says the vet. Brian wonders later if the touch at her undefended back might have called up the terror of the coyote attack. I take it as one last NO! from a fierce, unquenchable spirit. Who knows.

She settles again into Brian's lap. I stroke her head, and cover my mouth with the other hand to silence my wailing. The vet shaves a small clearing on her foreleg. She doesn't react, either to the buzz or the touch. He inserts the hypodermic. Not a twitch. A little of her blood swirls into the chamber and mixes with the clear liquid. He depresses the plunger. In less than a minute our Smudge stops breathing. No struggle this time, none that we can see or feel. Steve listens through the stethoscope. "She's gone." Brian shudders, sobbing.

As Steve and Amanda put on their coats, Brian says, "She just breathed."

"Sorry," says Steve, "I should have mentioned that. It's just air leaving the lungs." The last gasp, giving up the ghost. The two of them depart. Smudge's body lies limp across Brian's lap. Her hair has greyed almost as much as his. Her eyes are open, but vacant.

We lay her on the floor, on her side, in the position she assumed in deepest sleep. After a while we wrap her in one of her blankets, tucking her legs and tail close to her. Brian builds a simple box, and we leave her body outside to freeze overnight. We can't dig a grave now, not until spring. Through the evening I worry that she'll be cold or frightened out there. We listen for the tap dance of her nails on the kitchen floor. On the edge of sleep I wonder – a last remnant of bargaining? – if we'll come out in the morning to find the box thrown open and our Smudge resurrected, gone off to start a new world religion.

Life does go on. The bird-feeder at the kitchen window has to be filled, the customers are lining up. Logs have to be split for the stove. Bills arrive in the mailbox. Work is due, and must be sought. The world is ruled by thugs, and we have to resist. Willy continues to assert his needs and wants. They're minimal, less than Smudge's, but still, he reminds us pointedly, they are imperatives. I wash Smudge's last pee from the sofa cover and from Brian's jeans. He dismantles her den. I put together an album of photos, relics of her life.

The day after Smudge died, Brian and I go out for a morning walk. Each of us pauses at the door, automatically, to see her safely down the steps. We walk across snowy fields to the pond, frozen now, where she used to chase frogs and sought refuge from the coyotes. I haven't been up this way since last summer, when she could no longer manage it. We have our limits too; twice today Brian has to stop and stretch his aging back. We have no illusions; this is where the bargain ends: anything that lives dies.

Two days after Smudge died, we ski up the lane, through the woods, around the abandoned field that's reverting, tree by tree, to cedar forest. It's the first time we've skied this year. Despite the rare phenomenon of ideal conditions almost unbroken since the beginning of December, my morning walks, on or off skis, were defined by Smudge. As long as she could plough through the snow, she insisted on staying in the lead and never minded tripping us up as she scrambled across our skis. Today we proceed without impediment.

In perspective, I know her death wasn't the monstrous slaughter of innocents through famine or war, nor the unforgivable extinction of whole species. This was one life, it was well lived, and it became unsupportable. At the same time, I know how terribly wrong the people were who chided friends of ours for fussing too much when their dog died. After all, these people said airily, it was only a dog. We have such big brains, how can we be so stupid? By setting ourselves on high like this, god-like over all other creatures, we ensure that the only good future for this planet is free of us.

When the snow melts, we'll bury Smudge's body in the woods, by an ancient, deeply crevassed maple that's home to several small creatures of the forest. She patrolled it faithfully every time we passed. We'll shed the box and blanket and give her body into the earth.

In the meantime, and beyond, Brian and I will live in the deep gap that this great little being left in her wake.

This, I've learned, is the final cost of loving.